KANT'S THEORY OF KNOWLEDGE

First published 1909
This edition published by Lector House in 2023

ISBN: 978-93-5614-854-3

Lector House LLP
Registered Office: H. No. 96, Block C, Tomar Colony,
Burari, Delhi – 110084, India
info@lectorhouse.com
www.lectorhouse.com

KANT'S THEORY OF KNOWLEDGE

HAROLD ARTHUR PRICHARD

2023

LECTOR HOUSE

LECTOR HOUSE LLP

KANT'S THEORY OF KNOWLEDGE

BY

H. A. PRICHARD

FELLOW OF TRINITY COLLEGE, OXFORD

PREFACE

This book is an attempt to think out the nature and tenability of Kant's Transcendental Idealism, an attempt animated by the conviction that even the elucidation of Kant's meaning, apart from any criticism, is impossible without a discussion on their own merits of the main issues which he raises.

My obligations are many and great: to Caird's *Critical Philosophy of Kant* and to the translations of Meiklejohn, Max Müller, and Professor Mahaffy; to Mr. J. A. Smith, Fellow of Balliol College, and to Mr. H. W. B. Joseph, Fellow of New College, for what I have learned from them in discussion; to Mr. A. J. Jenkinson, Fellow of Brasenose College, for reading and commenting on the first half of the MS.; to Mr. H. H. Joachim, Fellow of Merton College, for making many important suggestions, especially with regard to matters of translation; to Mr. Joseph, for reading the whole of the proofs and for making many valuable corrections; and, above all, to my wife for constant and unfailing help throughout, and to Professor Cook Wilson, to have been whose pupil I count the greatest of philosophical good fortunes. Some years ago it was my privilege to be a member of a class with which Professor Cook Wilson read a portion of Kant's *Critique of Pure Reason*, and subsequently I have had the advantage of discussing with him several of the more important passages. I am especially indebted to him in my discussion of the following topics: the distinction between the Sensibility and the Understanding (pp. 14-16, 78-80, 87-89), the term 'form of perception' (pp. 19, 21, 71 fin.-72), the *Metaphysical Exposition of Space* (pp. 22-25), Inner Sense (Ch. V, and pp. 73-74), the *Metaphysical Deduction of the Categories* (pp. 80-82), Kant's account of 'the reference of representations to an object' (pp. 96-100), an implication of perspective (p. 47), the impossibility of a 'theory' of knowledge (p. 131), and the points considered, pp. 107 med.-108 med., 115 med.-116 med., and 117. The views expressed in the pages referred to originated from Professor Cook Wilson, though it must not be assumed that he would accept them in the form in which they are there stated.

REFERENCES

A	=	First edition of the *Critique of Pure Reason.*
B	=	Second edition of the *Critique of Pure Reason.*
Prol.	=	Kant's *Prolegomena to any future Metaphysic.*
M	=	Meiklejohn's Translation of the *Critique of Pure Reason.*
Mah.	=	Mahaffy. Translation of Kant's *Prolegomena to any future Metaphysic.* (The pages referred to are those of the first edition; these are also to be found in the text of the second edition.)
Caird	=	Caird's *Critical Philosophy of Kant.*

CONTENTS

CHAPTER IX

CHAPTER X

CHAPTER XI

CHAPTER XII

CHAPTER XIII

NOTE

CHAPTER I

THE PROBLEM OF THE CRITIQUE

THE problem of the *Critique* may be stated in outline and approximately in Kant's own words as follows.

Human reason is called upon to consider certain questions, which it cannot decline, as they are presented by its own nature, but which it cannot answer. These questions relate to God, freedom of the will, and immortality. And the name for the subject which has to deal with these questions is metaphysics. At one time metaphysics was regarded as the queen of all the sciences, and the importance of its aim justified the title. At first the subject, propounding as it did a dogmatic system, exercised a despotic sway. But its subsequent failure brought it into disrepute. It has constantly been compelled to retrace its steps; there has been fundamental disagreement among philosophers, and no philosopher has successfully refuted his critics. Consequently the current attitude to the subject is one of weariness and indifference. Yet humanity cannot really be indifferent to such problems; even those who profess indifference inevitably make metaphysical assertions; and the current attitude is a sign not of levity but of a refusal to put up with the illusory knowledge offered by contemporary philosophy. Now the objects of metaphysics, God, freedom, and immortality, are not objects of experience in the sense in which a tree or a stone is an object of experience. Hence our views about them cannot be due to experience; they must somehow be apprehended by pure reason, i. e. by thinking and without appeal to experience. Moreover, it is in fact by thinking that men have always tried to solve the problems concerning God, freedom, and immortality. What, then, is the cause of the unsatisfactory treatment of these problems and men's consequent indifference? It must, in some way, lie in a failure to attain the sure scientific method, and really consists in the neglect of an inquiry which should be a preliminary to all others in metaphysics. Men ought to have begun with a critical investigation of pure reason itself. Reason should have examined its own nature, to ascertain in general the extent to which it is capable of attaining knowledge without the aid of experience. This examination will decide whether reason is able to deal with the problems of God, freedom, and immortality at all; and without it no discussion of these problems will have a solid foundation. It is this preliminary investigation which the *Critique of Pure Reason* proposes to undertake. Its aim is to answer the question, 'How far can reason go, without the material presented and the aid furnished by experience?' and the result furnishes the solution, or at least the key to the solution, of all metaphysical problems.

Kant's problem, then, is similar to Locke's. Locke states[1] that his purpose is to inquire into the original, certainty, and extent of human knowledge; and he says, "If, by this inquiry into the nature of the understanding I can discover the powers thereof; how far they reach, to what things they are in any degree proportionate, and where they fail us; I suppose it may be of use to prevail with the busy mind of man, to be more cautious in meddling with things exceeding its comprehension; to stop when it is at the utmost extent of its tether; and to sit down in a quiet ignorance of those things, which, upon examination, are found to be beyond the reach of our capacities." Thus, to use Dr. Caird's analogy,[2] the task which both Locke and Kant set themselves resembled that of investigating a telescope, before turning it upon the stars, to determine its competence for the work.

The above outline of Kant's problem is of course only an outline. Its definite formulation is expressed in the well-known question, 'How are *a priori* synthetic judgements possible?'[3] To determine the meaning of this question it is necessary to begin with some consideration of the terms '*a priori*' and 'synthetic'.

While there is no difficulty in determining what Kant would have recognized as an *a priori* judgement, there is difficulty in determining what he meant by calling such a judgement *a priori*. The general account is given in the first two sections of the Introduction. An *a priori* judgement is introduced as something opposed to an *a posteriori* judgement, or a judgement which has its source in experience. Instances of the latter would be 'This body is heavy', and 'This body is hot'. The point of the word 'experience' is that there is direct apprehension of some individual, e. g. an individual body. To say that a judgement has its source in experience is of course to imply a distinction between the judgement and experience, and the word 'source' may be taken to mean that the judgement depends for its validity upon the experience of the individual thing to which the judgement relates. An *a priori* judgement, then, as first described, is simply a judgement which is not *a posteriori*. It is independent of all experience; in other words, its validity does not depend on the experience of individual things. It might be illustrated by the judgement that all three-sided figures must have three angles. So far, then, no positive meaning has been given to *a priori*.[4]

Kant then proceeds, not as we should expect, to state the positive meaning of *a priori*, but to give tests for what is *a priori*. Since a test implies a distinction between itself and what is tested, it is implied that the meaning of *a priori* is already

[1] Locke's *Essay*, i, 1, §§ 2, 4.

[2] Caird, i, 10.

[3] B. 19, M. 12.

[4] Kant is careful to exclude from the class of *a priori* judgements proper what may be called relatively *a priori* judgements, viz. judgements which, though not independent of all experience, are independent of experience of the facts to which they relate. "Thus one would say of a man who undermined the foundations of his house that he might have known *a priori* that it would fall down, i. e. that he did not need to wait for the experience of its actual falling down. But still he could not know this wholly *a priori*, for he had first to learn through experience that bodies are heavy and consequently fall, if their supports are taken away." (B. 2, M. 2.)

known.[5]

The tests given are necessity and strict universality.[6] Since judgements which are necessary and strictly universal cannot be based on experience, their existence is said to indicate another source of knowledge. And Kant gives as illustrations, (1) any proposition in mathematics, and (2) the proposition 'Every change must have a cause.'

So far Kant has said nothing which determines the positive meaning of *a priori*. A clue is, however, to be found in two subsequent phrases. He says that we may content ourselves with having established as a fact the pure use of our faculty of knowledge.[7] And he adds that not only in judgements, but even in conceptions, is an *a priori* origin manifest.[8] The second statement seems to make the *a priori* character of a judgement consist in its origin. As this origin cannot be experience, it must, as the first statement implies, lie in our faculty of knowledge. Kant's point is that the existence of universal and necessary judgements shows that we must possess a faculty of knowledge capable of yielding knowledge without appeal to experience. The term *a priori*, then, has some reference to the existence of this faculty; in other words, it gives expression to a doctrine of 'innate ideas'. Perhaps, however, it is hardly fair to press the phrase '*test* of *a priori* judgements'. If so, it may be said that on the whole, by *a priori* judgements Kant really means judgements which are universal and necessary, and that he regards them as implying a faculty which gives us knowledge without appeal to experience.

We may now turn to the term 'synthetic judgement'. Kant distinguishes analytic and synthetic judgements thus. In any judgement the predicate B either belongs to the subject A, as something contained (though covertly) in the conception A, or lies completely outside the conception A, although it stands in relation to it. In the former case the judgement is called analytic, in the latter synthetic.[9] 'All

[5] It may be noted that in this passage (Introduction, §§ 1 and 2) Kant is inconsistent in his use of the term 'pure'. Pure knowledge is introduced as a species of *a priori* knowledge: "*A priori* knowledge, if nothing empirical is mixed with it, is called pure". (B. 3, M. 2, 17.) And in accordance with this, the proposition 'every change has a cause' is said to be *a priori* but impure, because the conception of change can only be derived from experience. Yet immediately afterwards, pure, being opposed in general to empirical, can only mean *a priori*. Again, in the phrase 'pure *a priori*' (B. 4 fin., M. 3 med.), the context shows that 'pure' adds nothing to '*a priori*', and the proposition 'every change must have a cause' is expressly given as an instance of pure *a priori* knowledge. The inconsistency of this treatment of the causal rule is explained by the fact that in the former passage he is thinking of the conception of change as empirical, while in the latter he is thinking of the judgement as not empirical. At bottom in this passage 'pure' simply means *a priori*.

[6] In reality, these tests come to the same thing, for necessity means the necessity of connexion between the subject and predicate of a judgement, and since empirical universality, to which strict universality is opposed, means numerical universality, as illustrated by the proposition 'All bodies are heavy', the only meaning left for strict universality is that of a universality reached not through an enumeration of instances, but through the apprehension of a necessity of connexion.

[7] B. 5, M. 4.

[8] Ibid.

[9] B. 10, M. 7.

bodies are extended' is an analytic judgement; 'All bodies are heavy' is synthetic. It immediately follows that only synthetic judgements extend our knowledge; for in making an analytic judgement we are only clearing up our conception of the subject. This process yields no new knowledge, for it only gives us a clearer view of what we know already. Further, all judgements based on experience are synthetic, for it would be absurd to base an analytical judgement on experience, when to make the judgement we need not go beyond our own conceptions. On the other hand, *a priori* judgements are sometimes analytic and sometimes synthetic. For, besides analytical judgements, all judgements in mathematics and certain judgements which underlie physics are asserted independently of experience, and they are synthetic.

Here Kant is obviously right in vindicating the synthetic character of mathematical judgements. In the arithmetical judgement 7 + 5 = 12, the thought of certain units as a group of twelve is no mere repetition of the thought of them as a group of five added to a group of seven. Though the same units are referred to, they are regarded differently. Thus the thought of them as twelve means either that we think of them as formed by adding one unit to a group of eleven, or that we think of them as formed by adding two units to a group of ten, and so on. And the assertion is that the same units, which can be grouped in one way, can also be grouped in another. Similarly, Kant is right in pointing out that the geometrical judgement, 'A straight line between two points is the shortest,' is synthetic, on the ground that the conception of straightness is purely qualitative,[10] while the conception of shortest distance implies the thought of quantity.

It should now be an easy matter to understand the problem expressed by the question, 'How are *a priori* synthetic judgements possible?' Its substance may be stated thus. The existence of *a posteriori* synthetic judgements presents no difficulty. For experience is equivalent to perception, and, as we suppose, in perception we are confronted with reality, and apprehend it as it is. If I am asked, 'How do I know that my pen is black or my chair hard?' I answer that it is because I see or feel it to be so. In such cases, then, when my assertion is challenged, I appeal to my experience or perception of the reality to which the assertion relates. My appeal raises no difficulty because it conforms to the universal belief that if judgements are to rank as knowledge, they must be made to conform to the nature of things, and that the conformity is established by appeal to actual experience of the things. But do *a priori* synthetic judgements satisfy this condition? Apparently not. For when I assert that every straight line is the shortest way between its extremities, I have not had, and never can have, experience of all possible straight lines. How then can I be sure that all cases will conform to my judgement? In fact, how can I anticipate my experience at all? How can I make an assertion about any individual until I have had actual experience of it? In an *a priori* synthetic judgement the mind in some way, in virtue of its own powers and independently of experience, makes an assertion to which it claims that reality must conform. Yet why should reality conform? *A priori* judgements of the other kind, viz. analytic judgements, offer no difficulty, since they are at bottom tautologies, and consequently denial of them is

[10] Straightness means identity of direction.

self-contradictory and meaningless. But there is difficulty where a judgement asserts that a term B is connected with another term A, B being neither identical with nor a part of A. In this case there is no contradiction in asserting that A is not B, and it would seem that only experience can determine whether all A is or is not B. Otherwise we are presupposing that things must conform to our ideas about them. Now metaphysics claims to make *a priori* synthetic judgements, for it does not base its results on any appeal to experience. Hence, before we enter upon metaphysics, we really ought to investigate our right to make *a priori* synthetic judgements at all. Therein, in fact, lies the importance to metaphysics of the existence of such judgements in mathematics and physics. For it shows that the difficulty is not peculiar to metaphysics, but is a general one shared by other subjects; and the existence of such judgements in mathematics is specially important because there their validity or certainty has never been questioned.[11] The success of mathematics shows that at any rate under certain conditions *a priori* synthetic judgements are valid, and if we can determine these conditions, we shall be able to decide whether such judgements are possible in metaphysics. In this way we shall be able to settle a disputed case of their validity by examination of an undisputed case. The general problem, however, is simply to show what it is which makes *a priori* synthetic judgements as such possible; and there will be three cases, those of mathematics, of physics, and of metaphysics.

The outline of the solution of this problem is contained in the Preface to the Second Edition. There Kant urges that the key is to be found by consideration of mathematics and physics. If the question be raised as to what it is that has enabled these subjects to advance, in both cases the answer will be found to lie in a change of method. "Since the earliest times to which the history of human reason reaches, mathematics has, among that wonderful nation the Greeks, followed the safe road of a science. Still it is not to be supposed that it was as easy for this science to strike into, or rather to construct for itself, that royal road, as it was for logic, in which reason has only to do with itself. On the contrary, I believe that it must have remained long in the stage of groping (chiefly among the Egyptians), and that this change is to be ascribed to a *revolution*, due to the happy thought of one man, through whose experiment the path to be followed was rendered unmistakable for future generations, and the certain way of a science was entered upon and sketched out once for all. . . . A new light shone upon the first man (Thales, or whatever may have been his name) who demonstrated the properties of the isosceles triangle; for he found that he ought not to investigate that which he saw in the figure or even the mere conception of the same, and learn its properties from this, but that he ought to produce the figure by virtue of that which he himself had thought into it *a priori* in accordance with conceptions and had represented (by means of a construction), and that in order to know something with certainty *a priori* he must not attribute to the figure any property other than that which necessarily follows from that which he has himself introduced into the figure, in accordance with his conception."[12]

[11] Kant points out that this certainty has usually been attributed to the analytic character of mathematical judgements, and it is of course vital to his argument that he should be successful in showing that they are really synthetic.

[12] B. x-xii, M. xxvi.

Here Kant's point is as follows. Geometry remained barren so long as men confined themselves either to the empirical study of individual figures, of which the properties were to be discovered by observation, or to the consideration of the mere conception of various kinds of figure, e. g. of an isosceles triangle. In order to advance, men had in some sense to produce the figure through their own activity, and in the act of constructing it to recognize that certain features were necessitated by those features which they had given to the figure in constructing it. Thus men had to make a triangle by drawing three straight lines so as to enclose a space, and then to recognize that three angles must have been made by the same process. In this way the mind discovered a general rule, which must apply to all cases, because the mind itself had determined the nature of the cases. A property B follows from a nature A; all instances of A must possess the property B, because they have solely that nature A which the mind has given them and whatever is involved in A. The mind's own rule holds good in all cases, because the mind has itself determined the nature of the cases.

Kant's statements about physics, though not the same, are analogous. Experiment, he holds, is only fruitful when reason does not follow nature in a passive spirit, but compels nature to answer its own questions. Thus, when Torricelli made an experiment to ascertain whether a certain column of air would sustain a given weight, he had previously calculated that the quantity of air was just sufficient to balance the weight, and the significance of the experiment lay in his expectation that nature would conform to his calculations and in the vindication of this expectation. Reason, Kant says, must approach nature not as a pupil but as a judge, and this attitude forms the condition of progress in physics.

The examples of mathematics and physics suggest, according to Kant, that metaphysics may require a similar revolution of standpoint, the lack of which will account for its past failure. An attempt should therefore be made to introduce such a change into metaphysics. The change is this. Hitherto it has been assumed that our knowledge must conform to objects. This assumption is the real cause of the failure to extend our knowledge *a priori,* for it limits thought to the analysis of conceptions, which can only yield tautological judgements. Let us therefore try the effect of assuming that objects must conform to our knowledge. Herein lies the Copernican revolution. We find that this reversal of the ordinary view of the relation of objects to the mind enables us for the first time to understand the possibility of *a priori* synthetic judgements, and even to demonstrate certain laws which lie at the basis of nature, e. g. the law of causality. It is true that the reversal also involves the surprising consequence that our faculty of knowledge is incapable of dealing with the objects of metaphysics proper, viz. God, freedom, and immortality, for the assumption limits our knowledge to objects of possible experience. But this very consequence, viz. the impossibility of metaphysics, serves to test and vindicate the assumption. For the view that our knowledge conforms to objects as things in themselves leads us into an insoluble contradiction when we go on, as we must, to seek for the unconditioned; while the assumption that objects must, as phenomena, conform to our way of representing them, removes the contradiction[13].

[13] Cf. pp. 53-54.

Further, though the assumption leads to the denial of speculative knowledge in the sphere of metaphysics, it is still possible that reason in its practical aspect may step in to fill the gap. And the negative result of the assumption may even have a positive value. For if, as is the case, the moral reason, or reason in its practical aspect, involves certain postulates concerning God, freedom, and immortality, which are rejected by the speculative reason, it is important to be able to show that these objects fall beyond the scope of the speculative reason. And if we call reliance on these postulates, as being presuppositions of morality, faith, we may say that knowledge must be abolished to make room for faith.

This answer to the main problem, given in outline in the Preface, is undeniably plausible. Yet examination of it suggests two criticisms which affect Kant's general position.

In the first place, the parallel of mathematics which suggests the 'Copernican' revolution does not really lead to the results which Kant supposes. Advance in mathematics is due to the adoption not of any conscious assumption but of a certain procedure, viz. that by which we draw a figure and thereby see the necessity of certain relations within it. To preserve the parallel, the revolution in metaphysics should have consisted in the adoption of a similar procedure, and advance should have been made dependent on the application of an at least quasi-mathematical method to the objects of metaphysics. Moreover, since these objects are God, freedom, and immortality, the conclusion should have been that we ought to study God, freedom, and immortality by somehow constructing them in perception and thereby gaining insight into the necessity of certain relations. Success or failure in metaphysics would therefore consist simply in success or failure to see the necessity of the relations involved. Kant, however, makes the condition of advance in metaphysics consist in the adoption not of a method of procedure but of an assumption, viz. that objects conform to the mind. And it is impossible to see how this assumption can assist what, on Kant's theory, it ought to have assisted, viz. the study of God, freedom, and immortality, or indeed the study of anything. In geometry we presuppose that individual objects conform to the universal rules of relation which we discover. Now suppose we describe a geometrical judgement, e. g. that two straight lines cannot enclose a space, as a mental law, because we are bound to think it true. Then we may state the presupposition by saying that objects, e. g. individual pairs of straight lines, must conform to such a mental law. But the explicit recognition of this presupposition and the conscious assertion of it in no way assist the solution of particular geometrical problems. The presupposition is really a condition of geometrical thinking at all. Without it there is no geometrical thinking, and the recognition of it places us in no better position for the study of geometrical problems. Similarly, if we wish to think out the nature of God, freedom, and immortality, we are not assisted by assuming that these objects must conform to the laws of our thinking. We must presuppose this conformity if we are to think at all, and consciousness of the presupposition puts us in no better position. What is needed is an insight similar to that which we have in geometry, i. e. an insight into the necessity of the relations under consideration such as would enable us to see, for example, that being a man, as such, involves living for ever.

Kant has been led into the mistake by a momentary change in the meaning given to 'metaphysics'. For the moment he is thinking of metaphysics, not as the inquiry concerned with God, freedom, and immortality, but as the inquiry which has to deal with the problem as to how we can know *a priori*. This problem is assisted, at any rate prima facie, by the assumption that things must conform to the mind. And this assumption can be said to be suggested by mathematics, inasmuch as the mathematician presupposes that particular objects must correspond to the general rules discovered by the mind. From this point of view Kant's only mistake, if the parallelism is to be maintained, is that he takes for an assumption which enables the mathematician to advance a metaphysical presupposition of the advance, on which the mathematician never reflects, and awareness of which would in no way assist his mathematics.

In the second place the 'Copernican' revolution is not strictly the revolution which Kant supposes it to be. He speaks as though his aim is precisely to reverse the ordinary view of the relation of the mind to objects. Instead of the mind being conceived as having to conform to objects, objects are to be conceived as having to conform to the mind. But if we consider Kant's real position, we see that these views are only verbally contrary, since the word object refers to something different in each case. On the ordinary view objects are something outside the mind, in the sense of independent of it, and the ideas, which must conform to objects, are something within the mind, in the sense of dependent upon it. The conformity then is of something within the mind to something outside it. Again, the conformity means that one of the terms, viz. the object, exists first and that then the other term, the idea, is fitted to or made to correspond to it. Hence the real contrary of this view is that ideas, within the mind, exist first and that objects outside the mind, coming into existence afterwards, must adapt themselves to the ideas. This of course strikes us as absurd, because we always think of the existence of the object as the presupposition of the existence of the knowledge of it; we do not think the existence of the knowledge as the presupposition of the existence of the object. Hence Kant only succeeds in stating the contrary of the ordinary view with any plausibility, because in doing so he makes the term object refer to something which like 'knowledge' is within the mind. His position is that objects within the mind must conform to our general ways of knowing. For Kant, therefore, the conformity is not between something within and something without the mind, but between two realities within the mind, viz. the individual object, as object of perception, i. e. a phenomenon, and our general ways of perceiving and thinking. But this view is only verbally the contrary of the ordinary view, and consequently Kant does not succeed in reversing the ordinary view that we know objects independent of or outside the mind, by bringing our ideas into conformity with them. In fact, his conclusion is that we do not know this object, i. e. the thing in itself, at all. Hence his real position should be stated by saying not that the ordinary view puts the conformity between mind and things in the wrong way, but that we ought not to speak of conformity at all. For the thing in itself being unknowable, our ideas can never be made to conform to it. Kant then only reaches a conclusion which is apparently the reverse of the ordinary view by substituting another object for the thing in itself, viz. the phenomenon or appearance of the thing in itself to us.

Further, this second line of criticism, if followed out, will be found to affect his statement of the problem as well as that of its solution. It will be seen that the problem is mis-stated, and that the solution offered presupposes it to be mis-stated. His statement of the problem takes the form of raising a difficulty which the existence of *a priori* knowledge presents to the ordinary view, according to which objects are independent of the mind, and ideas must be brought into conformity with them. In a synthetic *a priori* judgement we claim to discover the nature of certain objects by an act of our thinking, and independently of actual experience of them. Hence if a supporter of the ordinary view is asked to justify the conformity of this judgement or idea with the objects to which it relates, he can give no answer. The judgement having *ex hypothesi* been made without reference to the objects, the belief that the objects must conform to it is the merely arbitrary supposition that a reality independent of the mind must conform to the mind's ideas. But Kant, in thus confining the difficulty to *a priori* judgements, implies that empirical judgements present no difficulty to the ordinary view; since they rest upon actual experience of the objects concerned, they are conformed to the objects by the very process through which they arise. He thereby fails to notice that empirical judgements present a precisely parallel difficulty. It can only be supposed that the conformity of empirical judgements to their objects is guaranteed by the experience upon which they rest, if it be assumed that in experience we apprehend objects as they are. But our experience or perception of individual objects is just as much mental as the thinking which originates *a priori* judgements. If we can question the truth of our thinking, we can likewise question the truth of our perception. If we can ask whether our ideas must correspond to their objects, we can likewise ask whether our perceptions must correspond to them. The problem relates solely to the correspondence between something within the mind and something outside it; it applies equally to perceiving and thinking, and concerns all judgements alike, empirical as well as *a priori*. Kant, therefore, has no right to imply that empirical judgements raise no problem, if he finds difficulty in *a priori* judgements. He is only able to draw a distinction between them, because, without being aware that he is doing so, he takes account of the relation of the object to the subject in the case of an *a priori* judgement, while in the case of an empirical judgement he ignores it. In other words, in dealing with the general connexion between the qualities of an object, he takes into account the fact that we are thinking it, but, in dealing with the perception of the coexistence of particular qualities of an object, he ignores the fact that we are perceiving it. Further, that the real problem concerns all synthetic judgements alike is shown by the solution which he eventually reaches. His conclusion turns out to be that while both empirical and *a priori* judgements are valid of phenomena, they are not valid of things in themselves; i. e. that of things in themselves we know nothing at all, not even their particular qualities. Since, then, his conclusion is that even empirical judgements are not valid of things in themselves, it shows that the problem cannot be confined to *a priori* judgements, and therefore constitutes an implicit criticism of his statement of the problem.

Must there not, however, be some problem peculiar to *a priori* judgements? Otherwise why should Kant have been led to suppose that his problem concerned them only? Further consideration will show that there is such a problem, and that it was only owing to the mistake indicated that Kant treated this problem as identical with that of which he actually offered a solution. In the universal judgements of mathematics we apprehend, as we think, general rules of connexion which must apply to all possible cases. Such judgements, then, presuppose a conformity between the connexions which we discover and all possible instances. Now Kant's treatment of this conformity as a conformity between our ideas and things has two implications. In the first place, it implies, as has been pointed out, that relation to the subject, as thinking, is taken into account in the case of the universal connexion, and that relation to the subject, as perceiving, is ignored in the case of the individual thing. In the second place, it implies that what is related to the subject as the object of its thought must be subjective or mental; that because we have to think the general connexion, the connexion is only our own idea, the conformity of things to which may be questioned. But the treatment, to be consistent, should take account of relation to the subject in both cases or in neither. If the former alternative be accepted, then the subjective character attributed by Kant in virtue of this relation to what is object of thought, and equally attributable to what is object of perception, reduces the problem to that of the conformity in general of all ideas, including perceptions, within the mind to things outside it; and this problem does not relate specially to *a priori* judgements. To discover the problem which relates specially to them, the other alternative must be accepted, that of ignoring relation to the subject in both cases. The problem then becomes 'What renders possible or is presupposed by the conformity of individual things to certain laws of connexion?' And, inasmuch as to deny the conformity is really to deny that there are laws of connexion,[14] the problem reduces itself to the question, 'What is the presupposition of the existence of definite laws of connexion in the world?' And the only answer possible is that reality is a system or a whole of connected parts, in other words, that nature is uniform. Thus it turns out that the problem relates to the uniformity of nature, and that the question 'How are *a priori* synthetic judgements possible?' has in reality nothing to do with the problem of the relation of reality to the knowing subject, but is concerned solely with the nature of reality.

Further, it is important to see that the alternative of ignoring relation to the subject is the right one, not only from the point of view of the problem peculiar to *a priori* judgements, but also from the point of view of the nature of knowledge in general. Perceiving and thinking alike presuppose that reality[15] is immediately object of the mind, and that the act of apprehension in no way affects or enters into the nature of what we apprehend about reality. If, for instance, I assert on the strength of perception that this table is round, I imply that I see the table, and that the shape which I judge it to have is not affected by the fact that I am perceiving it; for I mean that the table really is round. If some one then convinces me that I have made a mistake owing to an effect of foreshortening, and that the table is really oval, I amend my assertion, not by saying that the table is round but only to my apprehension, but by saying that it looks round. Thereby I cease to predicate

[14] To object that the laws in question, being laws which we have thought, may not be the true laws, and that therefore there may still be other laws to which reality conforms, is of course to reintroduce relation to the thinking subject.

[15] Cf. Bosanquet, *Logic*, vol. ii, p. 2.

roundness of the table altogether; for I mean that while it still looks round, it is not really so. The case of universal judgements is similar. The statement that a straight line is the shortest distance between its extremities means that it really is so. The fact is presupposed to be in no way altered by our having apprehended it. Moreover, reality is here just as much implied to be directly object of the mind as it is in the case of the singular judgement. Making the judgement consists, as we say, in *seeing* the connexion between the direction between two points and the shortest distance between them. The connexion of real characteristics is implied to be directly object of thought.[16] Thus both perceiving and thinking presuppose that the reality to which they relate is directly object of the mind, and that the character of it which we apprehend in the resulting judgement is not affected or altered by the fact that we have had to perceive or conceive the reality.[17]

Kant in the formulation of his problem implicitly admits this presupposition in the case of perception. He implies that empirical judgements involve no difficulty, because they rest upon the perception or experience of the objects to which they relate. On the other hand, he does not admit the presupposition in the case of conception, for he implies that in *a priori* judgements we are not confronted with reality but are confined to our own ideas. Hence we ought to ask why Kant is led to adopt an attitude in the latter case which he does not adopt in the former. The answer appears to be twofold. In the first place, there is an inveterate tendency to think of universals, and therefore of the connexions between them, as being not objective realities[18] but mere ideas. In other words, we tend to adopt the conceptualist attitude, which regards individuals as the only reality, and universals as mental fictions. In consequence, we are apt to think that while in perception, which is of the individual, we are confronted by reality, in universal judgements, in which we apprehend connexions between universals, we have before us mere ideas. Kant may fairly be supposed to have been unconsciously under the influence of this tendency. In the second place, we apprehend a universal connexion by the operation of thinking. Thinking is essentially an activity; and since activity in the ordinary sense in which we oppose action to knowledge originates something, we tend to think of the activity of thinking as also originating something, viz. that which is our object when we think. Hence, since we think of what is real as independent of us and therefore as something which we may discover but can in no sense make, we tend to think of the object of thought as only an idea. On the other hand, what is ordinarily called perception, though it involves the activity of

[16] In saying that a universal judgement is an immediate apprehension of fact, it is of course not meant that it can be actualized by itself or, so to say, *in vacuo*. Its actualization obviously presupposes the presentation of individuals in perception or imagination. Perception or imagination thus forms the necessary occasion of a universal judgement, and in that sense mediates it. Moreover, the universal judgement implies an act of abstraction by which we specially attend to those universal characters of the individuals perceived or imagined, which enter into the judgement. But, though our apprehension of a universal connexion thus implies a process, and is therefore mediated, yet the connexion, when we apprehend it, is immediately our object. There is nothing between it and us.

[17] For a fuller discussion of the subject see Chh. IV and VI.

[18] i. e. as not having a place in the reality which, as we think, exists independently of the mind.

thinking, also involves an element in respect of which we are passive. This is the fact pointed to by Kant's phrase 'objects are *given* in perception'. In virtue of this passive element we are inclined to think that in perception we simply stand before the reality in a passive attitude. The reality perceived is thought to be, so to say, there, existing independently of us; relation to the subject is unnoticed because of our apparently wholly passive attitude. At times, and especially when he is thinking of the understanding as a faculty of spontaneity, Kant seems to have been under the influence of this second tendency.

The preceding summary of the problem of the *Critique* represents the account given in the two Prefaces and the Introduction. According to this account, the problem arises from the unquestioned existence of *a priori* knowledge in mathematics and physics and the problematic existence of such knowledge in metaphysics, and Kant's aim is to determine the range within which *a priori* knowledge is possible. Thus the problem is introduced as relating to *a priori* knowledge as such, no distinction being drawn between its character in different cases. Nevertheless the actual discussion of the problem in the body of the *Critique* implies a fundamental distinction between the nature of *a priori* knowledge in mathematics and its nature in physics, and in order that a complete view of the problem may be given, this distinction must be stated.

The 'Copernican' revolution was brought about by consideration of the facts of mathematics. Kant accepted as an absolute starting-point the existence in mathematics of true universal and necessary judgements. He then asked, 'What follows as to the nature of the objects known in mathematics from the fact that we really know them?' Further, in his answer he accepted a distinction which he never examined or even questioned, viz. the distinction between things in themselves and phenomena.[19] This distinction assumed, Kant inferred from the truth of mathematics that things in space and time are only phenomena. According to him mathematicians are able to make the true judgements that they do make only because they deal with phenomena. Thus Kant in no way sought to *prove* the truth of mathematics. On the contrary, he argued from the truth of mathematics to the nature of the world which we thereby know. The phenomenal character of the world being thus established, he was able to reverse the argument and to regard the phenomenal character of the world as *explaining* the validity of mathematical judgements. They are valid, because they relate to phenomena. And the consideration which led Kant to take mathematics as his starting-point seems to have been the self-evidence of mathematical judgements. As we directly apprehend their necessity, they admit of no reasonable doubt.[20]

On the other hand, the general principles underlying physics, e. g. that every change must have a cause, or that in all change the quantum of matter is constant, appeared to Kant in a different light. Though certainly not based on experience,

---

[19] Cf. Ch. IV. This distinction should of course have been examined by one whose aim it was to determine how far our knowledge can reach.

[20] For the self-evidence of mathematics to Kant compare B. 120, M. 73 and B. 200, M. 121.

they did not seem to him self-evident.[21] Hence,[22] in the case of these principles, he sought to give what he did not seek to give in the case of mathematical judgements, viz. a proof of their truth.[23] The nerve of the proof lies in the contention that these principles are involved not merely in any general judgement in physics, e. g. 'All bodies are heavy,' but even in any singular judgement, e. g. 'This body is heavy,' and that the validity of singular judgements is universally conceded. Thus here the fact upon which he takes his stand is not the admitted truth of the universal judgements under consideration, but the admitted truth of any singular judgement in physics. His treatment, then, of the universal judgements of mathematics and that of the principles underlying physics are distinguished by the fact that, while he accepts the former as needing no proof, he seeks to prove the latter from the admitted validity of singular judgements in physics. At the same time the acceptance of mathematical judgements and the proof of the *a priori* principles of physics have for Kant a common presupposition which distinguishes mathematics and physics from metaphysics. Like universal judgements in mathematics, singular judgements in physics, and therefore the principles which they presuppose, are true only if the objects to which they relate are phenomena. Both in mathematics and physics, therefore, it is a condition of *a priori* knowledge that it relates to phenomena and not to things in themselves. But, just for this reason, metaphysics is in a different position; since God, freedom, and immortality can never be objects of experience, *a priori* knowledge in metaphysics, and therefore metaphysics itself, is impossible. Thus for Kant the very condition, the realization of which justifies the acceptance of mathematical judgements and enables us to prove the principles of physics, involves the impossibility of metaphysics.

Further, the distinction drawn between *a priori* judgements in mathematics and in physics is largely responsible for the difficulty of understanding what Kant means by *a priori*. His unfortunate tendency to explain the term negatively could be remedied if it could be held either that the term refers solely to mathematical judgements or that he considers the truth of the law of causality to be apprehended in the same way that we see that two and two are four. For an *a priori* judgement could then be defined as one in which the mind, on the presentation of an individual in perception or imagination, and in virtue of its capacity of thinking, apprehends the necessity of a specific relation. But this definition is precluded by Kant's view that the law of causality and similar principles, though *a priori*, are not self-evident.

[21] This is stated B. 200, M. 121. It is also implied B. 122, M. 75, B. 263-4, M. 160, and by the argument of the *Analytic* generally.

[22] This appears to be the real cause of the difference of treatment, though it is not the reason assigned by Kant himself, cf. B. 120, M. 73-4.

[23] His remarks about pure natural science in B. 20, M. 13 and Prol. § 4 sub fin., do not represent the normal attitude of the *Critique*.

CHAPTER II

THE SENSIBILITY AND THE UNDERSTANDING

THE distinction between the sensibility and the understanding[24] is to Kant fundamental both in itself and in relation to the conclusions which he reaches. An outline, therefore, of this distinction must precede any statement or examination of the details of his position. Unfortunately, in spite of its fundamental character, Kant never thinks of questioning or criticizing the distinction in the form in which he draws it, and the presence of certain confusions often renders it difficult to be sure of his meaning.

The distinction may be stated in his own words thus: "There are two stems of human knowledge, which perhaps spring from a common but to us unknown root, namely sensibility and understanding."[25] "Our knowledge springs from two fundamental sources of the mind; the first receives representations[26] (receptivity for impressions); the second is the power of knowing an object by means of these representations (spontaneity of conceptions). Through the first an object is *given* to us; through the second the object is *thought* in relation to the representation (which is a mere determination of the mind). Perception and conceptions constitute, therefore, the elements of all our knowledge, so that neither conceptions without a perception in some way corresponding to them, nor perception without conceptions can yield any knowledge. . . . Neither of these qualities has a preference over the other. Without sensibility no object would be given to us, and without understanding no object would be thought. Thoughts without content are empty, perceptions without conceptions are blind. Hence it is as necessary for the mind to make its conceptions sensuous (i. e. to add to them the object in perception) as to make its perceptions intelligible (i. e. to bring them under conceptions). Neither of these powers or faculties can exchange its function. The understanding cannot perceive, and the senses cannot think. Only by their union can knowledge arise."[27]

The distinction so stated appears straightforward and, on the whole,[28] sound. And it is fairly referred to by Kant as the distinction between the faculties of per-

---

[24] Cf. B. 1, 29, 33, 74-5, 75, 92-4; M. 1, 18, 21, 45-46, 57.

[25] B. 29, M. 18

[26] For the sake of uniformity *Vorstellung* has throughout been translated by 'representation', though sometimes, as in the present passage, it would be better rendered by 'presentation'.

[27] B. 74-5, M. 45-6.

[28] Cf. p. 15, note 29.

ceiving and conceiving or thinking, provided that the terms perceiving and conceiving or thinking be taken to indicate a distinction within perception in the ordinary sense of the word. His meaning can be stated thus: 'All knowledge requires the realization of two conditions; an individual must be presented to us in perception, and we as thinking beings must bring this individual under or recognize it as an instance of some universal. Thus, in order to judge 'This is a house' or 'That is red' we need the presence of the house or of the red colour in perception, and we must 'recognize' the house or the colour, i. e. apprehend the individual as a member of a certain kind. Suppose either condition unrealized. Then if we suppose a failure to conceive, i. e. to apprehend the individual as a member of some kind, we see that our perception—if it could be allowed to be anything at all—would be blind i. e. indeterminate, or a mere 'blur'. What we perceived would be for us as good as nothing. In fact, we could not even say that we were perceiving. Again, if we suppose that we had merely the conception of a house, and neither perceived nor had perceived an individual to which it applied, we see that the conception, being without application, would be neither knowledge nor an element in knowledge. Moreover, the content of a conception is derived from perception; it is only through its relation to perceived individuals that we become aware of a universal. To know the meaning of 'redness' we must have experienced individual red things; to know the meaning of 'house' we must at least have had experience of individual men and of their physical needs. Hence 'conceptions' without 'perceptions' are void or empty. The existence of conceptions presupposes experience of corresponding individuals, even though it also implies the activity of thinking in relation to these individuals.'[29]

Further, it is true to say that as perceiving we are passive; we do not do anything. This, as has been pointed out, is the element of truth contained in the statement that objects are *given* to us. On the other hand, it may be truly said that as conceiving, in the sense of bringing an individual under a universal, we are essentially active. This is presupposed by the notice or attention involved in perception ordinarily so called, i. e. perception in the full sense in which it includes conceiving as well as perceiving.[30] Kant, therefore, is justified in referring to the sensibility as a 'receptivity' and to the understanding as a 'spontaneity'.

The distinction, so stated, appears, as has been already said, intelligible and, in the main[31], valid. Kant, however, renders the elucidation of his meaning difficult by combining with this view of the distinction an incompatible and unwarranted theory of perception. He supposes,[32] without ever questioning the supposition, that perception is due to the operation of things outside the mind, which act upon our sensibility and thereby produce sensations. On this supposition, what we perceive is not, as the distinction just stated implies, the thing itself, but a sensation produced by it. Consequently a problem arises as to the meaning on this suppo-

[29] Kant's account implies that he has in view only empirical knowledge; in any case it only applies to empirical conceptions.

[30] This distinction within perception is of course compatible with the view that the elements so distinguished are inseparable.

[31] See p. 15, note 29.

[32] Cf. B. 1, M. 1.

sition of the statements 'by the sensibility objects are given to us' and 'by the understanding they are thought'. The former statement must mean that when a thing affects us there is a sensation. It cannot mean that by the sensibility we know that there exists a thing which causes the sensation, for this knowledge would imply the activity of thinking; nor can it mean that in virtue of the sensibility the thing itself is presented to us. The latter statement must mean that when sensation arises, the understanding judges that there is something causing it; and this assertion must really be *a priori*, because not dependent upon experience. Unfortunately the two statements so interpreted are wholly inconsistent with the account of the functions of the sensibility and the understanding which has just been quoted.

Further, this theory of perception has two forms. In its first form the theory is physical rather than metaphysical, and is based upon our possession of physical organs. It assumes that the reality to be apprehended is the world of space and time, and it asserts that by the action of bodies upon our physical organs our sensibility is affected, and that thereby sensations are originated in us. Thereupon a problem arises. For if the contribution of the sensibility to our knowledge of the physical world is limited to a succession of sensations, explanation must be given of the fact that we have succeeded with an experience confined to these sensations in acquiring knowledge of a world which does not consist of sensations.[33] Kant, in fact, in the *Aesthetic* has this problem continually before him, and tries to solve it. He holds that the mind, by means of its forms of perception and its conceptions of the understanding, superinduces upon sensations, as data, spatial and other relations, in such a way that it acquires knowledge of the spatial world.

An inherent difficulty, however, of this 'physical' theory of perception leads to a transformation of it. If, as the theory supposes, the cause of sensation is outside or beyond the mind, it cannot be known. Hence the initial assumption that this cause is the physical world has to be withdrawn, and the cause of sensation comes to be thought of as the thing in itself of which we can know nothing. This is undoubtedly the normal form of the theory in Kant's mind.

It may be objected that to attribute to Kant at any time the physical form of the theory is to accuse him of an impossibly crude confusion between things in themselves and the spatial world, and that he can never have thought that the cause of sensation, being as it is outside the mind, is spatial. But the answer is to be found in the fact that the problem just referred to as occupying Kant's attention in the *Aesthetic* is only a problem at all so long as the cause of sensation is thought of as a physical body. For the problem 'How do we, beginning with mere sensation, come to know a spatial and temporal world?' is only a problem so long as it is supposed that the cause of sensation is a spatial and temporal world or a part of it, and that this world is what we come to know. If the cause of sensation, as being beyond the mind, is held to be unknowable and so not known to be spatial or temporal, the problem has disappeared. Corroboration is given by certain passages[34] in the *Critique* which definitely mention 'the senses', a term which refers to bodily

[33] Cf. B. 1 init., M. 1 init.; B. 34, M. 21 sub fin.

[34] E. g. B. 1 init., M. 1 init., and B. 75 fin., M. 46, lines 12, 13 [for 'the sensuous faculty' should be substituted 'the senses'].

organs, and by others[35] to which meaning can be given only if they are taken to imply that the objects which affect our sensibility are not unknown things in themselves, but things known to be spatial. Even the use of the plural in the term 'things in themselves' implies a tendency to identify the unknowable reality beyond the mind with bodies in space. For the implication that different sensations are due to different things in themselves originates in the view that different sensations are due to the operation of different spatial bodies.

It is now necessary to consider how the distinction between the sensibility and the understanding contributes to articulate the problem 'How are *a priori* synthetic judgements possible?' As has been pointed out, Kant means by this question, 'How is it possible that the mind is able, in virtue of its own powers, to make universal and necessary judgements which anticipate its experience of objects?' To this question his general answer is that it is possible and only possible because, so far from ideas, as is generally supposed, having to conform to things, the things to which our ideas or judgements relate, viz. phenomena, must conform to the nature of the mind. Now, if the mind's knowing nature can be divided into the sensibility and the understanding, the problem becomes 'How is it possible for the mind to make such judgements in virtue of its sensibility and its understanding?' And the answer will be that it is possible because the things concerned, i. e. phenomena, must conform to the sensibility and the understanding, i. e. to the mind's perceiving and thinking nature. But both the problem and the answer, so stated, give no clue to the particular *a priori* judgements thus rendered possible nor to the nature of the sensibility and the understanding in virtue of which we make them. It has been seen, however, that the judgements in question fall into two classes, those of mathematics and those which form the presuppositions of physics. And it is Kant's aim to relate these classes to the sensibility and the understanding respectively. His view is that mathematical judgements, which, as such, deal with spatial and temporal relations, are essentially bound up with our perceptive nature, i. e. with our sensibility, and that the principles underlying physics are the expression of our thinking nature, i. e. of our understanding. Hence if the vindication of this relation between our knowing faculties and the judgements to which they are held to give rise is approached from the side of our faculties, it must be shown that our sensitive nature is such as to give rise to mathematical judgements, and that our understanding or thinking nature is such as to originate the principles underlying physics. Again, if the account of this relation is to be adequate, it must be shown to be exhaustive, i. e. it must be shown that the sensibility and the understanding give rise to no other judgements. Otherwise there may be other *a priori* judgements bound up with the sensibility and the understanding which the inquiry will have ignored. Kant, therefore, by his distinction between the sensibility and the understanding, sets himself another problem, which does not come into sight in the first formulation of the general question 'How are *a priori* synthetic judgements possible?' He has to determine what *a priori* judgements are related to the sensibility and to the understanding respectively. At the same time the distinction gives rise

[35] E. g. B. 42, lines 11, 12; M. 26, line 13; A. 100, Mah. 195 ('even in the absence of the object'). Cf. B. 182-3, M. 110-1 (see pp. 137-138, and note 356, p. 138), and B. 207-10, M. 126-8 (see pp. 141-143).

to a division within the main problem. His chief aim is to discover how it is that *a priori* judgements are universally applicable. But, as Kant conceives the issue, the problem requires different treatment according as the judgements in question are related to the sensibility or to the understanding. Hence arises the distinction between the *Transcendental Aesthetic* and the *Transcendental Analytic*, the former dealing with the *a priori* judgements of mathematics, which relate to the sensibility, and the latter dealing with the *a priori* principles of physics, which originate in the understanding. Again, within each of these two divisions we have to distinguish two problems, viz. 'What *a priori* judgements are essentially related to the faculty in question?' and 'How is it that they are applicable to objects?'

It is important, however, to notice that the distinction between the sensibility and the understanding, in the form in which it serves as a basis for distinguishing the *Aesthetic* and the *Analytic*, is not identical with or even compatible with the distinction, as Kant states it when he is considering the distinction in itself and is not thinking of any theory which is to be based upon it. In the latter case the sensibility and the understanding are represented as inseparable faculties involved in *all* knowledge.[36] Only from the union of both can knowledge arise.[37] But, regarded as a basis for the distinction between the *Aesthetic* and the *Analytic*, they are implied to be the source of different kinds of knowledge, viz. mathematics and the principles of physics. It is no answer to this to urge that Kant afterwards points out that space as an object presupposes a synthesis which does not belong to sense. No doubt this admission implies that even the apprehension of spatial relations involves the activity of the understanding. But the implication is really inconsistent with the existence of the *Aesthetic* as a distinct part of the subject dealing with a special class of *a priori* judgements.

[36] B. 74-5, M. 45-6; cf. pp. 14-15.

[37] B. 160 note, M. 98 note.

CHAPTER III

SPACE

It is the aim of the *Aesthetic* to deal with the *a priori* knowledge which relates to the sensibility. This knowledge, according to Kant, is concerned with space and time. Hence he has to show *firstly* that our apprehension of space and time is *a priori*, i. e. that it is not derived from experience but originates in our apprehending nature; and *secondly* that within our apprehending nature this apprehension belongs to the sensibility and not to the understanding, or, in his language, that space and time are forms of perception or sensibility. Further, if his treatment is to be exhaustive, he should also show *thirdly* that space and time are the only forms of perception. This, however, he makes no attempt to do except in one passage,[38] where the argument fails. The first two points established, Kant is able to develop his main thesis, viz. that it is a condition of the validity of the *a priori* judgements which relate to space and time that these are characteristics of phenomena, and not of things in themselves.

It will be convenient to consider his treatment of space and time separately, and to begin with his treatment of space. It is necessary, however, first of all to refer to the term 'form of perception'. As Kant conceives a form of perception, it involves three antitheses.

(1) As a *form* of perception it is opposed, as a way or mode of perceiving, to particular perceptions.

(2) As a form or mode of *perception* it is opposed to a form or mode of *conception*.

(3) As a form of *perception* it is also opposed, as a way in which we apprehend things, to a way in which things are.

While we may defer consideration of the second and third antitheses, we should at once give attention to the nature of the first, because Kant confuses it with two other antitheses. There is no doubt that in general a *form* of perception means for Kant a general capacity of perceiving which, as such, is opposed to the actual perceptions in which it is manifested. For according to him our spatial perceptions are not foreign to us, but manifestations of our general perceiving nature; and this view finds expression in the assertion that space is a form of perception or of sensibility.[39]

---

[38] B. 58, M. 35.

[39] Cf. B. 43 init., M. 26 med.

Unfortunately, however, Kant frequently speaks of this form of perception as if it were the same thing as the actual perception of empty space.[40] In other words, he implies that such a perception is possible, and confuses it with a potentiality, i. e. the power of perceiving that which is spatial. The confusion is possible because it can be said with some plausibility that a perception of empty space—if its possibility be allowed—does not inform us about actual things, but only informs us what must be true of things, if there prove to be any; such a perception, therefore, can be thought of as a possibility of knowledge rather than as actual knowledge.

The second confusion is closely related to the first, and arises from the fact that Kant speaks of space not only as a form of *perception*, but also as the form of *phenomena* in opposition to sensation as their matter. "That which in the phenomenon corresponds to[41] the sensation I term its matter; but that which effects that the manifold of the phenomenon can be arranged under certain relations I call the form of the phenomenon. Now that in which alone our sensations can be arranged and placed in a certain form cannot itself be sensation. Hence while the matter of all phenomena is only given to us *a posteriori*, their form [i. e. space] must lie ready for them all together *a priori* in the mind."[42] Here Kant is clearly under the influence of his theory of perception.[43] He is thinking that, given the origination of sensations in us by the thing in itself, it is the business of the mind to arrange these sensations spatially in order to attain knowledge of the spatial world.[44] Space being, as it were, a kind of empty vessel in which sensations are arranged, is said to be the form of phenomena.[45] Moreover, if we bear in mind that ultimately bodies in space are for Kant only spatial arrangements of sensations,[46] we see that the assertion that space is the form of phenomena is only Kant's way of saying that all bodies are spatial.[47] Now Kant, in thus asserting that space is the form of phenomena, is clearly confusing this assertion with the assertion that space is a form of perception, and he does so in consequence of the first confusion, viz. that between a capacity of perceiving and an actual perception of empty space. For in the passage last quoted he continues thus: "I call all representations[48] *pure* (in

[40] e. g. B. 34, 35, M. 22; B. 41, M. 25; *Prol.* §§ 9-11. The commonest expression of the confusion is to be found in the repeated assertion that space is a pure perception.

[41] 'Corresponds to' must mean 'is'.

[42] B. 34, M. 21.

[43] Cf. pp. 15-17.

[44] It is impossible, of course, to see how such a process can give us knowledge of the spatial world, for, whatever bodies in space are, they are not arrangements of sensations. Nevertheless, Kant's theory of perception really precludes him from holding that bodies are anything else than arrangements of sensations, and he seems at times to accept this view explicitly, e. g. B. 38, M. 23 (quoted p. 22), where he speaks of our representing sensations as external to and next to each other, and, therefore, as in different places.

[45] It may be noted that it would have been more natural to describe the particular shape of the phenomenon (i. e. the particular spatial arrangement of the sensations) rather than space as the form of the phenomenon; for the matter to which the form is opposed is said to be sensation, and that of which it is the matter is said to be the phenomenon, i. e. a body in space.

[46] Cf. note 44, p. 20.

[47] Cf. *Prol.* § 11 and p. 73.

[48] Cf. p. 22, note 51.

the transcendental sense) in which nothing is found which belongs to sensation. Accordingly there will be found *a priori* in the mind the pure form of sensuous perceptions in general, wherein all the manifold of phenomena is perceived in certain relations. This pure form of sensibility will also itself be called *pure perception*. Thus, if I abstract from the representation of a body that which the understanding thinks respecting it, such as substance, force, divisibility, &c., and also that which belongs to sensation, such as impenetrability, hardness, colour, &c., something is still left over for me from this empirical perception, viz. extension and shape. These belong to pure perception, which exists in the mind *a priori*, even without an actual object of the senses or a sensation, as a mere form of sensibility." Here Kant has passed, without any consciousness of a transition, from treating space as that in which the manifold of sensation is arranged to treating it as a capacity of perceiving. Moreover, since Kant in this passage speaks of space as a perception, and thereby identifies space with the perception of it,[49] the confusion may be explained thus. The form of phenomena is said to be the space in which all sensations are arranged, or in which all bodies are; space, apart from all sensations or bodies, i. e. empty, being the object of a pure perception, is treated as identical with a pure perception, viz. the perception of empty space; and the perception of empty space is treated as identical with a capacity of perceiving that which is spatial.[50]

The existence of the confusion, however, is most easily realized by asking, 'How did Kant come to think of space and time as the *only* forms of perception?' It would seem obvious that the perception of *anything* implies a form of perception in the sense of a mode or capacity of perceiving. To perceive colours implies a capacity for seeing; to hear noises implies a capacity for hearing. And these capacities may fairly be called forms of perception. As soon as this is realized, the conclusion is inevitable that Kant was led to think of space and time as the only forms of perception, because in this connexion he was thinking of each as a form of phenomena, i. e. as something in which all bodies or their states are, or, from the point of view of our knowledge, as that in which sensuous material is to be arranged; for there is nothing except space and time in which such arrangement could plausibly be said to be carried out.

As has been pointed out, Kant's argument falls into two main parts, one of which prepares the way for the other. The aim of the former is to show *firstly* that our apprehension of space is *a priori*, and *secondly* that it belongs to perception and not to conception. The aim of the latter is to conclude from these characteristics of our apprehension of space that space is a property not of things in themselves but only of phenomena. These arguments may be considered in turn.

The really valid argument adduced by Kant for the *a priori* character of our apprehension of space is based on the nature of geometrical judgements. The universality of our judgements in geometry is not based upon experience, i. e. upon the observation of individual things in space. The necessity of geometrical relations is apprehended directly in virtue of the mind's own apprehending nature.

---

[49] Cf. p. 26, note 70.

[50] The same confusion (and due to the same cause) is implied *Prol.* § 11, and B. 42 (b), M. 26 (b) first paragraph. Cf. B. 49 (b), M. 30 (b).

Unfortunately in the present context Kant ignores this argument and substitutes two others, both of which are invalid.

1. "Space is no empirical conception[51] which has been derived from external[52] experiences. For in order that certain sensations may be related to something external to me (that is, to something in a different part of space from that in which I am), in like manner, in order that I may represent them as external to and next to each other, and consequently as not merely different but as in different places, the representation of space must already exist as a foundation. Consequently, the representation of space cannot be borrowed from the relations of external phenomena through experience; but, on the contrary, this external experience is itself first possible only through the said representation."[53] Here Kant is thinking that in order to apprehend, for example, that A is to the right of B we must first apprehend empty space. He concludes that our apprehension of space is *a priori*, because we apprehend empty space *before* we become aware of the spatial relations of individual objects in it.

To this the following reply may be made. (*a*) The term *a priori* applied to an apprehension should mean, not that it arises prior to experience, but that its validity is independent of experience. (*b*) That to which the term *a priori* should be applied is not the apprehension of empty space, which is individual, but the apprehension of the nature of space in general, which is universal. (*c*) We do not apprehend empty space before we apprehend individual spatial relations of individual bodies or, indeed, at any time. (*d*) Though we come to apprehend *a priori* the nature of space in general, the apprehension is not prior but posterior in time to the apprehension of individual spatial relations. (*e*) It does not follow from the temporal priority of our apprehension of individual spatial relations that our apprehension of the nature of space in general is 'borrowed from experience', and is therefore not *a priori.*

2. "We can never represent to ourselves that there is no space, though we can quite well think that no objects are found in it. It must, therefore, be considered as the condition of the possibility of phenomena, and not as a determination dependent upon them, and it is an *a priori* representation, which necessarily underlies external phenomena."[54]

Here the premise is simply false. If 'represent' or 'think' means 'believe', we can no more represent or think that there are no objects in space than that there is no space. If, on the other hand, 'represent' or 'think' means 'make a mental picture of', the assertion is equally false. Kant is thinking of empty space as a kind of receptacle for objects, and the *a priori* character of our apprehension of space lies, as before, in the supposed fact that in order to apprehend objects in space we must

[51] *Begriff* (conception) here is to be understood loosely not as something opposed to *Anschauung* (perception), but as equivalent to the genus of which *Anschauung* and *Begriff* are species, i. e. *Vorstellung,* which maybe rendered by 'representation' or 'idea', in the general sense in which these words are sometimes used to include 'thought' and 'perception'.

[52] The next sentence shows that 'external' means, not 'produced by something external to the mind', but simply 'spatial'.

[53] B. 38, M. 23-4.

[54] B. 38, M. 24.

begin with the apprehension of empty space.

The examination of Kant's arguments for the *perceptive* character of our apprehension of space is a more complicated matter. By way of preliminary it should be noticed that they presuppose the possibility in general of distinguishing features of objects which belong to the perception of them from others which belong to the conception of them. In particular, Kant holds that our apprehension of a body as a substance, as exercising force and as divisible, is due to our understanding as conceiving it, while our apprehension of it as extended and as having a shape is due to our sensibility as perceiving it.[55] The distinction, however, will be found untenable in principle; and if this be granted, Kant's attempt to distinguish in this way the extension and shape of an object from its other features can be ruled out on general grounds. In any case, it must be conceded that the arguments fail by which he seeks to show that space in particular belongs to perception.

There appears to be no way of distinguishing perception and conception as the apprehension of different realities[56] except as the apprehension of the individual and of the universal respectively. Distinguished in this way, the faculty of perception is that in virtue of which we apprehend the individual, and the faculty of conception is that power of reflection in virtue of which a universal is made the explicit object of thought.[57] If this be granted, the only test for what is perceived is that it is individual, and the only test for what is conceived is that it is universal. These are in fact the tests which Kant uses. But if this be so, it follows that the various characteristics of objects cannot be divided into those which are perceived and those which are conceived. For the distinction between universal and individual is quite general, and applies to all characteristics of objects alike. Thus, in the case of colour, we can distinguish colour in general and the individual colours of individual objects; or, to take a less ambiguous instance, we can distinguish a particular shade of redness and its individual instances. Further, it may be said that perception is of the individual shade of red of the individual object, and that the faculty by which we become explicitly aware of the particular shade of red in general is that of conception. The same distinction can be drawn with respect to hardness, or shape, or any other characteristic of objects. The distinction, then, between perception and conception can be drawn with respect to any characteristic of objects, and does not serve to distinguish one from another.

Kant's arguments to show that our apprehension of space belongs to perception are two in number, and both are directed to show not, as they should, that space is a *form* of perception, but that it is a *perception*.[58] The first runs thus: "Space

[55] B. 35, M. 22 (quoted pp. 20-21). It is noteworthy (1) that the passage contains no *argument* to show that extension and shape are not, equally with divisibility, *thought* to belong to an object, (2) that impenetrability, which is here said to belong to sensation, obviously cannot do so, and (3) that (as has been pointed out, pp. 20-21) the last sentence of the paragraph in question presupposes that we have a perception of empty space, and that this is a *form* of perception.

[56] And *not* as mutually involved in the apprehension of any individual reality.

[57] This distinction is of course different to that previously drawn *within* perception in the full sense between perception in a narrow sense and conception (pp. 14-15).

[58] Kant uses the phrase 'pure perception'; but 'pure' can only mean 'not containing

is no discursive, or, as we say, general conception of relations of things in general, but a pure perception. For, in the first place, we can represent to ourselves only one space, and if we speak of many spaces we mean thereby only parts of one and the same unique space. Again, these parts cannot precede the one all-embracing space as the component parts, as it were, out of which it can be composed, but can be thought only in it. Space is essentially one; the manifold in it, and consequently the general conception of spaces in general, rests solely upon limitations."[59]

Here Kant is clearly taking the proper test of perception. Its object, as being an individual, is unique; there is only one of it, whereas any conception has a plurality of instances. But he reaches his conclusion by supposing that we first perceive empty space and then become aware of its parts by dividing it. Parts of space are essentially limitations of the one space; therefore to apprehend them we must first apprehend space. And since space is *one*, it must be object of perception; in other words, space, in the sense of the one all-embracing space, i. e. the totality of individual spaces, is something perceived.

The argument appears open to two objections. In the *first* place, we do *not* perceive space as a whole, and then, by dividing it, come to apprehend individual spaces. We perceive individual spaces, or, rather, individual bodies occupying individual spaces.[60] We then apprehend that these spaces, as spaces, involve an infinity of other spaces. In other words, it is reflection on the general nature of space, the apprehension of which is involved in our apprehension of individual spaces or rather of bodies in space, which gives rise to the apprehension of the totality[61] of spaces, the apprehension being an act, not of perception, but of thought or conception. It is necessary, then, to distinguish (*a*) individual spaces, which we perceive; (*b*) the nature of space in general, of which we become aware by reflecting upon the character of perceived individual spaces, and which we conceive; (*c*) the totality of individual spaces, the thought of which we reach by considering the nature of space in general.

In the *second* place, the distinctions just drawn afford no ground for distinguishing space as something perceived from any other characteristic of objects as something conceived; for any other characteristic admits of corresponding distinctions. Thus, with respect to colour it is possible to distinguish (*a*) individual colours which we perceive; (*b*) colouredness in general, which we conceive by reflecting on the common character exhibited by individual colours and which involves various kinds or species of colouredness; (*c*) the totality of individual colours, the thought of which is reached by considering the nature of colouredness in general.[62]

Both in the case of colour and in that of space there is to be found the distinc-

---

sensation', and consequently adds nothing relevant.

[59] B. 39, M. 24. The concluding sentences of the paragraph need not be considered.

[60] This contention is not refuted by the objection that our distinct apprehension of an individual space is always bound up with an indistinct apprehension of the spaces immediately surrounding it. For our indistinct apprehension cannot be supposed to be of the whole of the surrounding space.

[61] It is here assumed that a whole or a totality can be infinite. Cf. p. 53.

[62] For a possible objection and the answer thereto, see note, p. 37.

tion between universal and individual, and therefore also that between conception and perception. It may be objected that after all, as Kant points out, there is only one space, whereas there are many individual colours. But the assertion that there is only one space simply means that all individual bodies in space are related spatially. This will be admitted, if the attempt be made to think of two bodies as in different spaces and therefore as not related spatially. Moreover, there is a parallel in the case of colour, since individual coloured bodies are related by way of colour, e. g. as brighter and duller; and though such a relation is different from a relation of bodies in respect of space, the difference is due to the special nature of the universals conceived, and does not imply a difference between space and colour in respect of perception and conception. In any case, space as a whole is not object of perception, which it must be if Kant is to show that space, as being one, is perceived; for space in this context must mean the totality of individual spaces.

Kant's second argument is stated as follows: "Space is represented as an infinite *given* magnitude. Now every conception must indeed be considered as a representation which is contained in an infinite number of different possible representations (as their common mark), and which therefore contains these *under itself*, but no conception can, as such, be thought of as though it contained *in itself* an infinite number of representations. Nevertheless, space is so conceived, for all parts of space *ad infinitum* exist simultaneously. Consequently the original representation of space is an *a priori perception* and not a *conception*." In other words, while a conception implies an infinity of individuals which come under it, the elements which constitute the conception itself (e. g. that of triangularity or redness) are not infinite; but the elements which go to constitute space are infinite, and therefore space is not a conception but a perception.

Though, however, space in the sense of the infinity of spaces may be said to contain an infinite number of spaces if it be meant that it *is* these infinite spaces, it does not follow, nor is it true, that space in this sense is object of perception.

The aim of the arguments just considered, and stated in § 2 of the *Aesthetic*, is to establish the two characteristics of our apprehension of space,[63] from which it is to follow that space is a property of things only as they appear to us and not as they are in themselves. This conclusion is drawn in § 4. §§ 2 and 4 therefore complete the argument. § 3, a passage added in the second edition of the *Critique*, interrupts the thought, for ignoring § 2, it once more establishes the *a priori* and perceptive character of our apprehension of space, and independently draws the conclusion drawn in § 4. Since, however, Kant draws the final conclusion in the same way in § 3 and in § 4, and since a passage in the *Prolegomena*,[64] of which § 3 is only a summary, gives a more detailed account of Kant's thought, attention should be concentrated on § 3, together with the passage in the *Prolegomena*.

It might seem at the outset that since the arguments upon which Kant bases the premises for his final argument have turned out invalid, the final argument itself need not be considered. The argument, however, of § 3 ignores the preceding arguments for the *a priori* and perceptive character of our apprehension of space.

[63] viz. that it is *a priori* and a pure perception.

[64] §§ 6-11.

It returns to the *a priori* synthetic character of geometrical judgements, upon which stress is laid in the Introduction, and appeals to this as the justification of the *a priori* and perceptive character of our apprehension of space.

The argument of § 3 runs as follows: "Geometry is a science which determines the properties of space synthetically and yet *a priori*. What, then, must be the representation of space, in order that such a knowledge of it may be possible? It must be originally perception, for from a mere conception no propositions can be deduced which go beyond the conception, and yet this happens in geometry. But this perception must be *a priori*, i. e. it must occur in us before all sense-perception of an object, and therefore must be pure, not empirical perception. For geometrical propositions are always apodeictic, i. e. bound up with the consciousness of their necessity (e. g. space has only three dimensions), and such propositions cannot be empirical judgements nor conclusions from them."

"Now how can there exist in the mind an external perception[65] which precedes[66] the objects themselves, and in which the conception of them can be determined *a priori*? Obviously not otherwise than in so far as it has its seat in the subject only, as the formal nature of the subject to be affected by objects and thereby to obtain *immediate representation*, i. e. *perception* of them, and consequently only as the form of the external sense in general."[67]

Here three steps are taken. From the *synthetic* character of geometrical judgements it is concluded that space is not something which we *conceive*, but something which we *perceive*. From their *a priori* character, i. e. from the consciousness of necessity involved, it is concluded that the perception of space must be *a priori* in a new sense, that of taking place *before* the perception of objects in it.[68] From the fact that we perceive space before we perceive objects in it, and thereby are able to anticipate the spatial relations which condition these objects, it is concluded that space is only a characteristic of our perceiving nature, and consequently that space is a property not of things in themselves, but only of things as perceived by us.[69]

Two points in this argument are, even on the face of it, paradoxical. Firstly, the term *a priori*, as applied not to geometrical judgements but to the perception of space, is given a temporal sense; it means not something whose validity is independent of experience and which is the manifestation of the nature of the mind, but something which takes place before experience. Secondly, the conclusion is not that the perception of space *is the manifestation of* the mind's perceiving nature, but that it *is* the mind's perceiving nature. For the conclusion is that space[70] is the

[65] 'External perception' can only mean perception of what is spatial.

[66] *Vorhergeht.*

[67] 'Formal nature *to be affected by objects*' is not relevant to the context.

[68] Cf. B. 42, M. 26 (a) fin., (b) second sentence.

[69] Cf. B. 43, M. 26-7.

[70] Kant draws no distinction between space and the perception of space, or, rather, habitually speaks of space as a perception. No doubt he considers that his view that space is only a characteristic of phenomena justifies the identification of space and the perception of it. Occasionally, however, he distinguishes them. Thus he sometimes speaks of the representation of space (e. g. B. 38-40, M. 23-4); in *Prol.*, § 11, he speaks of a pure perception of space and time; and in B. 40, M. 25, he says that our representation of space must be per-

formal nature of the subject to be affected by objects, and therefore the form of the external sense in general. Plainly, then, Kant here confuses an actual perception and a form or way of perceiving. These points, however, are more explicit in the corresponding passage in the *Prolegomena*.[71]

It begins thus: "Mathematics carries with it thoroughly apodeictic certainty, that is, absolute necessity, and, therefore, rests on no empirical grounds, and consequently is a pure product of reason, and, besides, is thoroughly synthetical. How, then, is it possible for human reason to accomplish such knowledge entirely *a priori*?. . . But we find that all mathematical knowledge has this peculiarity, that it must represent its conception previously in *perception*, and indeed *a priori*, consequently in a perception which is not empirical but pure, and that otherwise it cannot take a single step. Hence its judgements are always *intuitive*. . . . This observation on the nature of mathematics at once gives us a clue to the first and highest condition of its possibility, viz. that there must underlie it *a pure perception* in which it can exhibit or, as we say, *construct* all its conceptions in the concrete and yet *a priori*. If we can discover this pure perception and its possibility, we may thence easily explain how *a priori* synthetical propositions in pure mathematics are possible, and consequently also how the science itself is possible. For just as empirical perception enables us without difficulty to enlarge synthetically in experience the conception which we frame of an object of perception through new predicates which perception itself offers us, so pure perception also will do the same, only with the difference that in this case the synthetical judgement will be *a priori* certain and apodeictic, while in the former case it will be only *a posteriori* and empirically certain; for the latter [i. e. the empirical perception on which the *a posteriori* synthetic judgement is based] contains only that which is to be found in contingent empirical perception, while the former [i. e. the pure perception on which the *a priori* synthetic judgement is based] contains that which is bound to be found in pure perception, since, as *a priori* perception, it is inseparably connected with the conception *before all experience* or individual sense-perception."

This passage is evidently based upon the account which Kant gives in the *Doctrine of Method* of the method of geometry.[72] According to this account, in or-

ception. But this language is due to the pressure of the facts, and not to his general theory; cf. pp. 72-73.

[71] §§ 6-11.

[72] B. 740 ff., M. 434 ff. Compare especially the following: "*Philosophical* knowledge is *knowledge of reason* by means of *conceptions*; mathematical knowledge is knowledge by means of the *construction* of conceptions. But the *construction* of a conception means the *a priori* presentation of a perception corresponding to it. The construction of a conception therefore demands a *non-empirical* perception, which, therefore, as a perception, is an *individual* object, but which none the less, as the construction of a conception (a universal representation), must express in the representation universal validity for all possible perceptions which come under that conception. Thus I construct a triangle by presenting the object corresponding to the conception, either by mere imagination in pure perception, or also, in accordance with pure perception, on paper in empirical perception, but in both cases completely *a priori*, without having borrowed the pattern of it from any experience. The individual drawn figure is empirical, but nevertheless serves to indicate the conception without prejudice to its universality, because in this empirical perception we always attend

der to apprehend, for instance, that a three-sided figure must have three angles, we must draw in imagination or on paper an individual figure corresponding to the conception of a three-sided figure. We then see that the very nature of the act of construction involves that the figure constructed must possess three angles as well as three sides. Hence, perception being that by which we apprehend the individual, a perception is involved in the act by which we form a geometrical judgement, and the perception can be called *a priori*, in that it is guided by our *a priori* apprehension of the necessary nature of the act of construction, and therefore of the figure constructed.

The account in the *Prolegomena*, however, differs from that of the *Doctrine of Method* in one important respect. It asserts that the perception involved in a mathematical judgement not only may, but must, be pure, i. e. must be a perception in which no spatial object is present, and it implies that the perception must take place *before* all experience of actual objects.[73] Hence *a priori*, applied to perception, has here primarily, if not exclusively, the temporal meaning that the perception takes place *antecedently to all experience*.[74]

The thought of the passage quoted from the *Prolegomena* can be stated thus: 'A mathematical judgement implies the perception of an individual figure antecedently to all experience. This may be said to be the first condition of the possibility of mathematical judgements which is revealed by reflection. There is, however, a prior or higher condition. The perception of an individual figure involves as its basis another pure perception. For we can only construct and therefore perceive an individual figure in empty space. Space is that *in which* it must be constructed and perceived. A perception[75] of empty space is, therefore, necessary. If, then, we can discover how this perception is possible, we shall be able to explain the possibility of *a priori* synthetical judgements of mathematics.'

Kant continues as follows: "But with this step the difficulty seems to increase rather than to lessen. For henceforward the question is '*How is it possible to perceive anything a priori?*' A perception is such a representation as would immediately depend upon the presence of the object. Hence it seems impossible *originally* to perceive *a priori*, because perception would in that case have to take place without an object to which it might refer, present either formerly or at the moment, and accordingly could not be perception. . . . How can *perception* of the object precede the object itself?"[76] Kant here finds himself face to face with the difficulty created by the preceding section. Perception, as such, involves the actual presence of an object; yet the pure perception of space involved by geometry—which, as pure, is the perception of empty space, and which, as the perception of empty space, is *a priori* in the sense of temporally prior to the perception of actual objects—presupposes that an object is not actually present.

only to the act of construction of the conception, to which many determinations, e. g. the magnitude of the sides and of the angles, are wholly indifferent, and accordingly abstract from these differences, which do not change the conception of the triangle."

[73] This becomes more explicit in § 8 and ff.

[74] This is also, and more obviously, implied in §§ 8-11.

[75] *Pure* perception only means that the space perceived is empty.

[76] *Prol.* § 8.

The solution is given in the next section. "Were our perception necessarily of such a kind as to represent things *as they are in themselves,* no perception would take place *a priori*, but would always be empirical. For I can only know what is contained in the object in itself, if it is present and given to me. No doubt it is even then unintelligible how the perception of a present thing should make me know it as it is in itself, since its qualities cannot migrate over into my faculty of representation; but, even granting this possibility, such a perception would not occur *a priori,* i. e. before the object was presented to me; for without this presentation, no basis of the relation between my representation and the object can be imagined; the relation would then have to rest upon inspiration. It is therefore possible only in one way for my perception to precede the actuality of the object and to take place as *a priori* knowledge, viz. *if it contains nothing but the form of the sensibility, which precedes in me, the subject, all actual impressions through which I am affected by objects*. For I can know *a priori* that objects of the senses can only be perceived in accordance with this form of the sensibility. Hence it follows that propositions which concern merely this form of sensuous perception will be possible and valid for objects of the senses, and in the same way, conversely, that perceptions which are possible *a priori* can never concern any things other than objects of our senses."

This section clearly constitutes the turning-point in Kant's argument, and primarily expresses, in an expanded form, the central doctrine of § 3 of the *Aesthetic,* that an external perception anterior to objects themselves, and in which our conceptions of objects can be determined *a priori,* is possible, if, and only if, it has its seat in the subject as its formal nature of being affected by objects, and consequently as the form of the external sense in general. It argues that, since this is true, and since geometrical judgements involve such a perception anterior to objects, space must be only the[77] form of sensibility.

Now why does Kant think that this conclusion follows? Before we can answer this question we must remove an initial difficulty. In this passage Kant unquestionably identifies a form of perception with an actual perception. It is at once an actual perception and a capacity of perceiving. This is evident from the words, "It is possible only in one way for my perception to precede the actuality of the object . . . viz. *if it contains nothing but the form of the sensibility*."[78] The identification becomes more explicit a little later. "A pure perception (of space and time) can underlie the empirical perception of objects, because it is nothing but the mere form of the sensibility, which precedes the actual appearance of the objects, in that it in fact first makes them possible. Yet this faculty of perceiving *a priori* affects not the matter of the phenomenon, i. e. that in it which is sensation, for this constitutes that which is empirical, but only its form, viz. space and time."[79] His argument, however, can be successfully stated without this identification. It is only necessary to re-write his cardinal assertion in the form 'the perception of space must be nothing but the *manifestation* of the form of the sensibility'. Given this modification, the question becomes, 'Why does Kant think that the perception of empty space, involved by geometrical judgements, can be only a manifestation of our perceiv-

[77] *The* and not *a,* because, for the moment, time is ignored.

[78] *Prol.,* § 9.

[79] *Prol.,* § 11.

ing nature, and not in any way the apprehension of a real quality of objects?' The answer must be that it is because he thinks that, while in empirical perception a real object is present, in the perception of empty space a real object is not present. He regards this as proving that the latter perception is only of something subjective or mental. "Space and time, by being pure *a priori* perceptions, prove that they are mere forms of our sensibility which must precede all empirical perception, i. e. sense-perception of actual objects."[80] His main conclusion now follows easily enough. If in perceiving empty space we are only apprehending a manifestation of our perceiving nature, what we apprehend in a geometrical judgement is really a law of our perceiving nature, and therefore, while it *must* apply to our perceptions of objects or to objects as perceived, it *cannot* apply to objects apart from our perception, or, at least, there is no ground for holding that it does so.

If, however, this fairly represents Kant's thought, it must be allowed that the conclusion which he should have drawn is different, and even that the conclusion which he does draw is in reality incompatible with his starting-point.

His starting-point is the view that the truth of geometrical judgements presupposes a perception of empty space, in virtue of which we can discover rules of spatial relation which must apply to all spatial objects subsequently perceived. His problem is to discover the presupposition of this presupposition. The proper answer must be, not that space is a form of sensibility or a way in which objects appear to us, but that space is the form of all objects, i. e. that all objects are spatial.[81] For in that case they must be subject to the laws of space, and therefore if we can discover these laws by a study of empty space, the only condition to be satisfied, if the objects of subsequent perception are to conform to the laws which we discover, is that all objects should be spatial. Nothing is implied which enables us to decide whether the objects are objects as they are in themselves or objects as perceived; for in either case the required result follows. If in empirical perception we apprehend things only as they appear to us, and if space is the form of them as they appear to us, it will no doubt be true that the laws of spatial relation which we discover must apply to things as they appear to us. But on the other hand, if in empirical perception we apprehend things as they are, and if space is their form, i. e. if things are spatial, it will be equally true that the laws discovered by geometry must apply to things as they are.

Again, Kant's starting-point really commits him to the view that space is a characteristic of things as they are. For—paradoxical though it may be—his problem is to explain the possibility of *perceiving a priori,* i. e. of *perceiving* the characteristics of an object anterior to the actual presence of the object in perception.[82] This implies that *empirical* perception, which involves the actual presence of the object, involves no difficulty; in other words, it is implied that empirical perception is of objects as they are. And we find Kant admitting this to the extent of allowing *for*

[80] *Prol.,* § 10.

[81] Kant expresses the assertion that space is the form of all objects by saying that space is the form of *phenomena.* This of course renders easy an unconscious transition from the thesis that space is the form of objects to the quite different thesis that space is the form of sensibility; cf. pp. 20-21.

[82] Cf. *Prol.,* Section 8.

the sake of argument that the perception of a present thing can make us know the thing as it is in itself.[83] But if empirical perception gives us things as they are, and if, as is the case, and as Kant really presupposes, the objects of empirical perception are spatial, then, since space is their form, the judgements of geometry must relate to things as they are. It is true that on this view Kant's first presupposition of geometrical judgements has to be stated by saying that we are able to perceive a real characteristic of things in space, before we perceive the things; and, no doubt, Kant thinks this impossible. According to him, when we perceive empty space no object is present, and therefore what is before the mind must be merely mental. But no greater difficulty is involved than that involved in the corresponding supposition required by Kant's own view. It is really just as difficult to hold that we can perceive a characteristic of things as they appear to us *before* they appear, as to hold that we can perceive a characteristic of them as they are in themselves *before* we perceive them.

The fact is that the real difficulty with which Kant is grappling in the *Prolegomena* arises, not from the supposition that spatial bodies are things in themselves, but from the supposed presupposition of geometry that we must be able to perceive empty space before we perceive bodies in it. It is, of course, impossible to defend the perception of empty space, but *if* it be maintained, the space perceived must be conceded to be not, as Kant thinks, something mental or subjective, but a real characteristic of things. For, as has been pointed out, the paradox of pure perception is reached solely through the consideration that, while in empirical perception we perceive objects, in pure perception we do not, and since the objects of empirical perception are spatial, space must be a real characteristic of them.

The general result of the preceding criticism is that Kant's conclusion does not follow from the premises by which he supports it. It should therefore be asked whether it is not possible to take advantage of this hiatus by presenting the argument for the merely phenomenal character of space without any appeal to the possibility of perceiving empty space. For it is clear that what was primarily before Kant, in writing the *Critique,* was the *a priori* character of geometrical judgements themselves, and not the existence of a perception of empty space which they were held to presuppose.[84]

If, then, the conclusion that space is only the form of sensibility can be connected with the *a priori* character of geometrical judgements without presupposing the existence of a perception of empty space, his position will be rendered more

[83] *Prol.,* § 9 (cf. p. 29).

[84] The difficulty with which Kant is struggling in the *Prolegomena,* §§ 6-11, can be stated from a rather different point of view by saying that the thought that geometrical judgements imply a perception of empty space led him to apply the term '*a priori*' to perception as well as to judgement. The term, *a priori,* applied to judgements has a valid meaning; it means, not that the judgement is made prior to all experience, but that it is not based upon experience, being originated by the mind in virtue of its own powers of thinking. Applied to perception, however, '*a priori*' must mean prior to all experience, and, since the object of perception is essentially individual (cf. B. 741, M. 435), this use of the term gives rise to the impossible task of explaining how a perception can take place prior to the actual experience of an individual in perception (cf. *Prol.,* § 8).

plausible.

This can be done as follows. The essential characteristic of a geometrical judgement is not that it takes place prior to experience, but that it is not based upon experience. Thus a judgement, arrived at by an activity of the mind in which it remains within itself and does not appeal to actual experience of the objects to which the judgement relates, is implied to hold good of those objects. If the objects were things as they are in themselves, the validity of the judgement could not be justified, for it would involve the gratuitous assumption that a necessity of thought is binding on things which *ex hypothesi* are independent of the nature of the mind. If, however, the objects in question are things as perceived, they will be through and through conditioned by the mind's perceiving nature; and, consequently, if a geometrical rule, e. g. that a three-sided figure must have three angles, is really a law of the mind's perceiving nature, all individual perceptions, i. e. all objects as perceived by us, will necessarily conform to the law. Therefore, in the latter case, and in that only, will the universal validity of geometrical judgements be justified. Since, then, geometrical judgements are universally valid, space, which is that of which geometrical laws are the laws, must be merely a form of perception or a characteristic of objects as perceived by us.

This appears to be the best form in which the substance of Kant's argument, stripped of unessentials, can be stated. It will be necessary to consider both the argument and its conclusion.

The argument, so stated, is undeniably plausible. Nevertheless, examination of it reveals two fatal defects. In the first place, its starting-point is false. To Kant the paradox of geometrical judgements lies in the fact that they are not based upon an appeal to experience of the things to which they relate. It is implied, therefore, that judgements which are based on experience involve no paradox, and for the reason that in experience we apprehend things as they are.[85] In contrast with this, it is implied that in geometrical judgements the connexion which we apprehend is not real, i. e. does not relate to things as they are. Otherwise, there would be no difficulty; if in geometry we apprehended rules of connexion relating to things as they are, we could allow without difficulty that the things must conform to them. No such distinction, however, can be drawn between *a priori* and empirical judgements. For the necessity of connexion, e. g. between being a three-sided figure and being a three-angled figure, is as much a characteristic of things as the empirically-observed shape of an individual body, e. g. a table. Geometrical judgements, therefore, cannot be distinguished from empirical judgements on the ground that in the former the mind remains within itself, and does not immediately apprehend fact or a real characteristic of reality.[86] Moreover, since in a geometrical judgement we do in fact think that we are apprehending a real connexion, i. e. a connexion which applies to things and to things as they are in themselves, to question the reality of the connexion is to question the validity of thinking altogether, and to do this is implicitly to question the validity of our thought about the nature of

[85] Cf. p. 9.

[86] For the reasons which led Kant to draw this distinction between empirical and *a priori* judgements, cf. pp. 11-12.

our own mind, as well as the validity of our thought about things independent of the mind. Yet Kant's argument, in the form in which it has just been stated, presupposes that our thought is valid at any rate when it is concerned with our perceptions of things, even if it is not valid when concerned with the things as they are in themselves.

This consideration leads to the second criticism. The supposition that space is only a form of perception, even if it be true, *in no way assists* the explanation of the universal validity of geometrical judgements. Kant's argument really confuses a *necessity* of relation with the *consciousness of a necessity* of relation. No doubt, if it be a law of our perceiving nature that, whenever we perceive an object as a three-sided figure, the object as perceived contains three angles, it follows that any object as perceived will conform to this law; just as if it be a law of things as they are in themselves that three-sided figures contain three angles, all three-sided figures will in themselves have three angles. But what has to be explained is the universal applicability, not of a law, but of a judgement about a law. For Kant's real problem is to explain why *our judgement* that a three-sided figure must contain three angles must apply to all three-sided figures. Of course, if it be granted that in the judgement we apprehend the true law, the problem may be regarded as solved. But how are we to know that what we judge *is* the true law? The answer is in no way facilitated by the supposition that the judgement relates to our perceiving nature. It can just as well be urged that what we think to be a necessity of our perceiving nature is not a necessity of it, as that what we think to be a necessity of things as they are in themselves is not a necessity of them. The best, or rather the only possible, answer is simply that that of which we apprehend the necessity must be true, or, in other words, that we *must* accept the validity of thought. Hence nothing is gained by the supposition that space is a form of sensibility. If what we judge to be necessary is, as such, valid, a judgement relating to things in themselves will be as valid as a judgement relating to our perceiving nature.[87]

This difficulty is concealed from Kant by his insistence on the *perception* of space involved in geometrical judgements. This leads him at times to identify the judgement and the perception, and, therefore, to speak of the judgement as a perception. Thus we find him saying that mathematical judgements are always *perceptive,*[88] and that "It is only possible for my perception to precede the actuality of the object and take place as *a priori* knowledge, if &c."[89] Hence, if, in addition, a geometrical judgement, as being a judgement about a necessity, be identified with a necessity of judging, the conformity of things to these universal judgements

[87] The same criticism can be urged against Kant's appeal to the necessity of *constructing* geometrical figures. The conclusion drawn from the necessity of construction is stated thus: "If the object (the triangle) were something in itself without relation to you the subject, how could you say that that which lies necessarily in your subjective conditions of constructing a triangle must also necessarily belong to the triangle in itself?" (B. 65, M. 39). Kant's thought is that the laws of the mind's constructing nature must apply to objects, if, and only if, the objects are the mind's own construction. Hence it is open to the above criticism if, in the criticism, 'construct' be substituted for 'perceive'.

[88] *Prol.*, § 7.

[89] *Prol.*, § 9.

will become the conformity of things to rules or necessities of our judging, i. e. of our perceiving nature, and Kant's conclusion will at once follow.[90] Unfortunately for Kant, a geometrical judgement, however closely related to a perception, must itself, as the apprehension of what is necessary and universal, be an act of thought rather than of perception, and therefore the original problem of the conformity of things to our mind can be forced upon him again, even after he thinks that he has solved it, in the new form of that of the conformity within the mind of perceiving to thinking.

The fact is simply that the universal validity of geometrical judgements can in no way be 'explained'. It is not in the least explained or made easier to accept by the supposition that objects are 'phenomena'. These judgements must be accepted as being what we presuppose them to be in making them, viz. the direct apprehension of necessities of relation between real characteristics of real things. To explain them by reference to the phenomenal character of what is known is really—though contrary to Kant's intention—to throw doubt upon their validity; otherwise, they would not need explanation. As a matter of fact, it is *impossible* to question their validity. In the act of judging, doubt is impossible. Doubt can arise only when we subsequently reflect and temporarily lose our hold upon the consciousness of necessity in judging.[91] The doubt, however, since it is non-existent in our geometrical consciousness, is really groundless,[92] and, therefore, the problem to which it gives rise is unreal. Moreover if, *per impossibile,* doubt could be raised, it could not be set at rest. No vindication of a judgement in which we are conscious of a necessity could do more than take the problem a stage further back, by basing it upon some other consciousness of a necessity; and since this latter judgement could be questioned for precisely the same reason, we should only be embarking upon an infinite process.

We may now consider Kant's conclusion in abstraction from the arguments by which he reaches it. It raises three main difficulties.

In the first place, it is not the conclusion to be expected from Kant's own standpoint. The phenomenal character of space is inferred, not from the fact that we make judgements at all, but from the fact that we make judgements of a particular kind, viz. *a priori* judgements. From this point of view empirical judgements present no difficulty. It should, therefore, be expected that the qualities which we attribute to things in empirical judgements are not phenomenal, but belong to things as they are. Kant himself implies this in drawing his conclusion concerning the nature of space. "Space does not represent any quality of things in themselves or things in relation to one another; that is, it does not represent any determination of things which would attach to the objects themselves and would remain, even though we abstracted from all subjective conditions of perception. For neither ab-

[90] Cf. (*Introduction,* B. xvii, M. xxix): "But if the object (as object of the senses) conforms to the nature of our faculty of perception, I can quite well represent to myself the possibility of *a priori* knowledge of it [i. e. mathematical knowledge]."

[91] Cf. Descartes, *Princ. Phil.* i. § 13, and *Medit.* v sub fin.

[92] The view that kinds of space other than that with which we are acquainted are possible, though usually held and discussed by mathematicians, belongs to them *qua* metaphysicians, and not *qua* mathematicians.

solute nor relative[93] determinations of objects can be perceived prior to the existence of the things to which they belong, and therefore not *a priori*."[94] It is, of course, implied that in experience, where we do not discover determinations of objects prior to the existence of the objects, we do apprehend determinations of things as they are in themselves, and not as they are in relation to us. Thus we should expect the conclusion to be, not that all that we know is phenomenal—which is Kant's real position—but that spatial (and temporal) relations alone are phenomenal, i. e. that they alone are the result of a transmutation due to the nature of our perceiving faculties.[95] This conclusion would, of course, be absurd, for what Kant considers to be the empirically known qualities of objects disappear, if the spatial character of objects is removed. Moreover, Kant is prevented by his theory of perception from seeing that this is the real solution of his problem, absurd though it may be. Since perception is held to arise through the origination of sensations by things in themselves, empirical knowledge is naturally thought of as knowledge about sensations, and since sensations are palpably within the mind, and are held to be due to things in themselves, knowledge about sensations can be regarded as phenomenal.

On the other hand, if we consider Kant's conclusion from the point of view, not of the problem which originates it, but of the distinction in terms of which he states it, viz. that between things as they are in themselves and things as perceived by us, we are led to expect the contrary result. Since perception is the being affected by things, and since the nature of the affection depends upon the nature of our capacity of being affected, in *all* perception the object will become distorted or transformed, as it were, by our capacity of being affected. The conclusion, therefore, should be that in all judgements, empirical as well as *a priori*, we apprehend things only as perceived. The reason why Kant does not draw this conclusion is probably that given above, viz. that by the time Kant reaches the solution of his problem empirical knowledge has come to relate to sensation only; consequently, it has ceased to occur to him that empirical judgements could possibly give us knowledge of things as they are. Nevertheless, Kant should not have retained in his formulation of the problem a distinction irreconcilable with his solution of it; and if he had realized that he was doing so he might have been compelled to modify his whole view.

[93] The first sentence shows that 'relative determinations' means, not 'determinations of objects in relation to us', but 'determinations of objects in relation to one another.' Cf. B. 37, M. 23; and B. 66 fin., 67 init., M. 40 (where these meanings are confused).

[94] B. 42, M. 26.

[95] This conclusion is also to be expected because, inconsistently with his real view, Kant is here (B. 41-2, M. 25-6) under the influence of the presupposition of our ordinary consciousness that in perception we are confronted by things in themselves, known to be spatial, and not by appearances produced by unknown things in themselves. Cf. (B. 41, M. 25) "and thereby of obtaining immediate representation of them [i. e. objects];" and (B. 42, M. 26) "the receptivity of the subject to be affected by objects necessarily precedes all perceptions of these objects." These sentences identify things in themselves and bodies in space, and thereby imply that in empirical perception we perceive things in themselves and as they *are*.

The second difficulty is more serious. If the truth of geometrical judgements presupposes that space is only a property of objects as perceived by us, it is a paradox that geometricians should be convinced, as they are, of the truth of their judgements. They undoubtedly think that their judgements apply to things as they are in themselves, and not merely as they appear to us. They certainly do not think that the relations which they discover apply to objects only as perceived. Not only, therefore, do they not think that bodies in space are phenomena, but they do not even leave it an open question whether bodies are phenomena or not. Hence, if Kant be right, they are really in a state of illusion, for on his view the true geometrical judgement should include in itself the phenomenal character of spatial relations; it should be illustrated by expressing Euclid I. 5 in the form that the equality of the angles at the base of an isosceles triangle belongs to objects as perceived. Kant himself lays this down. "The proposition 'all objects are beside one another in space' is valid under[96] the limitation that these things are taken as objects of our sensuous perception. If I join the condition to the perception, and say 'all things, as external phenomena, are beside one another in space', the rule is valid universally, and without limitation."[97] Kant, then, is in effect allowing that it is possible for geometricians to make judgements, of the necessity of which they are convinced, and yet to be wrong; and that, therefore, the apprehension of the necessity of a judgement is no ground of its truth. It follows that the truth of geometrical judgements can no longer be accepted as a starting-point of discussion, and, therefore, as a ground for inferring the phenomenal character of space.

There seems, indeed, one way of avoiding this consequence, viz. to suppose that for Kant it was an absolute starting-point, which nothing would have caused him to abandon, that only those judgements of which we apprehend the necessity are true. It would, of course, follow that geometricians would be unable to apprehend the necessity of geometrical judgements, and therefore to make such judgements, until they had discovered that things as spatial were only phenomena. It would not be enough that they should think that the phenomenal or non-phenomenal character of things as spatial must be left an open question for the theory of knowledge to decide. In this way the necessity of admitting the illusory character of geometry would be avoided. The remedy, however, is at least as bad as the disease. For it would imply that geometry must be preceded by a theory of knowledge, which is palpably contrary to fact. Nor could Kant accept it; for he avowedly bases his theory of knowledge, i. e. his view that objects as spatial are phenomena, upon the truth of geometry; this procedure would be circular if the making of true geometrical judgements was allowed to require the prior adoption of his theory of knowledge.

The third difficulty is the most fundamental. Kant's conclusion (and also, of course, his argument) presupposes the validity of the distinction between phenomena and things in themselves. If, then, this distinction should prove untenable in principle, Kant's conclusion with regard to space must fail on general grounds, and it will even have been unnecessary to consider his arguments for it. The importance of the issue, however, requires that it should be considered in a separate

[96] A. reads 'only under'

[97] B. 43, M. 27.

chapter.

NOTE TO PAGE 24.

The argument is not affected by the contention that, while the totality of spaces is infinite, the totality of colours or, at any rate, the totality of instances of some other characteristic of objects is finite; for this difference will involve no difference in respect of perception and conception. In both cases the apprehension that there is a totality will be reached in the same way, i. e. through the *conception* of the characteristic in general, and the apprehension in the one case that the totality is infinite and in the other that it is finite will depend on the apprehension of the special nature of the characteristic in question.

CHAPTER IV

PHENOMENA AND THINGS IN THEMSELVES

THE distinction between phenomena and things in themselves can be best approached by considering Kant's formulation of the alternative views of the nature of space and time. "What are space and time? Are they real existences? Or are they merely determinations or relations of things, such, however, as would also belong to them in themselves, even if they were not perceived, or are they attached to the form of perception only, and consequently to the subjective nature of our mind, without which these predicates can never be attributed to any thing?"[98]

Of these three alternatives, the first can be ignored. It is opposed to the second, and is the view that space and time are things rather than relations between things. This opposition falls within the first member of the wider opposition between things as they are in themselves and things as they are as perceived, and Kant, and indeed any one, would allow that if space and time belong to things as they are in themselves and not to things only as perceived, they are relations between things rather than things. The real issue, therefore, lies between the second and third alternatives. Are space and time relations between things which belong to them both in themselves and also as perceived by us, or are they relations which belong to things only as perceived?

To this question we may at once reply that, inasmuch as it involves an impossible antithesis, it is wholly unreal. The thought of a property or a relation which belongs to things as perceived involves a contradiction. To take Plato's example, suppose that we are looking at a straight stick, partially immersed in water. If we have not previously seen the stick, and are ignorant of the laws of refraction, we say that the stick is bent. If, however, we learn the effect of refraction, and observe the stick from several positions, we alter our assertion. We say that the stick is not really bent, but only looks or appears bent to us. But, if we reflect at all, we do not express our meaning by saying that the stick *is* bent to us as perceiving, though not in reality.[99] The word 'is' essentially relates to what really is. If, therefore, the phrase 'to us as perceiving' involves an opposition to the phrase 'in reality', as it must if it is to be a real qualification of 'is', it cannot rightly be added to the word 'is'. To put the matter more explicitly, the assertion that something *is* so and so implies that it is so and so in itself, whether it be perceived or not, and therefore

[98] B. 37, M. 23.

[99] Similarly, we do not say—if we mean what we say—of a man who is colour blind that an object which others call blue *is* pink to him or to his perception, but that it *looks* pink to him.

the assertion that something is so and so to us as perceiving, though not in itself, is a contradiction in terms. The phrase 'to us as perceiving', as a restriction upon the word 'is', merely takes back the precise meaning of the word 'is'. That to which the phrase can be added is not the word 'is', but the word 'looks' or 'appears'. We can rightly say that the stick looks or appears bent to us as perceiving. But even then the addition only helps to make explicit the essential meaning of 'appears', for 'appears' really means 'appears to us', and 'as perceiving' only repeats the meaning of 'appears' from the side of the perceiving subject as opposed to that of the object perceived. The essential point, however, is thereby brought out that the phrase 'to us as perceiving' essentially relates not to what a thing is, but to what it looks or appears to us.

What, then, is the proper statement of Kant's view that space is a determination of things only as they appear to us, and not as they are in themselves? It should be said that things are not in reality spatial, but only look or appear spatial to us. It should not be said that they *are* spatial for our perception, though not in themselves. Thus the view properly stated implies that space is an illusion, inasmuch as it is not a real property of things at all. This implication, however, is precisely the conclusion which Kant wishes to avoid. He takes infinite trouble to explain that he does not hold space and time to be illusions.[100] Though *transcendentally ideal* (i. e. though they do not belong to things in themselves), they are *empirically real*. In other words, space and time are real relations of *something*, though not of things in themselves.

How, then, does Kant obtain something of which space and time can be regarded as really relations? He reaches it by a transition which at first sight seems harmless. In stating the fact of perception he substitutes for the assertion that things appear so and so to us the assertion that things produce appearances in us. In this way, instead of an assertion which relates to the thing and states what it is not but only appears, he obtains an assertion which introduces a second reality distinct from the thing, viz. an appearance or phenomenon, and thereby he gains something other than the thing to which space can be attached as a real predicate. He thus gains something in respect of which, with regard to spatial relations we can be said to have *knowledge* and not illusion. For the position now is that space, though not a property of things in themselves, *is* a property of phenomena or appearances; in other words, that while things in themselves are not spatial, phenomena and appearances *are* spatial. As evidence of this transition, it is enough to point out that, while he states the *problem* in the form 'Are things in themselves spatial or are they only spatial as appearing to us?'[101] he usually states the *conclusion* in the form 'Space is the form of phenomena', i. e. phenomena are spatial. A transition is thereby implied from 'things as appearing' to 'appearances'. At the same time, it is clear that Kant is not aware of the transition, but considers the expressions equivalent, or, in other words, fails to distinguish them. For both modes of stating the conclusion are to be found even in the same sentence. "This predicate [space] is applied to things only in so far as they appear to us, i. e. are objects of sensibility [i.

[100] B. 44, 52, 53-4, 62-3, 69-70; M. 27, 31-2, 37-8, 41-2; *Prol.*, § 13, Remark iii.

[101] This is Kant's way of putting the question which should be expressed by asking, 'Are things spatial, or do they only look spatial?'

e. phenomena]."[102] Again, the common phrase 'things as phenomena' implies the same confusion. Moreover, if Kant had realized that the transition was more than one of phraseology he must have seen that it was necessary to recast his argument.

It may be said, then, that Kant is compelled to end with a different distinction from that with which he begins. He begins with the distinction between things as they are in themselves and things as they appear to us, the distinction relating to one and the same reality regarded from two different points of view. He ends with the distinction between two different realities, things-in-themselves,[103] external to, in the sense of independent of, the mind, and phenomena or appearances within it. Yet if his *argument* is to be valid, the two distinctions should be identical, for it is the first distinction to which the argument appeals.[104] In fact, we find him expressing what is to him the same distinction now in the one way and now in the other as the context requires.

The final form of Kant's conclusion, then, is that while things in themselves are not, or, at least, cannot be known to be spatial, 'phenomena,' or the appearances produced in us by things in themselves, are spatial. Unfortunately, the conclusion in this form is no more successful than it is in the former form, that things are spatial only as perceived. Expressed by the formula 'phenomena are spatial', it has, no doubt, a certain plausibility; for the word 'phenomena' to some extent conceals the essentially mental character of what is asserted to be spatial. But the plausibility disappears on the substitution of 'appearances'—the true equivalent of Kant's *Erscheinungen*—for 'phenomena'. Just as it is absurd to describe the fact that the stick only looks bent by saying that, while the stick is not bent, the appearance which it produces is bent, so it is, even on the face of it, nonsense to say that while things are not spatial, the appearances which they produce in us are spatial. For an 'appearance', being necessarily something mental, cannot possibly be said to be extended. Moreover, it is really an abuse of the term 'appearance' to speak of appearances *produced by* things, for this phrase implies a false severance of the appearance from the things which appear. If there are 'appearances' at all, they are appearances *of* things and not appearances *produced by* them. The importance of the distinction lies in the difference of implication. To speak of appearances produced by things is to imply that the object of perception is merely something mental, viz. an appearance. Consequently, access to a non-mental reality is excluded; for a perception of which the object is something belonging to the mind's own being cannot justify an inference to something beyond the mind, and the result is inevitably solipsism. On the other hand, the phrase 'appearances of things', whatever defects it may have, at least implies that it is a non-mental reality which appears, and therefore that in perception we are in direct relation to it; the phrase, therefore, does not imply from the very beginning that the apprehension of a non-mental reality is impossible.

The objection will probably be raised that this criticism is much too summary. We do, it will be said, distinguish in ordinary consciousness between appearance

[102] B. 43, M. 26. Cf. *Prol.*, § 9 fin. with § 10 init.

[103] It should be noticed that 'things-in-themselves' and 'things as they are in themselves' have a different meaning.

[104] Cf. p. 29 and ff.

and reality. Consequently there must be some form in which Kant's distinction between things in themselves and phenomena and the conclusion based upon it are justified. Moreover, Kant's reiterated assertion that his view does not imply that space is an illusion, and that the distinction between the real and the illusory is possible *within* phenomena, requires us to consider more closely whether Kant may not after all be entitled to hold that space is not an illusion.[105]

This objection is, of course, reasonable. No one can satisfy himself of the justice of the above criticisms until he has considered the real nature of the distinction between appearance and reality. This distinction must, therefore, be analysed. But before this is done it is necessary, in order to discover the real issue, to formulate the lines on which Kant may be defended. 'The reality,' it may be urged, 'which ideally we wish to know must be admitted to exist *in itself*, in the sense of independently of the perception, and consequently its nature must be admitted to be independent of perception. Ideally, then, our desire is to know things[106] as they are in themselves, a desire sufficiently expressed by the assertion that we desire to know things, for to know them is to know them as they are, i. e. as they are independently of perception. Again, since the reality which we desire to know consists of individuals, and since the apprehension of an individual implies perception, knowledge of reality requires perception. If in perception we apprehended reality as it is, no difficulty would arise. But we do not, for we are compelled to distinguish what things are, and what they look or appear; and what they appear essentially relates to perception. We perceive them as they look or appear and, therefore, not as they are, for what they look and what they are are *ex hypothesi* distinguished. And this fact constitutes a fatal obstacle to knowledge in general. We cannot know anything as it *is*. At least the negative side of Kant's position must be justified. We never can know things as they are in themselves. What then do we know? Two alternative answers may be given. It may be held that the positive side of Kant's position, though indefensible in the form that we know things as they appear to us, is valid in the form that we know what things look or appear. This, no doubt, implies that our ordinary beliefs about reality are illusory, for what things look is *ex hypothesi* different from what they are. But the implication does not constitute an important departure from Kant's view. For in any case only that is knowledge proper which relates to things as they are, and therefore the supposed knowledge of things as they appear may be discarded without serious loss. On the other hand, it may be held that the positive side of Kant's position can be vindicated in the form that, while we do not know things in themselves,[107] we do know the appearances which they produce in us. It is true that this view involves

[105] Cf. p. 49 and ff.

[106] 'Things' is substituted for 'the reality which we believe to exist independently of perception' in order to conform to Kant's language. The substitution, of course, has the implication—which Kant took for granted—that the reality consists of a plurality of individuals.

[107] 'Things in themselves' has here to be substituted for 'things as they are in themselves' in the statement of the negative side of the position, in order to express the proper antithesis, which is now that between two things, the one known and the other unknown, and not that between two points of view from which one and the same thing is known and not known respectively.

the difficulty of maintaining that appearances are spatial, but the difficulty is not insuperable. Moreover, in this form the doctrine has the advantage that, unlike the former, it does not imply that the knowledge which we have is only of illusions, for instead of implying that our knowledge is merely knowledge of what things look but really are not, it implies that we know the real nature of realities of another kind, viz. of appearances. Again, in this form of the view, it may be possible to vindicate Kant's doctrine that the distinction between the real and the illusory is tenable within what we know, for it may be possible to distinguish within appearances between a 'real' appearance[108] and an 'illusory' appearance.[109]'

An implication of this defence should be noticed. The issue relates to the nature of space[110], and may be stated in terms of it. For, since space is a presupposition of all other properties which the non-philosophical consciousness attributes to physical things, it makes no difference whether we say that things *only appear* heavy, hard, in motion, &c., or whether we say that things *only appear* spatial. In the same way it is a matter of indifference whether we say that, though things are not heavy, hard, &c., their appearances are so, or whether we say that, though things are not spatial, their appearances are so. The issue, then, concerns the possibility of maintaining either that things only appear spatial, or that the appearances which they produce are spatial, while the things themselves are not, or, at least cannot be known to be, spatial.

The tenability of these alternative positions has to be considered apart from the argument of the *Aesthetic*, for this, as we have seen, breaks down. At the outset it is important to realize that these positions are the product of philosophical reflection, and constitute general theories of knowledge. As has been pointed out, the distinction between appearance and reality first arises in our ordinary or scientific consciousness.[111] In this consciousness we are compelled to distinguish between appearance and reality with respect to the details of a reality which, as a whole, or, in principle, we suppose ourselves to know. Afterwards in our philosophical consciousness we come to reflect upon this distinction and to raise the question whether it is not applicable to reality as a whole. We ask with respect to knowledge in general, and not merely with respect to certain particular items of knowledge, whether we know or can know reality, and not merely appearance. The two positions just stated are alternative ways of answering the question in the negative. They are, then, philosophical views based upon a distinction found in our ordinary consciousness. Consequently, in order to decide whether the distinction will bear the superstructure placed upon it by the philosophical consciousness, it is necessary to examine the distinction as it exists in our ordinary consciousness.

The distinction is applied in our ordinary consciousness both to the primary and to the secondary qualities of matter, i. e. to the size, shape, position and motion of physical bodies, and to their colour, warmth, &c. We say, for instance, that

[108] *Erscheinung.*

[109] *Schein.*

[110] We might add time also; but, for a reason which will appear later (p. 74), it can be neglected.

[111] I. e. the consciousness for which the problems are those of science as opposed to philosophy.

the moon looks[112] or appears as large as the sun, though really it is much smaller. We say that railway lines, though parallel, look convergent, just as we say that the straight stick in water looks bent. We say that at sunset the sun, though really below the horizon, looks above it. Again, we say that to a person who is colour blind the colour of an object looks different to what it really is, and that the water into which we put our hand may be warmer than it appears to our touch.

The case of the primary qualities may be considered first. Since the instances are identical in principle, and only differ in complexity, it will be sufficient to analyse the simplest, that of the apparent convergence of the railway lines.

Two points at once force themselves upon our notice. In the first place, we certainly suppose that we perceive the reality which we wish to know, i. e. the reality which, as we suppose, exists independently of our perception, and not an 'appearance' of it. It is, as we say, the real lines which we see. Even the term 'convergent', in the assertion that the lines look convergent, conveys this implication. For 'convergent' is essentially a characteristic not of an appearance but of a reality, in the sense in which something independent of perception may be opposed as a reality to an 'appearance', which, as such, presupposes perception. We can say neither that an appearance is convergent, nor that the appearance of the lines is convergent. Only a reality similar to the lines, e. g. two roads, can be said to be convergent. Our ordinary thought, therefore, furnishes no ground for the view that the object of perception is not the thing, but merely an appearance of or produced by it. In the second place, the assertion that the lines *look* convergent implies considerable knowledge of the real nature of the reality to which the assertion relates. Both the terms 'lines' and 'convergent' imply that the reality *is* spatial. Further, if the context is such that we mean that, while the lines look convergent, we do not know their real relation, we imply that the lines really possess some characteristic which falls within the genus to which convergence belongs, i. e. we imply that they are convergent, divergent, or parallel. If, on the other hand, the context is such that we mean that the lines only look convergent, we imply that the lines are parallel, and therefore presuppose complete knowledge in respect of the very characteristic in regard to which we state what is only appearance. The assertion, then, in respect of a primary quality, that a thing looks so and so implies knowledge of its general character as spatial, and ignorance only of a detail; and the assertion that a thing only looks or appears so and so implies knowledge of the detail in question.

Attention may now be drawn to a general difficulty which may be raised with respect to the use of the terms 'looks' and 'appears'. It may be stated thus: 'If the lines are not convergent, how is it possible even to say that they *look* convergent? Must it not be implied that at least under *certain* circumstances we should perceive the lines as they are? Otherwise, why should we use the words 'look' or 'appear' at all? Moreover, this implication can be pushed further; for if we maintain that we perceive the real lines, we may reasonably be asked whether we must not under *all* circumstances perceive them as they are. It seems as though a reality cannot be perceived except as it is.' It is the view to which this difficulty gives rise which is

[112] 'Looks' means 'appears to sight', and 'looks' is throughout used as synonymous with 'appear', where the instance under discussion relates to visual perception.

mainly responsible for the doctrine that the object of perception is not the reality, but an appearance. Since we do distinguish between what things look and what they are, it would seem that the object of perception cannot be the thing, but only an appearance produced by it. Moreover, the doctrine gains in plausibility from the existence of certain illusions in the case of which the reality to which the illusion relates seems non-existent. For instance, if we look steadily at the flame of a candle, and then press one eyeball with a finger, we see, as we say, two candles;[113] but since *ex hypothesi* there is only one candle, it seems that what we see must be, not the candle, but two images or appearances produced by it.

This difficulty is raised in order to draw attention to the fact that, in the case of the railway lines, where it can be met on its own ground[114], this is because, and only because, we believe space to be 'real', i. e. to be a characteristic of reality, and because we understand its nature. The distinction between the actual and the apparent angle made by two straight lines presupposes a limiting case in which they coincide. If the line of sight along which we observe the point of intersection of two lines is known to be at right angles to both lines, we expect, and rightly expect, to see the angle of intersection as it is. Again, if we look at a short portion of two railway lines from a point known to be directly above them, and so distant that the effects of perspective are imperceptible, we can say that the lines look what they are, viz. parallel. Thus, from the point of view of the difficulty which has been raised, there is this justification in general for saying that two lines *look* parallel or *look* at right angles, that we know that in certain cases what they look is identical with what they are. In the same way, assertions of the type that the moon *looks* as large as the sun receive justification from our knowledge that two bodies of equal size and equally distant from the observer *are* what they look, viz. of the same size. And in both cases the justification presupposes knowledge of the reality of space and also such insight into its nature as enables us to see that in certain cases there must be an identity between what things look and what they are in respect of certain spatial relations. Again, in such cases we see that so far is it from being necessary to think that a thing must be perceived as it is, that it is not only possible but necessary to distinguish what a thing looks from what it is, and precisely in consequence of the nature of space. The visual perception of spatial relations from its very nature presupposes a particular point of view. Though the perception itself cannot be spatial, it presupposes a particular point in space as a standpoint or point of view,[115] and is therefore subject to conditions of perspective. This is best realized by considering the supposition that perfect visual powers would enable us to see the whole of a body at once, and that this perception would be possible if we had eyes situated all round the body. The supposition obviously breaks down through the impossibility of combining two or more points of view in one perception. But if visual perception is necessarily subject to conditions of perspective, the spatial relations of bodies can never look what they are except in the limiting case

[113] Cf. Dr. Stout, on 'Things and Sensations' (*Proceedings of the British Academy,* vol. ii).

[114] Cf., however, p. 46 and pp. 46-48.

[115] This is, of course, not refuted by the reminder that we see with two eyes, and that these are in different places.

referred to. Moreover, this distinction is perfectly intelligible, as we should expect from the necessity which we are under of drawing it. We understand perfectly why it is that bodies must, in respect of their spatial relations, look different to what they are, and we do so solely because we understand the nature of space, and therefore also the conditions of perspective involved in the perception of what is spatial. It is, therefore, needless to make the assertion 'Two lines appear convergent' intelligible by converting the verb 'appears' into a substantive, viz. an 'appearance', and then making the assertion relate to an 'appearance'. For—apart from the fact that this would not achieve the desired end, since no suitable predicate could be found for the appearance—the assertion that the lines *look* or *appear* convergent is perfectly intelligible in itself, though not capable of being stated in terms of anything else.[116] If we generalize this result, we may say that the distinction between appearance and reality, drawn with regard to the primary qualities of bodies, throughout presupposes the reality of space, and is made possible, and indeed necessary, by the nature of space itself.

We may now turn to the way in which we draw the distinction with respect to the secondary qualities of physical things. It must, it seems, be admitted that in our ordinary consciousness we treat these qualities as real qualities of bodies. We say that a bell is noisy; that sugar is sweet; that roses smell; that a mustard plaster is hot; that the sky is blue. It must also be admitted that in our ordinary consciousness we draw a distinction between appearance and reality *within* these qualities, just as we do *within* the primary qualities. Just as we speak of the right or real shape of a body, so we speak of its right or real colour, taste, &c., and distinguish these from its apparent colours, taste, &c., to some individual. We thereby imply that these qualities are real qualities of bodies, and that the only difficulty is to determine the particular character of the quality in a given case. Yet, as the history of philosophy shows, it takes but little reflection to throw doubt on the reality of these qualities. The doubt arises not merely from the apparent impossibility of finding a principle by which to determine the right or real quality in a given case, but also and mainly from misgivings as to the possible reality of heat, smell, taste, noise, and colour apart from a percipient. It must also be admitted that this misgiving is well founded; in other words, that these supposed real qualities do presuppose a percipient, and therefore cannot be qualities of things, since the qualities of a thing must exist independently of the perception of the thing.[117] This will readily be allowed in the case of all the secondary qualities except colour. No one, it may reasonably be said, who is familiar with and really faces the issue, will maintain that sounds, smells, tastes, and sensations of touch exist apart from a sensitive subject. So much is this the case, that when once the issue is raised, it is difficult and, in the end, impossible to use the word 'appear' in connexion with these qualities. Thus it is difficult and,

[116] It is important to notice that the proper formula to express what is loosely called 'an appearance' is 'A looks or appears B', and that this cannot be analysed into anything more simple and, in particular, into a statement about 'appearances'. Even in the case of looking at the candle, there is no need to speak of two 'appearances' or 'images'. Before we discover the truth, the proper assertion is 'The body which we perceive looks as if it were two candles', and, after we discover the truth, the proper assertion is 'The candle looks as if it were in two places'.

[117] Cf. pp. 38-39, and 48.

in the end, impossible to say that a bell *appears* noisy, or that sugar *appears* sweet. We say, rather, that the bell and the sugar produce certain sensations[118] in us.

The case of colour, however, is more difficult. From the closeness of its relation to the shape of bodies, it seems to be a real quality of bodies, and not something relative to a sensitive subject like the other secondary qualities. In fact, so intimate seems the relation of colour to the shape of bodies, that it would seem—as has, of course, often been argued—that if colour be relative to a sensitive subject, the primary qualities of bodies must also be relative to a sensitive subject, on the ground that shape is inseparable from colour.[119] Yet whether this be so or not, it must, in the end, be allowed that colour does presuppose a sensitive subject in virtue of its own nature, and quite apart from the difficulty—which is in itself insuperable—of determining the right colour of individual bodies. It must, therefore, be conceded that colour is not a quality of bodies. But if this be true, the use of the term 'look' or 'appear' in connexion with colour involves a difficulty which does not arise when it is used in connexion with the primary qualities. Bodies undoubtedly look or appear coloured. Now, as has already been suggested,[120] the term 'look' seems to presuppose some identity between what a thing is and what it looks, and at least the possibility of cases in which they are what they look—a possibility which, as we have seen, is realized in the case of the primary qualities. Yet, if colour is not a quality of bodies, then, with respect to colour, things look what they never are, or, in other words, are wholly different from what they look;[121] and since it seems impossible to hold that colour is really a property of bodies, this conclusion must, in spite of its difficulty, be admitted to be true.

There remain, however, to be noticed two respects in which assertions concerning what things look in respect of colour agree with corresponding assertions in respect of the primary qualities. They imply that what we perceive is a reality, in the sense already explained.[122] Thus the assertion that the grass looks green implies that it is a reality which looks green, or, in other words, that the object of perception is a reality, and not an 'appearance'. Again, such assertions imply that the reality about which the assertion is made is spatial. The term 'grass' implies extension, and only what is extended can be said to look coloured. If it be urged that what looks coloured need only *look* extended, it may be replied that the two considerations which lead us to think that things only *look* coloured presuppose that they *are* spatial. For the two questions, the consideration of which leads to this conclusion, are, 'What is the right or real colour of an individual thing?' and 'Has it really any colour at all, or does it only look coloured?' and neither question is significant unless the thing to which it refers is understood to be spatial.

We may now return to the main issue. Is it possible to maintain either (1) the position that only appearances are spatial and possess all the qualities which imply space, or (2) the position that things only appear spatial and only appear

[118] *Not* 'appearances'.

[119] Cf. p. 48 note.

[120] Cf. p. 43.

[121] It is assumed that there is not even plausibility in the supposition of continuity or identity between colour proper and its physical conditions in the way of light vibrations.

[122] I. e. in the sense of something which exists independently of perception.

or look as if they possessed the qualities which imply space? It may be urged that these questions have already been implicitly answered in the negative. For the division of the qualities of things into primary and secondary is exhaustive, and, as has been shown, the distinction between 'appearance' and 'reality', when drawn with respect to the primary qualities and to colour—the only secondary quality with respect to which the term 'appears' can properly be used[123]—presupposes the reality of space. Consequently, since we do draw the distinction, we must accept the reality of that which is the condition of drawing it at all. But even though this be conceded—and the concession is inevitable—the problem cannot be regarded as solved until we have discovered what it is in the nature of space which makes both positions untenable. Moreover, the admission that in the case of colour there is no identity between what things look and what they are removes at a stroke much of the difficulty of one position, viz. that we only know what things look or appear, and not what they are. For the admission makes it impossible to maintain as a general principle that there must be some identity between what they look and what they are. Consequently, it seems *possible* that things should be wholly different from what they appear, and, if so, the issue cannot be decided on general grounds. What is in substance the same point may be expressed differently by saying that just as things only *look* coloured, so things may only *look* spatial. We are thus again[124] led to see that the issue really turns on the nature of space and of spatial characteristics in particular.

In discussing the distinction between the real and the apparent shape of bodies, it was argued that while the nature of space makes it necessary to distinguish in general between what a body looks and what it is, yet the use of the term *look* receives justification from the existence of limiting cases in which what a thing looks and what it is are identical. The instances considered, however, related to qualities involving only two dimensions, e. g. convergence and bentness, and it will be found that the existence of these limiting cases is due solely to this restriction. If the assertion under consideration involves a term implying three dimensions, e. g. 'cubical' or 'cylindrical', there are no such limiting cases. Since our visual perception is necessarily subject to conditions of perspective, it follows that although we can and do see a cube, we can never see it as it *is*. It *is*, so to say, in the way in which a child draws the side of a house, i. e. with the effect of perspective eliminated; but it never can be seen in this way. No doubt, our unreflective knowledge of the nature of perspective enables us to allow for the effect of perspective, and to ascertain the real shape of a solid object from what it looks when seen from different points. In fact, the habit of allowing for the effect of perspective is so thoroughly ingrained in human beings that the child is not aware that he is making this allowance, but thinks that he draws the side of the house as he sees it. Nevertheless, it is true that we never see a cube as it is, and if we say that a thing looks cubical, we ought only to mean that it looks precisely what a thing looks which is a cube.

It is obvious, however, that two dimensions are only an abstraction from three, and that the spatial relations of bodies, considered fully, involve three dimensions; in other words, spatial characteristics are, properly speaking, three-dimensional. It

[123] Cf. pp. 45-46.
[124] Cf. p. 42.

follows that terms which fully state spatial characteristics can never express what things look, but only what they are. A body may be cylindrical, and we may see a cylindrical body; but such a body can never, strictly speaking, *look* cylindrical. The opposition, however, between what a thing *is* and what it *looks* implies that what it *is* is independent of a percipient, for it is precisely correlation to a percipient which is implied by 'looking' or 'appearing'. In fact, it is the view that what a thing really is it is, independently of a percipient, that forms the real starting-point of Kant's thought. It follows, then, that the spatial characteristics of things, and therefore space itself, must belong to what they are in themselves apart from a percipient, and not to what they look.[125] Consequently, it is so far from being true that we only know what things look and not what they are, that in the case of spatial relations we actually know what things are, even though they never look what they are.

This conclusion, however, seems to present a double difficulty. It is admitted that we perceive things as they look, and not as they are. How, then, is it possible for the belief that things *are* spatial to arise? For how can we advance from knowledge of what they look to knowledge of what they are but do not look? Again, given that the belief has arisen, may it not after all be illusion? No vindication seems possible. For how can it be possible to base the knowledge of what things are, independently of perception, upon the knowledge of what they look? Nevertheless, the answer is simple. In the case of the perception of what is spatial there is no transition *in principle* from knowledge of what things look to knowledge of what things are, though there is continually such a transition *in respect of details*. It is, of course, often necessary, and often difficult, to determine the precise position, shape, &c., of a thing, and if we are to come to a decision, we must appeal to what the thing looks or appears under various conditions. But, from the very beginning, our consciousness of what a thing appears in respect of spatial characteristics implies the consciousness of it as spatial and therefore also as, in particular, three-dimensional. If we suppose the latter consciousness absent, any assertion as to what a thing appears in respect of spatial characteristics loses significance. Thus, although there is a process by which we come to learn that railway lines are really parallel, there is no process by which we come to learn that they are really spatial. Similarly, although there is a process by which we become aware that a body is a cube, there is no process by which we become aware that it has a solid shape of some kind; the process is only concerned with the determination of the precise shape of the body. The second difficulty is, therefore, also removed. For if asser-

[125] This consideration disposes of the view that, if colour is relative to perception, the primary qualities, as being inseparable from colour, must also be relative to perception; for it implies that the primary qualities cannot from their very nature be relative to perception. Moreover, if the possibility of the separation of the primary qualities from colour is still doubted, it is only necessary to appeal to the blind man's ability to apprehend the primary qualities, though he may not even know what the word 'colour' means. Of course, it must be admitted that some sensuous elements are involved in the apprehension of the primary qualities, but the case of the blind man shows that these may relate to sight instead of to touch. Moreover, it, of course, does not follow from the fact that sensuous elements are inseparable from our perception of bodies that they belong to, and are therefore inseparable from, the bodies perceived.

tions concerning the apparent shape, &c. of things presuppose the consciousness that the things *are* spatial, to say that this consciousness may be illusory is to say that all statements concerning what things *appear*, in respect of spatial relations, are equally illusory. But, since it is wholly impossible to deny that we can and do state what things appear in this respect, the difficulty must fall to the ground.

There remains to be answered the question whether Kant's position is tenable in its other form, viz. that while we cannot say that reality is spatial, we can and must say that the appearances which it produces are spatial. This question, in view of the foregoing, can be answered as soon as it is stated. We must allow that reality is spatial, since, as has been pointed out, assertions concerning the apparent shape of things presuppose that they are spatial. We must equally allow that an appearance cannot be spatial. For on the one hand, as has just been shown, space and spatial relations can only qualify something the existence of which is not relative to perception, since it is impossible to perceive what is spatial as it is; and on the other hand an appearance, as being *ex hypothesi* an appearance to some one, i. e. to a percipient, must be relative to perception.

We may say, then, generally, that analysis of the distinction between appearance and reality, as it is actually drawn in our ordinary consciousness, shows the falsity of both forms of the philosophical agnosticism which appeals to the distinction. We know things; not appearances. We know what things are; and not merely what they appear but are not. We may also say that Kant cannot possibly be successful in meeting, at least in respect of space, what he calls 'the easily foreseen but worthless objection that the ideality of space and of time would turn the whole sensible world into pure illusion'.[126] For space, according to him, is not a property of things in themselves; it cannot, as has been shown, be a property of appearances; to say that it is a property of things as they appear to us is self-contradictory; and there is nothing else of which it can be said to be a property.

In conclusion, it may be pointed out that the impossibility that space[127] and spatial characteristics should qualify appearances renders untenable Kant's attempt to draw a distinction between reality and appearance *within* 'phenomena' or 'appearances'. The passage in which he tries to do so runs as follows:

"We generally indeed distinguish in appearances that which essentially belongs to the perception of them, and is valid for every human sense in general, from that which belongs to the same perception accidentally, as valid not for the sensibility in general, but for a particular state or organization of this or that sense. Accordingly, we are accustomed to say that the former is knowledge which represents the object itself, whilst the latter represents only the appearance of the same. This distinction, however, is only empirical. If we stop here (as is usual) and do not again regard that empirical perception as itself a mere phenomenon (as we ought to do), in which nothing which concerns a thing in itself is to be found, our transcendental distinction is lost; and in that case we are after all believing that we

[126] *Prol.*, § 13, Remark iii. (Cf. p. 52 note 134.) Cf. the confused note B. 70, M. 42. (See Dr. Vaihinger's Commentary on the *Critique*, ii, 488 ff.)

[127] The case of time can be ignored, since, as will be seen later (pp. 59-61), the contention that space is 'ideal' really involves the admission that time is real.

know things in themselves, although in the world of sense, investigate its objects as profoundly as we may, we have to do with nothing but appearances. Thus we call the rainbow a mere appearance during a sunny shower, but the rain the thing in itself; and this is right, if we understand the latter conception only physically as that which in universal experience and under all different positions with regard to the senses is in perception so and so determined and not otherwise. But if we consider this empirical element[128] in general, and inquire, without considering its agreement with every human sense, whether it represents an object in itself (not the raindrops, for their being phenomena by itself makes them empirical objects), the question of the relation of the representation to the object is transcendental; and not only are the raindrops mere appearances, but even their circular form, nay, even the space in which they fall, are nothing in themselves but mere modifications or fundamental dispositions of our sensuous perception; the transcendental object, however, remains unknown to us."[129]

Kant's meaning is plain. He is anxious to justify the physical distinction made in our ordinary or non-philosophical consciousness between a thing in itself and a mere appearance,[130] but at the same time to show that it falls within appearances, in respect of the philosophical distinction between things in themselves and appearances or phenomena. The physical distinction is the first of which we become aware, and it arises through problems connected with our senses. Owing, presumably, to the contradictions which would otherwise ensue, the mind is forced to distinguish between things and the 'appearances' which they produce, and to recognize that they do not correspond. The discrepancy is due to the fact that our perceptions are conditioned by the special positions of our physical organs with regard to the object of perception, and we discover its real nature by making allowance for these special positions. We thereby advance in knowledge to the extent of overcoming an obstacle due to the nature of our senses. But, this obstacle overcome, philosophical reflection forces upon us another. The thing which we distinguish in our ordinary consciousness from its appearances is, after all, only another appearance; and although the physical problem is solved concerning its accordance with our special senses, there remains the philosophical problem as to whether this appearance need correspond to what in the end is the real thing, viz. that which exists in itself and apart from all perception. The only possible answer is that it need not. We therefore can only know appearances and not reality; in other words, we cannot have knowledge proper. At the same time, our knowledge of appearances is objective to the extent that the appearances in question are the same for every one, and for us on various occasions; for the effects due to special positions of our senses have been removed. If, therefore, we return to the physical distinction, we see that the 'things' to which it refers are only a special kind of appearance, viz. that which is the same for every one, and for us at all times. The physical distinction, then, being a distinction between one kind of appearance and

[128] *Dieses Empirische.*

[129] B. 62-3, M. 37-8. *Erscheinung* is here translated 'appearance'.

[130] It should be noticed that the passage is, in the main, expressed in terms of the distinction between 'things' and 'appearances', and not, as it should be, in terms of the distinction between what things are and what things appear or look.

another, falls within 'phenomena' or 'appearances'.

Now the obvious objection to this line of thought is that the result of the second or metaphysical application of the distinction between reality and appearance is to destroy or annul the first or physical application of it. To oppose the rain, i. e. the raindrops as the thing in itself to the rainbow as a mere appearance is to imply that the rain is not an appearance. For though what is opposed to a *mere* appearance may still be an appearance, it cannot be called an appearance at all if it be described as the thing in itself. If it be only another appearance, it is the same in principle as that to which it is opposed, and consequently cannot be opposed to it. Thus, if Kant means by the rain, in distinction from the rainbow, the appearance when, as we say, we see the circular raindrops, the title of this appearance to the term thing in itself is no better than that of the rainbow; it is, in fact, if anything, worse, for the appearance is actual only under exceptional circumstances. We may never see the raindrops thus, or in Kant's language, have this 'appearance'; and therefore, in general, an appearance of this kind is not actual but only possible. The truth is that we can only distinguish something as the thing in itself from an appearance, so long as we mean by the thing in itself what Kant normally means by it, viz. something which exists independently of perception and is not an appearance at all.[131] That of which Kant is really thinking, and which he *calls* the appearance which is the thing, in distinction from a mere appearance, is not an appearance; on the contrary, it is the raindrops themselves, which he describes as circular and as falling through space, and which, as circular and falling, must exist and have these characteristics in themselves apart from a percipient. Kant's formula for an empirical thing, i. e. a thing which is an appearance, viz. 'that which in universal experience and under all different positions with regard to the senses is in perception so and so determined', is merely an attempt to achieve the impossible, viz. to combine in one the characteristics of a thing and an appearance. While the reference to *perception* and to *position with regard to the senses* implies that what is being defined is an appearance, the reference to *universal* experience, to *all* positions with regard to the senses, and to that which *is so and so determined* implies that it is a thing. But, plainly, mention of position with regard to the senses, if introduced at all, should refer to the *differences* in perception due to the different position of the object in particular cases. There is nothing of which it can be said that we perceive it in the same way or that it looks the same from *all* positions. When Kant speaks of that which under *all* different positions with regard to the senses is so and so determined, he is really referring to something in the consideration of which all reference to the senses has been discarded; it is what should be described as that which *in reality and apart from* all positions with regard to the senses is so and so determined; and this, as such, cannot be an appearance. Again, the qualification of 'is so and so determined' by 'in perception' is merely an attempt to treat

[131] Hence Kant's protest (B. 45, M. 27), against illustrating the ideality of space by the 'inadequate' examples of colour, taste, &c., must be unavailing. For his contention is that, while the assertion that space is not a property of things means that it is not a property of things in themselves, the assertion that colour, for example, is not a property of a rose only means that it is not a property of a thing in itself in an empirical sense, i. e. of an appearance of a special kind.

as relative to perception, and so as an appearance, what is essentially independent of perception.[132] Kant, no doubt, is thinking of a real presupposition of the process by which we distinguish between the real and the apparent qualities of bodies, i. e. between what they are and what they appear. We presuppose that that quality is really, and not only apparently, a quality of a body, which we and every one, judging from what it looks under various conditions (i. e. 'in universal experience'), must believe it to possess in itself and independently of all perception. His mistake is that in formulating this presupposition he treats as an appearance, and so as relative to perception, just that which is being distinguished from what, as an appearance, is relative to perception.

Underlying the mistake is the identification of perception with judgement. Our apprehension of what things *are* is essentially a matter of thought or judgement, and not of perception. We do not *perceive*[133] but *think* a thing as it is. It is true that we can follow Kant's language so far as to say that our judgement that the portion of the great circle joining two points on the surface of a sphere is the shortest way between them *via* the surface belongs essentially to the thinking faculty of every intelligent being, and also that it is valid for all intelligences, in the sense that they must all hold it to be true; and we can contrast this judgement with a perception of the portion of the great circle as something which, though it cannot be said to be invalid, still differs for different beings according to the position from which they perceive it. Kant, however, treats the judgement as a *perception*; for if we apply his general assertion to this instance, we find him saying that what we judge the portion of the great circle to be essentially belongs to the *perception* of it, and is valid for the *sensuous* faculty of every human being, and that thereby it can be distinguished from what belongs to the same perception of a great circle accidentally, e. g. its apparent colour, which is valid only for a particular organization of this or that sense.[134] In this way he correlates what the great circle really is, as well as what it looks, with perception, and so is able to speak of what it is for perception. But, in fact, what the great circle is, is correlated with thought, and not with perception; and if we raise Kant's transcendental problem in reference not to perception but to thought, it cannot be solved in Kant's agnostic manner. For it is a presupposition of thinking that things are in themselves what we think them to be; and from the nature of the case a presupposition of thinking not only cannot be rightly questioned, but cannot be questioned at all.

---

[132] Cf. pp. 38-39.

[133] Cf. pp. 38-39.

[134] In the *Prol.*, § 13, Remark iii, Kant carefully distinguishes judgement from perception, but destroys the effect of the distinction by regarding judgement as referring to what is relative to perception, viz. appearances.

NOTE

THE FIRST ANTINOMY

KANT holds that the antinomy or contradiction which arises when we consider the character of the world as spatial and temporal, viz. that we are equally bound to hold that the world is infinite in space and time, and that it is finite in space and time, is due to regarding the world as a thing in itself. He holds that the contradiction disappears, as soon as it is recognized that the world is only a phenomenon, for then we find that we need only say that the world is *capable* of being extended infinitely in respect of time and space.[135] Objects in space and time are only phenomena, and, as such, are actual only in perception. When we say that a past event, or that a body which we do not perceive, is real, we merely assert the possibility of a 'perception'. "All events from time immemorial prior to my existence mean nothing else than the possibility of prolonging the chain of experience from the present perception upwards to the conditions which determine this perception according to time."[136] "That there may be inhabitants of the moon, although no one has ever seen them, must certainly be admitted, but this assertion only means that we could come upon them in the possible progress of experience."[137] The contradictions, therefore, can be avoided by substituting for the actual infinity of space and time, as relating to things in themselves, the possible infinity of a series of 'perceptions'.

This contention, if successful, is clearly important. If it could be shown that the treatment of the world as a thing in itself is the source of a contradiction, we should have what at least would seem a strong, if not conclusive, ground for holding that the world is a phenomenon, and, consequently, that the distinction between phenomena and things in themselves is valid.

Professor Cook Wilson has, however, pointed out that Kant's own doctrine does not avoid the difficulty. For, though, according to Kant, the infinity of actual representations of spaces and times is only possible, yet the possibilities of these representations will be themselves infinite, and, as such, will give rise to contradictions similar to those involved in the infinity of space and time. Moreover, as Professor Cook Wilson has also pointed out, there is no contradiction involved in the thought of the world as spatial and temporal; for, as we see when we reflect, we always presuppose that space and time are infinite, and we are only tempted to think that they must be finite, because, when maintaining that the world must be

[135] B. 532-3, M. 315.
[136] B. 523, M. 309.
[137] B. 521, M. 308.

a whole, we are apt to make the false assumption, without in any way questioning it, that any whole must be finite.

CHAPTER V

TIME AND INNER SENSE

THE arguments by which Kant seeks to show that time is not a determination of things in themselves but only a form of perception are, *mutatis mutandis*, identical with those used in his treatment of space.[138] They are, therefore, open to the same criticisms, and need no separate consideration.

Time, however, according to Kant, differs from space in one important respect. It is the form not of outer but of inner sense; in other words, while space is the form under which we perceive things, time is the form under which we perceive ourselves. It is upon this difference that attention must be concentrated. The existence of the difference at all is upon general grounds surprising. For since the arguments by which Kant establishes the character of time as a form of perception run *pari passu* with those used in the case of space, we should expect time, like space, to be a form under which we perceive things; and, as a matter of fact, it will be found that the only *argument* used to show that time is the form of inner, as opposed to outer, sense is not only independent of Kant's general theory of forms of sense, but is actually inconsistent with it.[139] Before, however, we attempt to decide Kant's right to distinguish between inner and outer sense, we must consider the facts which were before Kant's mind in making the distinction.

These facts and, to a large extent, the frame of mind in which Kant approached them, find expression in the passage in Locke's *Essay*, which explains the distinction between 'ideas of sensation' and 'ideas of reflection'.

"Whence has it [i. e. the mind] all the materials of reason and knowledge? To this I answer, in one word, from experience. . . . Our observation, employed either about external, sensible objects, or about the internal operations of our minds, perceived and reflected on, by ourselves, is that which supplies our understandings with all the materials of thinking. These two are the fountains of knowledge. . . ."

"First, Our senses, conversant about particular sensible objects, do convey into

[138] Cf. B. 46-9, §§ 4, 5 and 6 (a), M. 28-30, §§ 5, 6 and 7 (a) with B. 38-42, § 2 (1-4), and § (3) to (a) inclusive, M. 23-6, §§ 2, 3, and 4 (a). The only qualification needed is that, since the parts of time cannot, like those of space, be said to exist simultaneously, B. § 4 (5), M. § 5, 5 is compelled to appeal to a different consideration from that adduced in the parallel passage on space (B. § 2 (4), M. § 2, 4). Since, however, B. § 4 (5), M. § 5, 5 introduces no new matter, but only appeals to the consideration already urged (B. § 4, 4, M. § 5, 4), this difference can be neglected. B. § 5, M. § 6 adds a remark about change which does not affect the main argument.

[139] B. 49 (b), M. 30 (b). See pp. 58-60.

the mind several distinct perceptions of things, according to those various ways, wherein those objects do affect them: and thus we come by those ideas we have of Yellow, White, Heat, Cold, Soft, Hard, Bitter, Sweet, and all those, which we call sensible qualities; which, when I say the senses convey into the mind, I mean, they, from external objects, convey into the mind what produces there those perceptions. This great source of most of the ideas we have, depending wholly upon our senses, and derived by them to the understanding, I call *sensation*."

"Secondly, The other fountain, from which experience furnisheth the understanding with ideas, is the perception of the operations of our own mind within us, as it is employed about the ideas it has got; which operations, when the soul comes to reflect on, and consider, do furnish the understanding with another set of ideas, which could not be had from things without; and such are Perception, Thinking, Doubting, Believing, Reasoning, Knowing, Willing, and all the different actings of our own minds; which we being conscious of, and observing in ourselves, do, from these, receive into our understandings as distinct ideas, as we do from bodies affecting our senses. This source of ideas every man has wholly in himself; and though it be not sense as having nothing to do with external objects, yet it is very like it, and might properly enough be called internal sense. But, as I call the other sensation, so I call this *reflection*; the ideas it affords being such only as the mind gets, by reflecting on its own operations within itself."[140]

Here Locke is thinking of the distinction between two attitudes of mind, which, however difficult it may be to state satisfactorily, must in some sense be recognized. The mind, undoubtedly, in virtue of its powers of perceiving and thinking—or whatever they may be—becomes through a temporal process aware of a spatial world in its varied detail. In the first instance, its attention is absorbed in the world of which it thus becomes aware; subsequently, however, it is in some way able to direct its attention away from this world to the activities in virtue of which it has become aware of this world, and in some sense to make itself its own object. From being conscious it becomes self-conscious. This process by which the mind turns its attention back upon itself is said to be a process of 'reflection'. While we should say that it is by perception that we become aware of things in the physical world, we should say that it is by reflection that we become aware of our activities of perceiving, thinking, willing, &c. Whatever difficulties the thought of self-consciousness may involve, and however inseparable, and perhaps even temporally inseparable, the attitudes of consciousness and self-consciousness may turn out to be, the distinction between these attitudes must be recognized. The object of the former is the world, and the object of the latter is in some sense the mind itself; and the attitudes may be described as that of our ordinary, scientific, or unreflecting consciousness and that of reflection.

The significance of Locke's account of this distinction lies for our purposes in its anticipation of Kant. He states the second attitude, as well as the first, in terms of sense. Just as in our apprehension of the world things external to, in the sense of existing independently of, the mind are said to act on our physical organs or 'senses', and thereby to produce 'perceptions' in the mind, so the mind is said to

[140] Locke, *Essay*, ii, 1, §§ 2-4.

become conscious of its own operations by 'sense'. We should notice, however, that Locke hesitates to use the word 'sense' in the latter case, on the ground that it involves no operation of external things (presumably upon our physical organs), though he thinks that the difficulty is removed by calling the sense in question 'internal'.

Kant is thinking of the same facts, and also states them in terms of sense, though allowance must be made for the difference of standpoint, since for him 'sense', in the case of the external sense, refers not to the affection of our physical organs by physical bodies, but to the affection of the mind by things in themselves. Things in themselves act on our minds and produce in them appearances, or rather sensations, and outer sense is the mind's capacity for being so affected by outer things, i. e. things independent of the mind. This is, in essentials, Kant's statement of the attitude of consciousness, i. e. of our apprehension of the world which exists independently of the mind, and which, for him, is the world of things in themselves. He also follows Locke in giving a parallel account of the attitude of self-consciousness. He asks, 'How can the subject perceive itself?' Perception *in man* is essentially passive; the mind must be *affected* by that which it perceives. Consequently, if the mind is to perceive itself, it must be affected by its own activity; in other words, there must be an inner sense, i. e. a capacity in virtue of which the mind is affected by itself.[141] Hence Kant is compelled to extend his agnosticism to the knowledge of ourselves. Just as we do not know things, but only the appearances which they produce in us,[142] so we do not know ourselves, but only the appearances which we produce in ourselves; and since time is a mode of relation of these appearances, it is a determination not of ourselves, but only of the appearances due to ourselves.

The above may be said to represent the train of thought by which Kant arrived at his doctrine of time and the inner sense. It was reached by combining recognition of the fact that we come to be aware not only of the details of the physical world, but also of the successive process on our part by which we have attained this knowledge, with the view that our apprehension of this successive process is based on 'sense', just as is our apprehension of the world. But the question remains whether Kant is, on his own principles, entitled to speak of an inner sense at all. According to him, knowledge begins with the production in us of sensations, or, as we ought to say in the present context, appearances by the action of things in themselves. These sensations or appearances can reasonably be ascribed to external sense. They may be ascribed to sense, because they arise through our being *affected* by things in themselves. The sense may be called external, because the object affecting it is external to the mind, i. e. independent of it. In conformity with this account, internal sense must be the power of being affected by something internal to the mind, i. e. dependent upon the mind itself, and since being affected implies the activity of affecting, it will be the power of being affected by the mind's own activity.[143] The activity will presumably be that of arranging spatially the sensa-

[141] Cf. B. 67 fin., M. 41 init.

[142] It is here assumed that this is Kant's normal view of the phenomenal character of our knowledge. Cf. p. 40.

[143] B. 68 init., M. 41 init.

tions or appearances due to things in themselves.[144] This activity must be said to produce an affection in us, the affection being an appearance due to ourselves. Lastly, the mind must be said to arrange these appearances temporally. Hence it will be said to follow that we know only the appearances due to ourselves and not ourselves, and that time is only a determination of these appearances.[145]

The weakness of the position just stated lies on the surface. It provides no means of determining whether any affection produced in us is produced by ourselves rather than by the thing in itself; consequently we could never say that a given affection was an appearance due to *ourselves,* and therefore to *inner* sense. On the contrary, we should ascribe all affections to things in themselves, and should, therefore, be unable to recognize an *inner* sense at all. In order to recognize an inner sense we must know that certain affections are due to *our* activity, and, to do this, we must know what the activity consists in—for we can only be aware that we are active by being aware of an activity of ours of a particular kind—and, therefore, we must know ourselves. Unless, then, we know ourselves, we cannot call any affections internal.

If, however, the doctrine of an internal sense is obviously untenable from Kant's own point of view, why does he hold it? The answer is that, inconsistently with his general view, he continues to think of the facts as they really are, and that he is deceived by an ambiguity into thinking that the facts justify a distinction between internal and external sense.

He brings forward only one argument to show that time is the form of the internal sense. "Time is nothing else than the form of the internal sense, i. e. of the perception of ourselves and our inner state. For time cannot be any determination of external phenomena; it has to do neither with a shape nor a position; on the contrary, it determines the relation of representations in our internal state."[146]

To follow this argument it is first necessary to realize a certain looseness and confusion in the expression of it. The term 'external', applied to phenomena, has a double meaning. It must mean (1) that of which the parts are external to one another, i. e. spatial; for the ground on which time is denied to be a determination of external phenomena is that it has nothing to do with a shape or a position. It must also mean (2) external to, in the sense of independent of, the mind; for it is contrasted with our internal state, and if 'internal', applied to 'our state', is not to be wholly otiose, it can only serve to emphasize the contrast between our state and something external to in the sense of independent of us. Again, 'phenomena,' in the phrase 'external phenomena', can only be an unfortunate expression for things independent of the mind, these things being here called phenomena owing to Kant's view that bodies in space are phenomena. Otherwise, 'phenomena' offers no contrast to 'our state' and to 'representations'. The passage, therefore, pre-

[144] The precise nature of the activity makes no difference to the argument.

[145] In B. 152 fin., M. 93 fin. Kant expresses his conclusion in the form that we know ourselves only as we appear to ourselves, and not as we are in ourselves (cf. p. 40). The above account, and the criticism which immediately follows, can be adapted, *mutatis mutandis,* to this form of the view.

[146] B. 49 (b), M. 30 (b).

supposes a distinction between states of ourselves and things in space, the former being internal to, or dependent upon, and the latter external to, or independent of, the mind.

It should now be easy to see that the argument involves a complete *non sequitur*. The conclusion which is justified is that time is a form not of things but of our own states. For the fact to which he appeals is that while things, as being spatial, are not related temporally, our states are temporally related; and if 'a form' be understood as a mode of relation, this fact can be expressed by the formula 'Time is a form not of things but of our own states', the corresponding formula in the case of space being 'Space is a form not of our states but of things'. But the conclusion which Kant desires to draw—and which he, in fact, actually draws—is the quite different conclusion that time is a form of *perception* of our states, the corresponding conclusion in the case of space being that space is a form of perception of things. For time is to be shown to be the form of inner sense, i. e. the form of the perception of what is internal to ourselves, i. e. of our own states.[147] The fact is that the same unconscious transition takes place in Kant's account of time which, as we saw,[148] takes place in his account of space. In the case of space, Kant passes from the assertion that space is a form of things, in the sense that all things are spatially related—an assertion which he expresses by saying that space is the form of phenomena—to the quite different assertion that space is a form of perception, in the sense of a way in which we perceive things as opposed to a way in which things are. Similarly, in the case of time, Kant passes from the assertion that time is the form of our internal states, in the sense that all our states are temporally related, to the assertion that time is a way in which we perceive our states as opposed to a way in which our states really are. Further, the two positions, which he thus fails to distinguish, are not only different, but incompatible. For if space is a form of things, and time is a form of our states, space and time cannot belong only to our mode of perceiving things and ourselves respectively, and not to the things and ourselves; for *ex hypothesi* things *are* spatially related, and our states *are* temporally related.

Kant's procedure, therefore, may be summed up by saying that he formulates a view which is true but at the same time inconsistent with his general position, the view, viz. that while things in space are not temporally related, the acts by which we come to apprehend them are so related; and further, that he is deceived by the verbally easy transition from a legitimate way of expressing this view, viz. that time is the form of our states, to the desired conclusion that time is the form of inner sense.

The untenable character of Kant's position with regard to time and the knowledge of ourselves can be seen in another way. It is not difficult to show that, in order to prove that we do not know *things*, but only the appearances which they produce, we must allow that we do know *ourselves*, and not appearances produced by ourselves, and, consequently, that time is real and not phenomenal. To show this, it is only necessary to consider the objection which Kant himself quotes against

[147] Cf. B. 49 (b) line 2, M. 30 (b) line 2.

[148] Cf. pp. 20-21.

his view of time. The objection is important in itself, and Kant himself remarks that he has heard it so unanimously urged by intelligent men that he concludes that it must naturally present itself to every reader to whom his views are novel. According to Kant, it runs thus: "Changes are real (this is proved by the change of our own representations, even though all external phenomena, together with their changes, be denied). Now changes are only possible in time; therefore time is something real."[149] And he goes on to explain why this objection is so unanimously brought, even by those who can bring no intelligible argument against the ideality of space. "The reason is that men have no hope of proving apodeictically the absolute reality of space, because they are confronted by idealism, according to which the reality of external objects is incapable of strict proof, whereas the reality of the object of our internal senses (of myself and my state) is immediately clear through consciousness. External objects might be mere illusion, but the object of our internal senses is to their mind undeniably something real."[150]

Here, though Kant does not see it, he is faced with a difficulty from which there is no escape. On the one hand, according to him, we do not know things in themselves, i. e. things independent of the mind. In particular, we cannot know that they are spatial; and the objection quoted concedes this. On the other hand, we do know phenomena or the appearances produced by things in themselves. Phenomena or appearances, however, as he always insists, are essentially states or determinations of the mind. To the question, therefore, 'Why are we justified in saying that we do know phenomena, whereas we do not know the things which produce them?' Kant could only answer that it is because phenomena are dependent upon the mind, as being its own states.[151] As the objector is made to say, 'the reality of the object of our internal senses (of myself and my state) is immediately clear through consciousness.' If we do not know things in themselves, because they are independent of the mind, we only know phenomena because they are dependent upon the mind. Hence Kant is only justified in denying that we know things in themselves if he concedes that we really know our own states, and not merely appearances which they produce.

Again, Kant must allow—as indeed he normally does—that these states of ours are related by way of succession. Hence, since these states are really our states and not appearances produced by our states, these being themselves unknown, time, as a relation of these states, must itself be real, and not a way in which we apprehend what is real. It must, so to say, be really in what we apprehend about ourselves, and not put into it by us as perceiving ourselves.

The objection, then, comes to this. Kant must at least concede that we undergo a succession of changing states, even if he holds that *things*, being independent of the mind, cannot be shown to undergo such a succession; consequently, he ought to allow that time is not a way in which we apprehend ourselves, but a real feature of our real states. Kant's answer[152] does not meet the point, and, in any case,

[149] B. 53, M. 32.
[150] B. 55, M. 33.
[151] Cf. p. 66.
[152] B. 55, M. 33 med.

proceeds on the untenable assumption that it is possible for the characteristic of a thing to belong to it as perceived, though not in itself.[153]

[153] Cf. pp. 37-39.

CHAPTER VI

KNOWLEDGE AND REALITY

KANT's theory of space, and, still more, his theory of time, are bewildering subjects. It is not merely that the facts with which he deals are complex; his treatment of them is also complicated by his special theories of 'sense' and of 'forms of perception'. Light, however, may be thrown upon the problems raised by the *Aesthetic*, and upon Kant's solution of them, in two ways. In the first place, we may attempt to vindicate the implication of the preceding criticism, that the very nature of knowledge presupposes the independent existence of the reality known, and to show that, in consequence, all idealism is of the variety known as subjective. In the second place, we may point out the way in which Kant is misled by failing to realize (1) the directness of the relation between the knower and the reality known, and (2) the impossibility of transferring what belongs to one side of the relation to the other.

The question whether any reality exists independently of the knowledge of it may be approached thus. The standpoint of the preceding criticism of Kant may be described as that of the plain man. It is the view that the mind comes by a temporal process to apprehend or to know a spatial world which exists independently of it or of any other mind, and that the mind knows it as it exists in the independence. 'Now this view,' it may be replied, 'is exposed to at least one fatal objection. It presupposes the possibility of knowing the thing in itself, i. e. something which exists independently of the mind which comes to know it. Whatever is true, this is not. Whatever be the criticism to which Kant's doctrine is exposed in detail, it contains one inexpugnable thesis, viz. that the thing in itself cannot be known. Unless the physical world stands in essential relation to the mind, it is impossible to understand how it can be known. This position being unassailable, any criticism of an idealistic theory must be compatible with it, and therefore confined to details. Moreover, Kant's view can be transformed into one which will defy criticism. Its unsatisfactory character lies in the fact that in regarding the physical world as dependent on the mind, it really alters the character of the world by reducing the world to a succession of 'appearances' which, as such, can only be mental, i. e. can only belong to the mind's own being. Bodies, as being really appearances in the mind, are regarded as on the level of transitory mental occurrences, and as thereby at least resembling feelings and sensations. This consequence, however, can be avoided by maintaining that the real truth after which Kant was groping was that knower and known form an inseparable unity, and that, therefore, any reality which is not itself a knower, or the knowing of a knower, presupposes a mind which knows it. In that case nothing is suggested as to the special nature of the reality known, and, in particular, it is not implied to be a transitory element of the mind's own being. The contention merely attributes to any reality, conceived to have the special nature ordinarily attributed to it, the additional characteristic that it is known. Consequently, on this view, the physical world can retain the permanence ordinarily attributed to it. To the objection that, at any rate, *our* knowledge is transitory, and that if the world is relative to it the world also must be transitory, it may be replied—though with some sense of uneasiness—that the world must be considered relative not to us as knowers, but to a knower who knows always and completely, and whose knowing is in some way identical with ours. Further, the view so transformed has two other advantages. In the first place, it renders it possible to dispense with what has been called the Mrs. Harris of philosophy, the thing in itself. As Kant states his position, the thing in itself must be retained, for it is impossible to believe that there is no reality other than what is mental. But if the physical world need not be considered to be a succession of mental occurrences, it can be considered to be the reality which is not mental. In the second place, knowledge proper is vindicated, for on this view we do not know 'only' phenomena; we know the reality which is not mental, and we know it as it is, for it is as object of knowledge.'

'Moreover, the contention must be true, and must form the true basis of idealism. For the driving force of idealism is furnished by the question, 'How can the mind and reality come into the relation which we call knowledge?' This question is unanswerable so long as reality is thought to stand in no essential relation to the knowing mind. Consequently, in the end, knowledge and reality must be considered inseparable. Again, even if it be conceded that the mind in some way gains access to an independent reality, it is impossible to hold that the mind can really know it. For the reality cannot in the relation of knowledge be what it is apart from this relation. It must become in some way modified or altered in the process. Hence the mind cannot on this view know the reality as it is. On the other hand, if the reality is essentially relative to a knower, the knower knows it as it is, for what it is is what it is in this relation.'

The fundamental objection, however, to this line of thought is that it contradicts the very nature of knowledge. Knowledge unconditionally presupposes that the reality known exists independently of the knowledge of it, and that we know it as it exists in this independence. It is simply *impossible* to think that any reality depends upon our knowledge of it, or upon any knowledge of it. If there is to be knowledge, there must first *be* something to be known. In other words, knowledge is essentially discovery, or the finding of what already is. If a reality could only be or come to be in virtue of some activity or process on the part of the mind, that activity or process would not be 'knowing', but 'making' or 'creating', and to make and to know must in the end be admitted to be mutually exclusive.[154]

This presupposition that what is known exists independently of being known is quite general, and applies to feeling and sensation just as much as to parts of the physical world. It must in the end be conceded of a toothache as much as of a

[154] Cf. pp. 126-127.

stone that it exists independently of the knowledge of it. There must be a pain to be attended to or noticed, which exists independently of our attention or notice. The true reason for asserting feeling and sensation to be dependent on the mind is that they presuppose not a knowing, but a feeling and a sentient subject respectively. Again, it is equally presupposed that knowing in no way alters or modifies the thing known. We can no more think that in apprehending a reality we do not apprehend it as it is apart from our knowledge of it, than we can think that its existence depends upon our knowledge of it. Hence, if 'things in themselves' means 'things existing independently of the knowledge of them', knowledge is essentially of 'things in themselves'. It is, therefore, unnecessary to consider whether idealism is assisted by the supposition of a non-finite knowing mind, correlated with reality as a whole. For reality must equally be independent of it. Consequently, if the issue between idealism and realism is whether the physical world is or is not dependent on the mind, it cannot turn upon a dependence in respect of knowledge.

That the issue does not turn upon knowledge is confirmed by our instinctive procedure when we are asked whether the various realities which we suppose ourselves to know depend upon the mind. Our natural procedure is not to treat them simply as realities and to ask whether, as realities, they involve a mind to know them, but to treat them as realities of the particular kind to which they belong, and to consider relation to the mind of some kind other than that of knowledge. We should say, for instance, that a toothache or an emotion, as being a feeling, presupposes a mind capable of feeling, whose feeling it is; for if the mind be thought of as withdrawn, the pain or the feeling must also be thought of as withdrawn. We should say that an act of thinking presupposes a mind which thinks. We should, however, naturally deny that an act of thinking or knowing, in order to be, presupposes that it is known either by the thinker whose act it is, or by any other mind. In other words, we should say that knowing presupposes a mind, not as something which *knows* the knowing, but as something which *does* the knowing. Again, we should naturally say that the shape or the weight of a stone is *not* dependent on the mind which perceives the stone. The shape, we should say, would disappear with the disappearance of the stone, but would not disappear with the disappearance of the mind which perceives the stone. Again, we should assert that the stone itself, so far from depending on the mind which perceives it, has an independent being of its own. We might, of course, find difficulty in deciding whether a reality of some particular kind, e. g. a colour, is dependent on a mind. But, in any case, we should think that the ground for decision lay in the special character of the reality in question, and should not treat it merely as a reality related to the mind as something known. We should ask, for instance, whether a colour, as a colour, involves a mind which sees, and not whether a colour, as a reality, involves its being known. Our natural procedure, then, is to divide realities into two classes, those which depend on a mind, and may therefore be called mental, and those which do not, and to conclude that some realities depend upon the mind, while others do not. We thereby ignore a possible dependence of realities on their being known; for not only is the dependence which we recognize of some other kind, e. g. in respect of feeling or sentience, but if the dependence were in respect of knowledge, we could not distinguish in respect of dependence between one reality and another.

Further, if reality be allowed to exist independently of knowledge, it is easy to see that, from the idealist's point of view, Kant's procedure was essentially right, and that all idealism, when pressed, must prove subjective; in other words, that the idealist must hold that the mind can only know what is mental and belongs to its own being, and that the so-called physical world is merely a succession of appearances. Moreover, our instinctive procedure[155] is justified. For, in the first place, since it is impossible to think that a reality depends for its existence upon being known, it is impossible to reach an idealistic conclusion by taking into account relation by way of knowledge; and if this be the relation considered, the only conclusion can be that all reality is independent of the mind. Again, since knowledge is essentially of reality as it is apart from its being known, the assertion that a reality is dependent upon the mind is an assertion of the kind of thing which it is in itself, apart from its being known.[156] And when we come to consider what we mean by saying of a reality that it depends upon the mind, we find we mean that it is in its own nature of such a kind as to disappear with the disappearance of the mind, or, more simply, that it is of the kind called mental. Hence, we can only decide that a particular reality depends upon the mind by appeal to its special character. We cannot treat it simply as a reality the relation of which to the mind is solely that of knowledge. And we can only decide that all reality is dependent upon the mind by appeal to the special character of all the kinds of reality of which we are aware. Hence, Kant in the *Aesthetic*, and Berkeley before him, were essentially right in their procedure. They both ignored consideration of the world simply as a reality, and appealed exclusively to its special character, the one arguing that in its special character as spatial and temporal it presupposed a percipient, and the other endeavouring to show that the primary qualities are as relative to perception as the secondary. Unfortunately for their view, in order to think of bodies in space as dependent on the mind, it is necessary to think of them as being in the end only certain sensations or certain combinations of sensations which may be called appearances. For only sensations or combinations of them can be thought of as at once dependent on the mind, and capable with any plausibility of being identified with bodies in space. In other words, in order to think of the world as dependent on the mind, we have to think of it as consisting only of a succession of appearances, and in fact Berkeley, and, at certain times, Kant, did think of it in this way.

That this is the inevitable result of idealism is not noticed, so long as it is supposed that the essential relation of realities to the mind consists in their being known; for, as we have seen, nothing is thereby implied as to their special nature. To say of a reality that it is essentially an object of knowledge is merely to add to the particular nature ordinarily attributed to the existent in question the further characteristic that it must be known.[157] Moreover, since in fact, though contrary to the theory, any reality exists independently of the knowledge of it, when the relation thought of between a reality and the mind is *solely* that of knowledge, the realities can be thought of as independent of the mind. Consequently, the physical

[155] Cf. p. 64.

[156] Though not apart from relation to the mind of some other kind.

[157] Cf. pp. 62-63.

world can be thought to have that independence of the mind which the ordinary man attributes to it, and, therefore, need not be conceived as only a succession of appearances. But the advantage of this form of idealism is really derived from the very fact which it is the aim of idealism in general to deny. For the conclusion that the physical world consists of a succession of appearances is only avoided by taking into account the relation of realities to the mind by way of knowledge, and, then, without being aware of the inconsistency, making use of the independent existence of the reality known.

Again, that the real contrary to realism is *subjective* idealism is confirmed by the history of the theory of knowledge from Descartes onwards. For the initial supposition which has originated and sustained the problem is that in knowledge the mind is, at any rate in the first instance, confined within itself. This supposition granted, it has always seemed that, while there is no difficulty in understanding the mind's acquisition of knowledge of what belongs to its own being, it is difficult, if not impossible, to understand how it can acquire knowledge of what does not belong to its own being. Further, since the physical world is ordinarily thought of as something which does not belong to the mind's own being, the problem has always been not 'How is it possible to know anything?' but 'How is it possible to know a particular kind of reality, viz. the physical world?' Moreover, in consequence of the initial supposition, any answer to this question has always presupposed that our apprehension of the physical world is indirect. Since *ex hypothesi* the mind is confined within itself, it can only apprehend a reality independent of it through something within the mind which 'represents' or 'copies' the reality; and it is perhaps Hume's chief merit that he showed that no such solution is possible, or, in other words, that, on the given supposition, knowledge of the physical world is impossible.

Now the essential weakness of this line of thought lies in the initial supposition that the mind can only apprehend what belongs to its own being. It is as much a fact of our experience that we directly apprehend bodies in space, as that we directly apprehend our feelings and sensations. And, as has already been shown,[158] what is spatial cannot be thought to belong to the mind's own being on the ground that it is relative to perception. Further, if it is legitimate to ask, 'How can we apprehend what does not belong to our being?' it is equally legitimate to ask, 'How can we apprehend what does belong to our own being?' It is wholly arbitrary to limit the question to the one kind of reality. If a question is to be put at all, it should take the form, 'How is it possible to apprehend anything?' But this question has only to be put to be discarded. For it amounts to a demand to *explain* knowledge; and any answer to it would involve the derivation of knowledge from what was not knowledge, a task which must be as impossible as the derivation of space from time or of colour from sound. Knowledge is *sui generis*, and, as such, cannot be explained.[159]

---

[158] Cf. pp. 46-48.

[159] This assertion, being self-evident, admits of no direct proof. A 'proof' can only take the form of showing that any supposed 'derivation' or 'explanation' of knowledge presupposes knowledge in that from which it derives it. Professor Cook Wilson has pointed out that we must understand what knowing is in order to explain anything at all, so that

Moreover, it may be noted that the support which this form of idealism sometimes receives from an argument which uses the terms 'inside' and 'outside' the mind is unmerited. At first sight it seems a refutation of the plain man's view to argue thus: 'The plain man believes the spatial world to exist whether any one knows it or not. Consequently, he allows that the world is outside the mind. But, to be known, a reality must be inside the mind. Therefore, the plain man's view renders knowledge impossible.' But, as soon as it is realized that 'inside the mind' and 'outside the mind' are metaphors, and, therefore, must take their meaning from their context, it is easy to see that the argument either rests on an equivocation or assumes the point at issue. The assertion that the world is outside the mind, being only a metaphorical expression of the plain man's view, should only mean that the world is something independent of the mind, as opposed to something inside the mind, in the sense of dependent upon it, or mental. But the assertion that, to be known, a reality must be inside the mind, if it is to be incontestably true, should only mean that a reality, to be apprehended, must really be object of apprehension. And in this case 'being inside the mind', since it only means 'being object of apprehension', is not the opposite of 'being outside the mind' in the previous assertion. Hence, on this interpretation, the second assertion is connected with the first only apparently and by an equivocation; there is really no argument at all. If, however, the equivocation is to be avoided, 'inside the mind' in the second assertion must be the opposite of 'outside the mind' in the first, and consequently the second must mean that a reality, to be known, must be dependent on the mind, or mental. But in that case the objection to the plain man's view is a *petitio principii*, and not an argument.

Nevertheless, the tendency to think that the only object or, at least, the only direct object of the mind is something mental still requires explanation. It seems due to a tendency to treat self-consciousness as similar to consciousness of the world. When in reflection we turn our attention away from the world to the activity by which we come to know it, we tend to think of our knowledge of the world as a reality to be apprehended similar to the world which we apprehended prior to reflection. We thereby implicitly treat this knowledge as something which, like the world, merely *is* and is not the knowledge of anything; in other words, we imply that, so far from being knowledge, i. e. the knowing of a reality, it is precisely that which we distinguish from knowledge, viz. a reality to be known, although—since knowledge must be mental—we imply that it is a reality of the special kind called mental. But if the knowledge upon which we reflect is thus treated as consisting in a mental reality which merely *is*, it is implied that in this knowledge the world is not, at any rate directly, object of the mind, for *ex hypothesi* a reality which merely *is* and is not the knowledge of anything has no object. Hence it comes to be thought that the only object or, at least, the only direct object of the mind is this mental reality itself, which is the object of reflection; in other words, that the only immediate object of the mind comes to be thought of as its own idea. The root of the mistake lies in the initial supposition—which, it may be noted, seems to underlie the whole treatment of knowledge by empirical psychology—that knowledge can be treated

any proposed explanation of knowing would necessarily presuppose that we understood what knowing is. For the general doctrine, cf. p. 131.

as a reality to be apprehended, in the way in which any reality which is not knowledge is a reality to be apprehended.

We may now revert to that form of idealism which maintains that the essential relation of reality to the mind is that of *being known*, in order to consider two lines of argument by which it may be defended.

According to the first of these, the view of the plain man either is, or at least involves, materialism; and materialism is demonstrably absurd. The plain man's view involves the existence of the physical world prior to the existence of the knowledge of it, and therefore also prior to the existence of minds which know it, since it is impossible to separate the existence of a knowing mind from its actual knowledge. From this it follows that mere matter, having only the qualities considered by the physicist, must somehow have originated or produced knowing and knowing minds. But this production is plainly impossible. For matter, possessing solely, as it does, characteristics bound up with extension and motion, cannot possibly have originated activities of a wholly different kind, or beings capable of exercising them.

It may, however, be replied that the supposed consequence, though absurd, does not really follow from the plain man's realism. Doubtless, it would be impossible for a universe consisting solely of the physical world to originate thought or beings capable of thinking. But the real presupposition of the coming into existence of human knowledge at a certain stage in the process of the universe is to be found in the pre-existence, not of a mind or minds which always actually knew, but simply of a mind or minds in which, under certain conditions, knowledge is necessarily actualized. A mind cannot be the product of anything or, at any rate, of anything but a mind. It cannot be a new reality introduced at some time or other into a universe of realities of a wholly different order. Therefore, the presupposition of the present existence of knowledge is the pre-existence of a mind or minds; it is not implied that its or their knowledge must always have been actual. In other words, knowing implies the ultimate or unoriginated existence of beings possessed of the capacity to know. Otherwise, knowledge would be a merely derivative product, capable of being stated in terms of something else, and in the end in terms of matter and motion. This implication is, however, in no wise traversed by the plain man's realism. For that implies, not that the existence of the physical world is prior to the existence of a mind, but only that it is prior to a mind's actual knowledge of the world.

The second line of thought appeals to the logic of relation. It may be stated thus. If a term is relative, i. e. is essentially 'of' or relative to another, that other is essentially relative to it. Just as a doctor, for instance, is essentially a doctor of a patient, so a patient is essentially the patient of a doctor. As a ruler implies subjects, so subjects imply a ruler. As a line essentially has points at its ends, so points are essentially ends of a line. Now knowledge is essentially 'of' or relative to reality. Reality, therefore, is essentially relative to or implies the knowledge of it. And this correlativity of knowledge and reality finds linguistic confirmation in the terms 'subject' and 'object'. For, linguistically, just as a subject is always the subject of an object, so an object is always the object of a subject.

Nevertheless, further analysis of the nature of relative terms, and in particular of knowledge, does not bear out this conclusion. To take the case of a doctor. It is true that if some one is healing, some one else is receiving treatment, i. e. is being healed; and 'patient' being the name for the recipient of treatment, we can express this fact by saying that a doctor is essentially the doctor of a patient. Further, it is true that a recipient of treatment implies a giver of it, as much as a giver of it implies a recipient. Hence we can truly say that since a doctor is the doctor of a patient, a patient is the patient of a doctor, meaning thereby that since that to which a doctor is relative is a patient, a patient must be similarly relative to a doctor. There is, however, another statement which can be made concerning a doctor. We can say that a doctor is a doctor of a human being who is ill, i. e. a sick man. But in this case we cannot go on to say that since a doctor is a doctor of a sick man, a sick man implies or is relative to a doctor. For we mean that the kind of reality capable of being related to a doctor as his patient is a sick man; and from this it does not follow that a reality of this kind does stand in this relation. Doctoring implies a sick man; a sick man does not imply that some one is treating him. We can only say that since a doctor is the doctor of a sick man, a sick man implies the possibility of doctoring. In the former case the terms, viz. 'doctor' and 'patient', are inseparable because they signify the relation in question in different aspects. The relation is one fact which has two inseparable 'sides', and, consequently, the terms must be inseparable which signify the relation respectively from the point of view of the one side and from the point of view of the other. Neither term signifies the nature of the elements which can stand in the relation. In the latter case, however, the terms, viz. 'doctor' and 'sick man', signify respectively the relation in question (in one aspect), and the nature of one of the elements capable of entering into it; consequently they are separable.

Now when it is said that knowledge is essentially knowledge of reality, the statement is parallel to the assertion that a doctor is essentially the doctor of a sick man, and not to the assertion that a doctor is essentially the doctor of a patient. It should mean that that which is capable of being related to a knower as his object is something which is or exists; consequently it cannot be said that since knowledge is of reality, reality must essentially be known. The parallel to the assertion that a doctor is the doctor of a patient is the assertion that knowledge is the knowledge of an object; for just as 'patient' means that which receives treatment from a doctor, so 'object' means that which is known. And here we *can* go on to make the further parallel assertion that since knowledge is essentially the knowledge of an object, an object is essentially an object of knowledge. Just as 'patient' means a recipient of treatment, or, more accurately, a sick man under treatment, so 'object' means something known, or, more accurately, a reality known. And 'knowledge' and 'object of knowledge', like 'doctor' and 'patient', indicate the same relation, though from different points of view, and, consequently, when we can use the one term, we can use the other. But to say that an object (i. e. a reality known) implies the knowledge of it is not to say that reality implies the knowledge of it, any more than to say that a patient implies a doctor is to say that a sick man implies a doctor.

But a doctor, it might be objected, is not a fair parallel to knowledge or a knower. A doctor, though an instance of a relative term, is only an instance of one kind of relative term, that in which the elements related are capable of existing apart from the relation, the relation being one in which they can come to stand and cease to stand. But there is another kind of relative term, in which the elements related presuppose the relation, and any thought of these elements involves the thought of the relation. A universal, e. g. whiteness, is always the universal of certain individuals, viz. individual whites; an individual, e. g. this white, is always an individual of a universal, viz. whiteness. A genus is the genus of a species, and vice versa. A surface is the surface of a volume, and a volume implies a surface. A point is the end of a line, and a line is bounded by points. In such cases the very being of the elements related involves the relation, and, apart from the relation, disappears. The difference between the two kinds of relative terms can be seen from the fact that only in the case of the former kind can two elements be found of which we can say significantly that their relation is of the kind in question. We can say of two men that they are related as doctor and patient, or as father and son, for we can apprehend two beings as men without being aware of them as so related. But of no two elements is it possible to say that their relation is that of universal and individual, or of genus and species, or of surface and volume; for to apprehend elements which are so related we must apprehend them so related.[160] To apprehend a surface is to apprehend a surface of a volume. To apprehend a volume is to apprehend a volume bounded by a surface. To apprehend a universal is to apprehend it as the universal of an individual, and vice versa.[161] In the case of relations of this kind, the being of either element which stands in the relation is relative to that of the other; neither can be real without the other, as we see if we try to think of one without the other. And it is at least possible that knowledge and reality or, speaking more strictly, a knower and reality, are related in this way.

What is, however, at least a strong presumption against this view is to be found in the fact that while relations of the second kind are essentially non-temporal, the relation of knowing is essentially temporal. The relation of a universal and its individuals, or of a surface and the volume which it bounds, does not either come to be, or persist, or cease. On the other hand, it is impossible to think of a knowing which is susceptible of no temporal predicates and is not bound up with a process; and the thought of knowing as something which comes to be involves the thought that the elements which become thus related exist independently of the relation. Moreover, the real refutation of the view lies in the fact that, when we

[160] It is, of course, possible to say significantly that two elements, A and B, are related as universal and individual, or as surface and volume, if we are trying to explain what we mean by 'universal and individual' or 'surface and volume'; but in that case we are elucidating the relationship through the already known relation of A and B, and are not giving information about the hitherto unknown relation of A and B.

[161] Professor Cook Wilson has pointed out that the distinction between these two kinds of relation is marked in language in that, for instance, while we speak of the 'relation *of* universal *and* individual', we speak of 'the relation *between* one man *and* another', or of 'the relation *of* one man *to* another', using, however, the phrase 'the relation *of* doctor *and* patient', when we consider two men only as in that relation.

I owe to him recognition of the fact that the use of the word 'relation' in connexion with such terms as 'universal and individual' is really justified.

consider what we really think, we find that we think that the relation between a knower and reality is not of the second kind. If we consider what we mean by 'a reality', we find that we mean by it something which is not correlative to a mind knowing it. It does not mean something the thought of which disappears with the thought of a mind actually knowing it, but something which, though it can be known by a mind, need not be actually known by a mind. Again, just as we think of a reality as something which *can* stand as object in the relation of knowledge, without necessarily being in this relation, so, as we see when we reflect, we think of a knowing mind as something which *can* stand as subject in this relation without necessarily being in the relation. For though we think of the capacities which constitute the nature of a knowing mind as only recognized through their actualizations, i. e. through actual knowing, we think of the mind which is possessed of these capacities as something apart from their actualization.

It is now possible to direct attention to two characteristics of perception and knowledge with which Kant's treatment of space and time conflicts, and the recognition of which reveals his procedure in its true light.

It has been already urged that both knowledge and perception—which, though not identical with knowledge, is presupposed by it—are essentially of *reality*. Now, in the *first* place, it is thereby implied that the relation between the mind and reality in knowledge or in perception is essentially direct, i. e. that there is no *tertium quid* in the form of an 'idea' or a 'representation' between us as perceiving or knowing and what we perceive or know. In other words, it is implied that Locke's view is wrong in principle, and, in fact, the contrary of the truth. In the *second* place, it is implied that while the whole fact of perception includes the reality perceived and the whole fact of knowledge includes the reality known, since both perception and knowledge are 'of', and therefore inseparable from a reality, yet the reality perceived or known is essentially distinct from, and cannot be stated in terms of, the perception or the knowledge. Just as neither perception nor knowledge can be stated in terms of the reality perceived or known from which they are distinguished, so the reality perceived or known cannot be stated in terms of the perception or the knowledge. In other words, the terms 'perception' and 'knowledge' ought to stand for the activities of perceiving and knowing respectively, and not for the reality perceived or known. Similarly, the terms 'idea' and 'representation'—the latter of which has been used as a synonym for Kant's *Vorstellung*—ought to stand not for something thought of or represented, but for the act of thinking or representing.

Further, this second implication throws light on the proper meaning of the terms 'form of perception' and 'form of knowledge or of thought'. For, in accordance with this implication, a 'form of perception' and a 'form of knowledge' ought to refer to the nature of our acts of perceiving and knowing or thinking respectively, and not to the nature of the realities perceived or known. Consequently, Kant was right in making the primary antithesis involved in the term 'form of perception' that between a way in which we perceive and a way in which things are, or, in other words, between a characteristic of our perceiving nature and a characteristic of the reality perceived. Moreover, Kant was also right in making this distinction a real antithesis and not a mere distinction within one and the same thing regarded from two points of view. That which is a form of perception cannot also be a form of the reality and vice versa. Thus we may illustrate a perceived form of perception by pointing out that our apprehension of the physical world (1) is a temporal process, and (2) is conditioned by perspective. Both the succession and the conditions of perspective belong to the act of perception, and do not form part of the nature of the world perceived. And it is significant that in our ordinary consciousness it never occurs to us to attribute either the perspective or the time to the reality perceived. Even if it be difficult in certain cases, as in that of colour, to decide whether something belongs to our act of perception or not, we never suppose that it can be *both* a form of perception *and* a characteristic of the reality perceived. We think that if it be the one, it cannot be the other.

Moreover, if we pass from perception to knowledge or thought—which in this context may be treated as identical—and seek to illustrate a form of knowledge or of thought, we may cite the distinction of logical subject and logical predicate of a judgement. The distinction as it should be understood—for it does not necessitate a difference of grammatical form—may be illustrated by the difference between the judgements 'Chess is the *most trying of games*' and '*Chess* is the most trying of games'. In the former case 'chess' is the logical subject, in the latter case it is the logical predicate. Now this distinction clearly does not reside in or belong to the reality about which we judge; it relates solely to the order of our approach in thought to various parts of its nature. For, to take the case of the former judgement, in calling 'chess' its subject, and 'most trying of games' its predicate, we are asserting that in this judgement we begin by apprehending the reality of which we are thinking as chess, and come to apprehend it as the most trying of games. In other words, the distinction relates solely to the order of our apprehension, and not to anything in the thing apprehended.

In view of the preceding, it is possible to make clear the nature of certain mistakes on Kant's part. In the first place, space, and time also, so far as we are thinking of the world, and not of our apprehension of it, as undergoing a temporal process, are essentially characteristics not of perception but of the reality perceived, and Kant, in treating space, and time, so regarded, as forms of perception, is really transferring to the perceiving subject that which in the whole fact 'perception of an object' or 'object perceived' belongs to the object.

Again, if we go on to ask how Kant manages to avoid drawing the conclusion proper to this transference, viz. that space and time are not characteristics of any realities at all, but belong solely to the process by which we come to apprehend them, we see that he does so because, in effect, he contravenes both the characteristics of perception referred to. For, in the first place, although in conformity with his theory he almost always *speaks* of space and time in terms of perception,[162] he consistently *treats* them as features of the reality perceived, i. e. of phenomena. Thus in arguing that space and time belong not to the understanding but to the sensibility, although he uniformly speaks of them as perceptions, his argument implies that they are objects of perception; for its aim, properly stated, is to show

[162] Cf. p. 26, note 70.

that space and time are not objects of thought but objects of perception. Consequently, in his treatment of space and time, he refers to what are both to him and in fact objects of perception in terms of perception, and thereby contravenes the second implication of perception to which attention has been drawn. Again, in the second place, if we go on to ask how Kant is misled into doing this, we see that it is because he contravenes the first implication of perception. In virtue of his theory of perception[163] he interposes a *tertium quid* between the reality perceived and the percipient, in the shape of an 'appearance'. This *tertium quid* gives him something which can plausibly be regarded as at once a perception and something perceived. For, though from the point of view of the thing in itself an appearance is an appearance or a perception of it, yet, regarded from the point of view of what it is in itself, an appearance is a reality perceived of the kind called mental. Hence space and time, being characteristics of an appearance, can be regarded as at once characteristics of our perception of a reality, viz. of a thing in itself, and characteristics of a reality perceived, viz. an appearance. Moreover, there is another point of view from which the treatment of bodies in space as appearances or phenomena gives plausibility to the view that space, though a form of perception, is a characteristic of a reality. When Kant speaks of space as the form of phenomena the fact to which he refers is that all bodies are spatial.[164] He means, not that space is a way in which we perceive something, but that it is a characteristic of things perceived, which he *calls* phenomena, and which *are* bodies. But, since in his statement of this fact he substitutes for bodies phenomena, which to him are perceptions, his statement can be put in the form 'space is *the form of perceptions*'; and the statement in this form is verbally almost identical with the statement that space is *a form of perception*. Consequently, the latter statement, which *should* mean that space is a way in which we perceive things, is easily identified with a statement of which the meaning is that space is a characteristic of something perceived.[165]

Again, Kant's account of time will be found to treat something represented or perceived as also a perception. We find two consecutive paragraphs[166] of which the aim is apparently to establish the contrary conclusions: (1) that time is only the form of our internal state and not of external phenomena, and (2) that time is the formal condition of all phenomena, external and internal.

To establish the first conclusion, Kant argues that time has nothing to do with shape or position, but, on the contrary, determines the relation of representations in our internal state. His meaning is that we have a succession of perceptions or representations of bodies in space,[167] and that while the bodies perceived are not related temporally, our perceptions or representations of them are so related. Here 'representations' refers to our apprehension, and is distinguished from what is

---

[163] Cf. pp. 15-16 and ff.

[164] Cf. pp. 20-21.

[165] It can be shown in the same way, *mutatis mutandis* (cp. p. 59), that the view that time, though the form of inner perception, is a characteristic of a reality gains plausibility from Kant's implicit treatment of our states as appearances due to ourselves.

[166] B. 49-50 (b) and (c), M. 30 (b) and (c).

[167] Kant here refers to bodies by the term 'phenomena', but their character as phenomena is not relevant to his argument.

represented, viz. bodies in space.

How, then, does Kant reach the second result? He remembers that bodies in space are 'phenomena', i. e. representations. He is, therefore, able to point out that all representations belong, as determinations of the mind, to our internal state, whether they have external things, i. e. bodies in space, for their objects or not, and that, consequently, they are subject to time. Hence time is concluded to be the form of all phenomena. In this second argument, however, it is clear that Kant has passed from his previous treatment of bodies in space as something represented or perceived to the treatment of them as themselves representations or perceptions.[168]

In conclusion, we may point out an insoluble difficulty in Kant's account of time. His treatment of space and time as the forms of outer and inner sense respectively implies that, while spatial relations apply to the realities which we perceive, temporal relations apply solely to our perceptions of them. Unfortunately, however, as Kant in certain contexts is clearly aware, time also belongs to the realities perceived. The moon, for instance, moves round the earth. Thus there are what may be called real successions as well as successions in our perception. Further, not only are we aware of this distinction in general, but in particular cases we succeed in distinguishing a succession of the one kind from a succession of the other. Yet from Kant's standpoint it would be impossible to distinguish them in particular cases, and even to be aware of the distinction in general. For the distinction is possible only so long as a distinction is allowed between our perceptions and the realities perceived. But for Kant this distinction has disappeared, for in the end the realities perceived are merely our perceptions; and time, if it be a characteristic of anything, must be a characteristic only of our perceptions.

---

[168] It may be noted that Kant's assertion (B. 50, M. 31) that time is the immediate condition of internal phenomena, and thereby also mediately the condition of external phenomena, does not help to reconcile the two positions.

CHAPTER VII

THE METAPHYSICAL DEDUCTION OF THE CATEGORIES

THE aim of the *Aesthetic* is to answer the first question of the *Critique* propounded in the Introduction, viz. 'How is pure mathematics possible?'[169] The aim of the *Analytic* is to answer the second question, viz. 'How is pure natural science possible?' It has previously[170] been implied that the two questions are only verbally of the same kind. Since Kant thinks of the judgements of mathematics as self-evident, and therefore as admitting of no reasonable doubt[171], he takes their truth for granted. Hence the question, 'How is pure mathematics possible?' means 'Granted the truth of mathematical judgements, what inference can we draw concerning the nature of the reality to which they relate?'; and the inference is to proceed from the truth of the judgements to the nature of the reality to which they relate. Kant, however, considers that the principles underlying natural science, of which the law of causality is the most prominent, are not self-evident, and consequently need proof.[172] Hence, the question, 'How is pure natural science possible?' means 'What justifies the assertion that the presuppositions of natural science are true?' and the inference is to proceed from the nature of the objects of natural science to the truth of the *a priori* judgements which relate to them.

Again, as Kant rightly sees, the vindication of the presuppositions of natural science, to be complete, requires the discovery upon a definite principle of *all* these presuppositions. The clue to this discovery he finds in the view that, just as the perceptions of space and time originate in the sensibility, so the *a priori* conceptions and laws which underlie natural science originate in the understanding; for, on this view, the discovery of all the conceptions and laws which originate in the understanding will be at the same time the discovery of all the presuppositions of natural science.

Kant therefore in the *Analytic* has a twofold problem to solve. He has firstly to discover the conceptions and laws which belong to the understanding as such, and secondly to vindicate their application to individual things. Moreover, although it is obvious that the conceptions and the laws of the understanding must be closely related,[173] he reserves them for separate treatment.

---

[169] B. 20, M. 13.

[170] pp. 12-13.

[171] Cf. p. 12, note 20.

[172] Cf. p. 13, notes 21 and 22.

[173] E. g. the conception of 'cause and effect', and the law that 'all changes take place

The *Analytic* is accordingly subdivided into the *Analytic of Conceptions* and the *Analytic of Principles*. The *Analytic of Conceptions*, again, is divided into the *Metaphysical Deduction of the Categories*, the aim of which is to discover the conceptions of the understanding, and the *Transcendental Deduction of the Categories*, the aim of which is to vindicate their validity, i. e. their applicability to individual things.

It should further be noticed that, according to Kant, it is the connexion of the *a priori* conceptions and laws underlying natural science with the *understanding* which constitutes the main difficulty of the vindication of their validity, and renders necessary an answer of a different kind to that which would have been possible, if the validity of mathematical judgements had been in question.

"We have been able above, with little trouble, to make comprehensible how the conceptions of space and time, although *a priori* knowledge, must necessarily relate to objects and render possible a synthetic knowledge of them independently of all experience. For since an object can appear to us, i. e. be an object of empirical perception, only by means of such pure forms of sensibility, space and time are pure perceptions, which contain *a priori* the condition of the possibility of objects as phenomena, and the synthesis in space and time has objective validity."

"On the other hand, the categories of the understanding do not represent the conditions under which objects are given in perception; consequently, objects can certainly appear to us without their necessarily being related to functions of the understanding, and therefore without the understanding containing *a priori* the conditions of these objects. Hence a difficulty appears here, which we did not meet in the field of sensibility, viz. how *subjective conditions of thought* can have *objective validity*, i. e. can furnish conditions of the possibility of all knowledge of objects; for phenomena can certainly be given us in perception without the functions of the understanding. Let us take, for example, the conception of cause, which indicates a peculiar kind of synthesis in which on A something entirely different B is placed[174] according to a law. It is not *a priori* clear why phenomena should contain something of this kind . . . and it is consequently doubtful *a priori*, whether such a conception is not wholly empty, and without any corresponding object among phenomena. For that objects of sensuous perception must conform to the formal conditions of the sensibility which lie *a priori* in the mind is clear, since otherwise they would not be objects for us; but that they must also conform to the conditions which the understanding requires for the synthetical unity of thought is a conclusion the cogency of which it is not so easy to see. For phenomena might quite well be so constituted that the understanding did not find them in conformity with the conditions of its unity, and everything might lie in such confusion that, e. g. in the succession of phenomena, nothing might present itself which would offer a rule of synthesis, and so correspond to the conception of cause and effect, so that this conception would be quite empty, null, and meaningless. Phenomena would none the less present objects to our perception, for perception does not in any way require the functions of thinking."[175]

according to the law of the connexion between cause and effect'.

[174] *Gesetzt.*

[175] B. 121-3, M. 75-6.

This passage, if read in connexion with that immediately preceding it,[176] may be paraphrased as follows: 'The argument of the *Aesthetic* assumes the validity of mathematical judgements, which as such relate to space and time, and thence it deduces the phenomenal character of space and time, and of what is contained therein. At the same time the possibility of questioning the validity of the law of causality, and of similar principles, may lead us to question even the validity of mathematical judgements. In the case of mathematical judgements, however, in consequence of their relation to perception, an answer is readily forthcoming. We need only reverse the original argument and appeal directly to the phenomenal character of space and time and of what is contained in them. Objects in space and time, being appearances, must conform to the laws according to which we have appearances; and since space and time are only ways in which we perceive, or have appearances, mathematical laws, which constitute the general nature of space and time, are the laws according to which we have appearances. Mathematical laws, then, constitute the general structure of appearances, and, as such, enter into the very being of objects in space and time. But the case is otherwise with the conceptions and principles underlying natural science. For the law of causality, for instance, is a law not of our perceiving but of our thinking nature, and consequently it is not presupposed in the presentation to us of objects in space and time. Objects in space and time, being appearances, need conform only to the laws of our perceiving nature. We have therefore to explain the possibility of saying that a law of our thinking nature must be valid for objects which, as conditioned merely by our perceiving nature, are independent of the laws of our thinking; for phenomena might be so constituted as not to correspond to the necessities of our thought.'

No doubt Kant's *solution* of this problem in the *Analytic* involves an emphatic denial of the central feature of this statement of it, viz. that phenomena may be given in perception without any help from the activity of the understanding.[177] Hence it may be urged that this passage merely expresses a temporary aberration on Kant's part, and should therefore be ignored. Nevertheless, in spite of this inconsistency, the view that phenomena may be given in perception without help from the activity of the understanding forms the basis of the difference of treatment which Kant thinks necessary for the vindication of the judgements underlying natural science and for that of the judgements of mathematics.

We may now consider how Kant 'discovers' the categories or conceptions which belong to the understanding as such.[178] His method is sound in principle. He begins with an account of the understanding in general. He then determines its essential differentiations. Finally, he argues that each of these differentiations involves a special conception, and that therefore these conceptions taken together constitute an exhaustive list of the conceptions which belong to the understanding.

His account of the understanding is expressed thus: "The understanding was explained above only negatively, as a non-sensuous faculty of knowledge. Now, independently of sensibility, we cannot have any perception; consequently, the

[176] B. 120-1, M. 73-4.

[177] Cf. B. 137-8, M. 85, and B. 160 note, M. 98 note.

[178] B. 91-105, M. 56-63.

understanding is no faculty of perception. But besides perception there is no other kind of knowledge, except through conceptions. Consequently, the knowledge of every understanding, or at least of every human understanding, is a knowledge through conceptions,—not perceptive, but discursive. All perceptions, as sensuous, depend on affections; conceptions, therefore, upon functions. By the word function, I understand the unity of the act of arranging different representations under one common representation. Conceptions, then, are based on the spontaneity of thinking, as sensuous perceptions are on the receptivity of impressions. Now the understanding cannot make any other use of these conceptions than to judge by means of them. Since no representation, except only the perception, refers immediately to the object, a conception is never referred immediately to an object, but to some other representation thereof, be that a perception or itself a conception. A judgement, therefore, is the mediate knowledge of an object, consequently the representation of a representation of it. In every judgement there is a conception which is valid for many representations, and among these also comprehends a given representation, this last being then immediately referred to the object. For example, in the judgement 'All bodies are divisible', our conception of the divisible refers to various other conceptions; among these, however, it is herein particularly referred to the conception of body, and this conception of body is referred to certain phenomena which present themselves to us. These objects, therefore, are mediately represented by the conception of divisibility. Accordingly, all judgements are functions of unity in our representations, since, instead of an immediate, a higher representation, which comprehends this and several others, is used for the knowledge of the object, and thereby many possible items of knowledge are collected into one. But we can reduce all acts of the understanding to judgements, so that the *understanding* in general can be represented as a *faculty of judging*."[179]

It is not worth while to go into all the difficulties of this confused and artificial passage. Three points are clear upon the surface. In the first place, the account of the understanding now given differs from that given earlier in the *Critique*[180] in that, instead of merely distinguishing, it separates the sensibility and the understanding, and treats them as contributing, not two inseparable factors involved in all knowledge, but two kinds of knowledge. In the second place, the guise of argument is very thin, and while Kant ostensibly *proves*, he really only *asserts* that the understanding is the faculty of judgement. In the third place, in describing judgement Kant is hampered by trying to oppose it as the mediate knowledge of an object to perception as the immediate knowledge of an object. A perception is said to relate immediately to an object; in contrast with this, a conception is said to relate immediately only to another conception or to a perception, and mediately to an object through relation to a perception, either directly or through another conception. Hence a judgement, as being the use of a conception, viz. the predicate of the judgement, is said to be the mediate knowledge of an object. But if this distinction be examined, it will be found that two kinds of immediate relation are involved, and that the account of perception is not really compatible with that of judgement.

[179] B. 92-4, M. 56-7.

[180] B. 74-6, M. 45-6.

When a perception is said to relate immediately to an object, the relation in question is that between a sensation or appearance produced by an object acting upon or affecting the sensibility and the object which produces it. But when a conception is said to relate immediately to another conception or to a perception, the relation in question is that of universal and particular, i. e. that of genus and species or of universal and individual. For the conception is said to be 'valid for' (i. e. to 'apply to') and to 'comprehend' the conception or perception to which it is immediately related; and again, when a conception is said to relate mediately to an object, the relation meant is its 'application' to the object, even though in this case the application is indirect. Now if a perception to which a conception is related—either directly or indirectly through another conception—were an appearance produced by an object, the conception could never be related to the object in the sense required, viz. that it applies to it; for an appearance does not *apply to* but is *produced* by the object. Consequently, when Kant is considering a conception, and therefore also when he is considering a judgement, which is the use of a conception, he is really thinking of the perception to which it is related as an *object of* perception, i. e. as a perceived individual, and he has ceased to think of a perception as an appearance produced by an object.[181] Hence in considering Kant's account of a conception and of judgement, we should ignore his account of perception, and therefore also his statement that judgement is the mediate knowledge of an object.

If we do so, we see that Kant's account of judgement simply amounts to this: 'Judgement is the use of a conception or 'universal'; the use of a conception or universal consists in bringing under it corresponding individuals or species. Consequently, judgement is a function producing unity. If, for instance, we judge 'All bodies are divisible', we thereby unify 'bodies' with other kinds of divisible things by bringing them under the conception of divisibility; and if we judge 'This body is divisible' we thereby unify this divisible body with others by bringing it and them under the conception of divisibility.'[182] Again, since 'the understanding in general can be represented as a *faculty of judging*', it follows that the activity of the understanding consists in introducing unity into our representations, by bringing individuals or species—both these being representations—under the corresponding universal or conception.[183]

---

[181] Kant, in *illustrating* the nature of a judgement, evades the difficulty occasioned by his account of perception, by illustrating a 'perception' by the 'conception of body', and 'objects' by 'certain phenomena'. He thereby covertly substitutes the relation of universal and individual for the relation of an appearance and the object which causes it.

[182] It is not Kant's general account of judgement given in this passage, but the account of perception incompatible with it, which leads him to confine his illustrations to universal judgements.

[183] We may note three minor points. (1) Kant's definition of function as 'the unity of the act of arranging [i. e. the act which produces unity by arranging] different representations under a common representation' has no justification in its immediate context, and is occasioned solely by the forthcoming description of judgement. (2) Kant has no right to distinguish the activity which *originates* conceptions, or upon which they depend, from the activity which *uses* conceptions, viz. judgement. For the act of arranging diverse representations under a common representation which originates conceptions is the act of judgement as Kant describes it. (3) It is wholly artificial to speak of judgement as 'the representation of

Having explained the nature of the understanding, Kant proceeds to take the next step. His aim being to connect the understanding with the categories, and the categories being a plurality, he has to show that the activity of judgement can be differentiated into several kinds, each of which must subsequently be shown to involve a special category. Hence, solely in view of the desired conclusion, and in spite of the fact that he has described the activity of judgement as if it were always of the same kind, he passes in effect from the singular to the plural and asserts that 'all the functions of the understanding can be discovered, when we can completely exhibit the functions of unity in judgements'. After this preliminary transition, he proceeds to assert that, if we abstract in general from all content of a judgement and fix our attention upon the mere form of the understanding, we find that the function of thinking in a judgement can be brought under four heads, each of which contains three subdivisions. These, which are borrowed with slight modifications from Formal Logic, are expressed as follows.[184]

I. *Quantity.*
Universal
Particular
Singular.

II. *Quality.*
Affirmative
Negative
Infinite.

III. *Relation.*
Categorical
Hypothetical
Disjunctive.

IV. *Modality.*
Problematic
Assertoric
Apodeictic.

These distinctions, since they concern only the form of judgements, belong, according to Kant, to the activity of judgement as such, and in fact constitute its essential differentiations.

Now, before we consider whether this is really the case, we should ask what answer Kant's account of judgement would lead us to expect to the question 'What are all the functions of unity in judgement?' The question must mean 'What are the kinds of unity produced by judgement?' To this question three alternative answers are prima facie possible. (1) There is only one kind of unity, that of a group of particulars unified through relation to the corresponding universal. The special unity produced will differ for different judgements, since it will depend upon the special universal involved. The kind or form of unity, however, will always be the same, viz. that of particulars related through the corresponding universal. For instance, 'plants' and 'trees' are unified respectively by the judgements 'This body is a plant' and 'This body is a tree'; for 'this body' is in the one case related to other 'plants' and in the other case to other 'trees'. And though the unity produced is different in each case, the kind of unity is the same; for plants and trees are, as members of a kind, unities of a special kind distinct from unities of another kind, such as the parts of a spatial or numerical whole. (2) There are as many kinds of unity as there are universals. Every group of particulars forms a unity of a special

a representation of an object'.

[184] B. 95, M. 58.

kind through relation to the corresponding universal. (3) There are as many kinds of unity as there are highest universals or *summa genera*. These *summa genera* are the most general sources of unity through which individuals are related in groups, directly or indirectly. The kinds of unity are therefore in principle the Aristotelian categories, i. e. the highest forms of being under which all individuals fall.

Nevertheless, it is easy to see that the second and third answers should be rejected in favour of the first. For though, according to Kant, a judgement unifies particulars by bringing them under a universal, the special universal involved in a given judgement belongs not to the judgement as such, but to the particulars unified. What belongs to the judgement as such is simply the fact that the particulars are brought under a universal. In other words, the judgement as such determines the kind of unity but not the particular unity. The judgements 'Gold is a metal' and 'Trees are green', considered merely as judgements and not as the particular judgements which they are, involve the same kind of unity, viz. that of particulars as particulars of a universal; for the distinction between 'metal' and 'green' is a distinction not of kinds of unity but of unities. Moreover, to anticipate the discussion of Kant's final conclusion, the moral is that Kant's account of judgement should have led him to recognize that judgement involves the reality, not of any special universals or—in Kant's language—conceptions, but of universality or conception as such. In other words, on his view of judgement the activity of the understanding implies simply that there *are* universals or conceptions; it does not imply the existence of special conceptions which essentially belong to the understanding, e. g. that of 'cause' or 'plurality'.[185]

If we now turn to the list of the activities of thought in judgement, borrowed from Formal Logic, we shall see that it is not in any way connected with Kant's account of judgement.[186] For if the kinds of judgement distinguished by Formal Logic are to be regarded as different ways of unifying, the plurality unified must be allowed to be not a special kind of group of particulars, but the two conceptions which constitute the terms of the judgement[187]; and the unity produced must be allowed to be in no case a special form of the unity of particulars related through the corresponding universal. Thus the particular judgement 'Some coroners are doctors' must be said to unify the conceptions of 'coroner' and of 'doctor', and presumably by means of the conception of 'plurality'. Again, the hypothetical judgement 'If it rains, the ground will be wet' must be said to unify the judgements 'It rains' and 'The ground will be wet', and presumably by means of the conception of 'reason and consequence'. In neither case can the act of unification be consid-

---

[185] To this failure in Kant's argument is due the difficulty in following his transition from 'function' to 'functions' of judgements. The judgement, as Kant describes it, always does one and the same thing; it unifies particulars by bringing them under a universal. This activity does not admit of differentiation.

[186] Moreover, the forms of judgement clearly lack the systematic character which Kant claims for them. Even if it be allowed that the subdivisions within the four main heads of quantity, quality, relation, and modality are based upon single principles of division, it cannot be said that the four heads themselves originate from a common principle.

[187] In the case of the third division, the plurality unified will be two prior judgements.

ered a special form of the act of recognizing particulars as particulars of the corresponding universal. The fact is that the distinctions drawn by Formal Logic are based on a view of judgement which is different from, and even incompatible with, Kant's, and they arise from the attempt to solve a different problem. The problem before Kant in describing judgement is to distinguish the understanding from the sensibility, i. e. thought from perception. Hence he regards judgement as the act of unifying a manifold given in perception, directly, or indirectly by means of a conception. But this is not the problem with which Formal Logic is occupied. Formal Logic assumes judgement to be an act which relates material given to it in the shape of 'conceptions' or 'judgements' by analysis of this material, and seeks to discover the various modes of relation thereby effected. The work of judgement, however, cannot consist *both* in relating particulars through a conception *and* in relating two conceptions or judgements.

It may be urged that this criticism only affects Kant's argument, but not his conclusion. Possibly, it may be said, the list of types of judgement borrowed from Formal Logic really expresses the essential differentiations of judgement, and, in that case, Kant's only mistake is that he bases them upon a false or at least inappropriate account of judgement.[188] Moreover, since this list furnishes Kant with the 'clue' to the categories, provided that it expresses the essential differentiations of judgement, the particular account of judgement upon which it is based is a matter of indifference.

This contention leads us to consider the last stage of Kant's argument, in which he deduces the categories in detail from his list of the forms of judgement. For it is clear that unless the forms of judgement severally involve the categories, it will not matter whether these forms are or are not the essential differentiations of judgement.

Kant's mode of connecting the categories in detail with the forms of judgement discovered by Formal Logic is at least as surprising as his mode of connecting the latter with the nature of judgement in general. Since the twelve distinctions within the form of judgement are to serve as a clue to the conceptions which belong to the understanding, we naturally expect that each distinction will be found directly to involve a special conception or category, and that therefore, to discover the categories, we need only look for the special conception involved in each form of judgement.[189] Again, since the plurality unified in a judgement of each form is the two conceptions or judgements which form the matter of the judgement, we should expect the conception involved in each form of judgement to be merely the type of relationship established between these conceptions or judgements. This expectation is confirmed by a cursory glance at the table of categories.[190]

[188] It may be noted that the account cannot be merely inappropriate to the general problem, if it be *incompatible* with that assumed by Formal Logic.

[189] This expectation is confirmed by Kant's view that judgement introduces unity into a plurality by means of a conception. This view leads us to expect that different forms of judgement—if there be any—will be distinguished by the different conceptions through which they unify the plurality; for it will naturally be the different conceptions involved which are responsible for the different kinds of unity effected.

[190] B. 106, M. 64.

I. *Of Quantity.*	II. *Of Quality.*
Unity	Reality
Plurality	Negation
Totality.	Limitation.

III. *Of Relation.*	IV. *Of Modality.*
Inherence and Subsistence (*Substantia et Accidens*)	Possibility—Impossibility
Causality and Dependence (*Cause and Effect*)	Existence—Non-existence
Community (*Reciprocity between the agent and patient.*)	Necessity—Contingence.

If we compare the first division of these categories with the first division of judgements we naturally think that Kant conceived singular, particular, and universal judgements to unify their terms by means of the conceptions of 'one', of 'some', and of 'all' respectively; and we form corresponding, though less confident, expectations in the case of the other divisions.

Kant, however, makes no attempt to show that each form of judgement distinguished by Formal Logic involves a special conception. In fact, his view is that the activities of thought studied by Formal Logic do not originate or use any special conceptions at all. For his actual deduction of the categories[191] is occupied in showing that although thought, when exercised under the conditions under which it is studied by Formal Logic, does not originate and use conceptions of its own, it is able under certain other conditions to originate and use such conceptions, i. e. categories.[192] Hence if we attend only to the professed procedure of the deduction, we are compelled to admit that the deduction not only excludes any use of the 'clue' to the categories, supposed to be furnished by Formal Logic, but even fails to deduce them at all. For it does not even nominally attempt to discover the categories in detail, but reverts to the prior task of showing merely that there are categories. Doubtless Kant thinks that the forms of judgement formulated by Formal Logic in some way *suggest* the conceptions which become operative in thought under these other conditions. Nevertheless, it is impossible to see how these forms of judgement can suggest these conceptions, unless they actually presuppose them.

It is clear, however, that the professed link[193] between the forms of judgement and the categories does not represent the actual process by which Kant reached his list of categories; for he could never have reached any list of categories by an argument which was merely directed to show that there are categories. Moreover, an inspection of the list shows that he actually reached it partly by noticing the conceptions which the forms of judgement seemed to presuppose, and partly by

[191] B. 102-5, M. 62-3.
[192] Cf. pp. 89-90.
[193] B. 102-5, M. 62-3.

bearing in mind the general conceptions underlying physics which it was his ultimate aim to vindicate. Since this is the case, and since the categories can only be connected with the forms of judgement by showing that they are presupposed in them, the proper question to be considered from the point of view of the metaphysical deduction is simply whether the forms of judgement really presuppose the categories.[194]

If, however, we examine the forms of judgement distinguished by Formal Logic, we find that they do not presuppose the categories. To see this, it is only necessary to examine the four main divisions of judgement *seriatim*.

The first division of judgements is said to be a division in respect of quantity into singular, particular, and universal. So stated, the division is numerical. It is a division of judgements according as they make an assertion about one, more than one, or all the members of a kind. Each species may be said to presuppose (1) the conception of quantity, and (2) a conception peculiar to itself: the first presupposing the conception of one member of a kind, the second that of more than one but less than all members of a kind, the third that of all members of a kind. Moreover, a judgement of each kind may perhaps be said to relate the predicate conception to the subject conception by means of one of these three conceptions.

The fundamental division, however, into which universal and singular judgements enter is not numerical at all, and ignores particular judgements altogether. It is that between such judgements as "Three-sided figures, as such, are three-angled' and 'This man is tall'. The essential distinction is that in the universal judgement the predicate term is apprehended to belong to the subject through our insight that it is necessitated by the nature of the subject term, while in the singular judgement our apprehension that the predicate term belongs to the subject is based upon the perception or experience of the coexistence of predicate and subject terms in a common subject. In other words, it is the distinction between an *a priori* judgement and a judgement of perception.[195] The merely numerically universal judgement, and the merely numerically particular judgement[196] are simply aggregates of singular judgements, and therefore are indistinguishable in principle from the singular judgement. If then we ask what conceptions are really presupposed by the kinds of judgement which Kant seeks to distinguish in the first division, we can only reply that the universal judgement presupposes the conception of a connected or systematic whole of attributes, and that the singular judgement presupposes the conception of the coexistence of two attributes in a common subject. Neither kind of judgement presupposes the conception of quantity or the conceptions of unity, plurality, and totality.

[194] As we shall see later, the real importance of the passage in which Kant professes to effect the transition from the forms of judgement to the categories (B. 102-5, M. 62-3) lies in its introduction of a new and important line of thought, on which the transcendental deduction turns. Consideration of it is therefore deferred to the next chapter.

[195] I owe this view of the distinction to Professor Cook Wilson's lectures on logic.

[196] 'Some coroners are doctors' of course in some contexts means, 'it is possible for a coroner to be a doctor,' and is therefore not numerical; but understood in this sense it is merely a weakened form of the universal judgement in which the connexion apprehended between subject and predicate terms is incomplete.

The second division of judgements is said to be a division in respect of quality into affirmative, negative, and infinite, i. e. into species which may be illustrated by the judgements, 'A college is a place of education,' 'A college is not a hotel,' and 'A college is a not-hotel'. The conceptions involved are said to be those of reality, of negation, and of limitation respectively. The conception of limitation may be ignored, since the infinite judgement said to presuppose it is a fiction. On the other hand, the conceptions of reality and negation, even if their existence be conceded, cannot be allowed to be the conceptions presupposed. For when we affirm or deny, we affirm or deny of something not mere being, but being of a particular kind. The conceptions presupposed are rather those of identity and difference. It is only because differences fall within an identity that we can affirm, and it is only because within an identity there are differences that we can deny.

The third division of judgements is said to be in respect of relation into categorical, hypothetical, and disjunctive judgements. Here, again, the conclusion which Kant desires is clearly impossible. The categorical judgement may be said to presuppose the conception of subject and attribute, but not that of substance and accident. The hypothetical judgement may be conceded to presuppose the conception of reason and consequence, but it certainly does not presuppose the conception of cause and effect.[197] Lastly, while the disjunctive judgement may be said to presuppose the conception of mutually exclusive species of a genus, it certainly does not presuppose the conception of reciprocal action between physical things.

The fourth division of judgement is said to be in respect of modality into assertoric, problematic, and apodeictic, the conceptions involved being respectively those of possibility and impossibility, of actuality and non-actuality, and of necessity and contingence. Now, from the point of view of Kant's argument, these conceptions, like those which he holds to be involved in the other divisions of judgement, must be considered to relate to reality and not to our attitude towards it. Considered in this way, they resolve themselves into the conceptions of—

(1) the impossible (impossibility);

(2) the possible but not actual (possibility, nonexistence);

(3) the actual but not necessary (existence, contingence);

(4) the necessary (necessity).

But since it must, in the end, be conceded that all fact is necessary, it is impossible to admit the reality of the conception of the possible but not actual, and of the actual but not necessary. There remain, therefore, only the conceptions of the necessary and of the impossible. In fact, however, the distinctions between the assertoric, the problematic, and the apodeictical judgement relate to our attitude to reality and not to reality, and therefore involve no different conceptions relating to reality. It must, therefore, be admitted that the 'metaphysical' deduction of the categories breaks down doubly. Judgement, as Kant describes it, does not involve the

[197] No doubt, as the schematism of the categories shows, Kant does not think that the hypothetical judgement *directly* involves the conception of cause and effect, i. e. of the relation of necessary succession between the various states of physical things. The point is, however, that the hypothetical judgement does not involve it at all.

forms of judgement borrowed from Formal Logic as its essential differentiations; and these forms of judgement do not involve the categories.

CHAPTER VIII

THE TRANSCENDENTAL DEDUCTION OF THE CATEGORIES

THE aim of the *Transcendental Deduction* is to show that the categories, though *a priori* as originating in the understanding, are valid, i. e. applicable to individual things. It is the part of the *Critique* which has attracted most attention and which is the most difficult to follow. The difficulty of interpretation is increased rather than diminished by the complete rewriting of this portion in the second edition. For the second version, though it does not imply a change of view, is undoubtedly even more obscure than the first. It indeed makes one new contribution to the subject by adding an important link in the argument,[198] but the importance of the link is nullified by the fact that it is not really the link which it professes to be. The method of treatment adopted here will be to consider only the minimum of passages necessary to elucidate Kant's meaning and to make use primarily of the first edition.

It is necessary, however, first to consider the passage in the *Metaphysical Deduction* which nominally connects the list of categories with the list of forms of judgement.[199] For its real function is to introduce a new and third account of knowledge, which forms the keynote of the *Transcendental Deduction*.[200]

In this passage, the meaning of which it is difficult to state satisfactorily, Kant's thought appears to be as follows: 'The activity of thought studied by Formal Logic relates by way of judgement conceptions previously obtained by an analysis of perceptions. For instance, it relates the conceptions of body and of divisibility, obtained by analysis of perceptions of bodies, in the judgement 'Bodies are divisible'. It effects this, however, merely by analysis of the conception 'body'. Consequently, the resulting knowledge or judgement, though *a priori,* is only analytic, and the conceptions involved originate not from thought but from the manifold previously analysed. But besides the conceptions obtained by analysis of a given manifold, there are others which belong to thought or the understanding as such, and in virtue of which thought originates synthetic *a priori* knowledge, this activity of thought being that studied by Transcendental Logic. Two questions therefore arise. Firstly, how do these conceptions obtain a matter to which they can apply

[198] Cf. p. 110-113.

[199] B. 102-5, M. 62-3. Cf. pp. 82-83.

[200] The first two accounts are (1) that of judgement given B. 92-4, M. 56-8, and (2) that of judgement implicit in the view that the forms of judgement distinguished by Formal Logic are functions of unity. In A. 126, Mah. 215, Kant seems to imply—though untruly—that this new account coincides with the other two, which he does not distinguish.

and without which they would be without content or empty? And, secondly, how does thought in virtue of these conceptions originate synthetic *a priori* knowledge? The first question is easily answered, for the manifolds of space and time, i. e. individual spaces and individual times, afford matter of the kind needed to give these conceptions content. As perceptions (i. e. as objects of perception), they are that to which a conception can apply, and as pure or *a priori* perceptions, they are that to which those conceptions can apply which are pure or *a priori*, as belonging to the understanding. The second question can be answered by considering the process by which this pure manifold of space and time enters into knowledge. All synthetic knowledge, whether empirical or *a priori*, requires the realization of three conditions. In the first place, there must be a manifold given in perception. In the second place, this manifold must be 'gone through, taken up, and combined'. In other words, if synthesis be defined as 'the act of joining different representations to one another and of including their multiplicity in one knowledge', the manifold must be subjected to an act of synthesis. This is effected by the imagination. In the third place, this synthesis produced by the imagination must be brought to a conception, i. e. brought under a conception which will constitute the synthesis a unity. This is the work of the understanding. The realization of *a priori* knowledge, therefore, will require the realization of the three conditions in a manner appropriate to its *a priori* character. There must be a pure or *a priori* manifold; this is to be found in individual spaces and individual times. There must be an act of pure synthesis of this manifold; this is effected by the pure imagination. Finally, this pure synthesis must be brought under a conception. This is effected by the pure understanding by means of its pure or a priori conceptions, i. e. the categories. This, then, is the process by which *a priori* knowledge is originated. The activity of thought or understanding, however, which unites two conceptions in a judgement by analysis of them—this being the act studied by Formal Logic—is the same as that which gives unity to the synthesis of the pure manifold of perception —this being the act studied by Transcendental Logic. Consequently, 'the same understanding, and indeed by the same activities whereby in dealing with conceptions it unifies them in a judgement by an act of analysis, introduces by means of the synthetical unity which it produces in the pure manifold of perception a content into its own conceptions, in consequence of which these conceptions are called pure conceptions of the understanding,'[201] and we are entitled to say *a priori* that these conceptions apply to objects because they are involved in the process by which we acquire *a priori* knowledge of objects.'

A discussion of the various difficulties raised by the general drift of this passage, as well as by its details,[202] is unnecessary, and would anticipate discussion of the *Transcendental Deduction*. But it is necessary to draw attention to three points.

In the first place, as has been said, Kant here introduces—and introduces without warning—a totally new account of knowledge. It has its origin in his theory

[201] An interpretation of B. 105 init., M. 63 fin.

[202] E. g. Kant's arbitrary assertion that the operation of counting presupposes the conception of that number which forms the scale of notation adopted as the source of the unity of the synthesis. This is of course refuted among other ways by the fact that a number of units less than the scale of notation can be counted.

of perception, according to which knowledge begins with the production of sensations in us by things in themselves. Since the spatial world which we come to know consists in a multiplicity of related elements, it is clear that the isolated data of sensation have somehow to be combined and unified, if we are to have this world before us or, in other words, to know it. Moreover, since these empirical data are subject to space and time as the forms of perception, individual spaces and individual times, to which the empirical data will be related, have also to be combined and unified. On this view, the process of knowledge consists in combining certain data into an individual whole and in unifying them through a principle of combination.[203] If the data are empirical, the resulting knowledge will be empirical; if the data are *a priori*, i. e. individual spaces and individual times, the resulting knowledge will be *a priori*.[204] This account of knowledge is new, because, although it treats knowledge as a process or act of unifying a manifold, it describes a different act of unification. As Kant first described the faculty of judgement,[205] it unifies a group of particulars through relation to the corresponding universal. As Formal Logic, according to Kant, treats the faculty of judgement, it unifies two conceptions or two prior judgements into a judgement. As Kant now describes the faculty of judgement or thought, it unifies an empirical or an *a priori* manifold of perception combined into an individual whole, through a conception which constitutes a principle of unity. The difference between this last account and the others is also shown by the fact that while the first two kinds of unification are held to be due to mere analysis of the material given to thought, the third kind of unification is held to be superinduced by thought, and to be in no way capable of being extracted from the material by analysis. Further, this new account of knowledge does not replace the others, but is placed side by side with them. For, according to Kant, there exist *both* the activity of thought which relates two conceptions in a judgement,[206] *and* the activity by which it introduces a unity of its own into a manifold of perception. Nevertheless, this new account of knowledge, or rather this account of a new kind of knowledge, must be the important one; for it is only the process now described for the first time which produces synthetic as opposed to analytic knowledge.

In the second place, the passage incidentally explains why, according to Kant, the forms of judgement distinguished by Formal Logic do not involve the categories.[207] For its doctrine is that while thought, if exercised under the conditions under which it is studied by Formal Logic, can only analyse the manifold given to it, and so has, as it were, to borrow from the manifold the unity through which

---

[203] Cf. A. 97, Mah. 193, 'Knowledge is a totality of compared and connected representations.'

[204] No doubt Kant would allow that at least some categories, e. g. the conception of cause and effect, are principles of synthesis of a manifold which at any rate contains an empirical element, but it *includes* just one of the difficulties of the passage that it implies that *a priori* knowledge either is, or involves, a synthesis of pure or *a priori* elements.

[205] B. 92-4, M. 56-8.

[206] Kant, of course, thinks of this activity of thought, as identical with that which brings particulars under a conception.

[207] Cf. pp. 82-83.

it relates the manifold,[208] yet if an *a priori* manifold be given to it, it can by means of a conception introduce into the manifold a unity of its own which could not be discovered by analysis of the manifold. Thus thought as studied by Formal Logic merely analyses and consequently does not and cannot make use of conceptions of its own; it can use conceptions of its own only when an *a priori* manifold is given to it to deal with.

In the third place, there is great difficulty in following the part in knowledge assigned to the understanding. The synthesis of the manifold of perception is assigned to the imagination, a faculty which, like the new kind of knowledge, is introduced without notice. The business of the understanding is to 'bring this synthesis to conceptions' and thereby to 'give unity to the synthesis'. Now the question arises whether 'the activity of giving unity to the synthesis' really means what it says, i. e. an activity which *unifies* or *introduces a unity into* the synthesis, or whether it only means an activity which *recognizes* a unity already given to the synthesis by the imagination. Prima facie Kant is maintaining that the understanding really unifies, or introduces the principle of unity. For the twice-repeated phrase 'give unity to the synthesis' seems unmistakable in meaning, and the important rôle in knowledge is plainly meant to be assigned to the understanding. Kant's language, however, is not decisive; for he speaks of the synthesis of the manifold as that which 'first produces a knowledge which indeed at first may be crude and confused and therefore needs *analysis*[209]', and he says of the conceptions which give unity to the synthesis that 'they consist solely in the *representation*[210] of this necessary synthetical unity'.[211] Again, 'to bring the synthesis to a conception' may well be understood to mean 'to recognize the synthesis as an instance of the conception'; and, since Kant is speaking of knowledge, 'to give unity to the synthesis' may only mean 'to give unity to the synthesis *for us*', i. e. 'to make us aware of its unity'. Moreover, consideration of what thought can possibly achieve with respect to a synthesis presented to it by the imagination renders it necessary to hold that the understanding only recognizes the unity of the synthesis. For if a synthesis has been effected, it must have been effected in accordance with a principle of construction or synthesis, and therefore it would seem that the only work left for the understanding is to discover the principle latent in the procedure of the imagination. At any rate, if the synthesis does not involve a principle of synthesis, it is impossible to see how thought can subsequently introduce a principle. The imagination, then, must be considered to have already introduced the principle of unity into the manifold by combining it in accordance with a conception or principle of combination, and the work of the understanding must be considered to consist in recognizing that the manifold has been thereby combined and unified through the conception. We are therefore obliged to accept one of two alternatives. *Either* the understanding merely renders the mind conscious of the procedure of a fac-

[208] In bringing perceptions under a conception, thought, according to Kant, finds the conception *in* the perceptions by analysis of them, and in relating two conceptions in judgement, it determines the particular form of judgement by analysis of the conceptions.

[209] The italics are mine.

[210] The italics are mine.

[211] Cf. the description of the imagination as 'blind'.

ulty different from itself, viz. the imagination, in which case the important rôle in knowledge, viz. the effecting of the synthesis according to a principle, is played by a faculty different from the understanding; *or* the imagination is the understanding working unreflectively, and the subsequent process of bringing the synthesis to a conception is merely a process by which the understanding becomes conscious of its own procedure. Moreover, it is the latter alternative which we must accept as more in accordance with the general tenor of Kant's thought. For the synthesis of the imagination is essentially the outcome of activity or spontaneity, and, as such, it belongs to the understanding rather than to the sensibility; in fact we find Kant in one place actually saying that 'it is one and the same spontaneity which at one time under the name of imagination, at another time under that of understanding, introduces connexion into the manifold of perception'.[212] Further, it should be noted that since the imagination must be the understanding working unreflectively, and since it must be that which introduces unity into the manifold, there is some justification for his use of language which implies that the understanding is the source of the unity, though it will not be so in the sense in which the passage under discussion might at first sight lead us to suppose.

We can now turn to the argument of the *Transcendental Deduction* itself. Kant introduces it in effect by raising the question, 'How is it that, beginning with the isolated data of sense, we come to acquire knowledge?' His aim is to show (1) that knowledge requires the performance of certain operations by the mind upon the manifold of sense; (2) that this process is a condition not merely of knowledge, but also of self-consciousness; and (3) that, since the manifold is capable of entering into knowledge, and since we are capable of being self-conscious, the categories, whose validity is implied by this process, are valid.

Kant begins by pointing out[213] that all knowledge, *a priori* as well as empirical, requires the manifold, produced successively in the mind, to be subjected to three operations.

1. Since the elements of the manifold are as given mere isolated units, and since knowledge is the apprehension of a unity of connected elements, the mind must first run through the multiplicity of sense and then grasp it together into a whole, i. e. into an image.[214] This act is an act of synthesis; it is called 'the synthesis of apprehension' and is ascribed to the imagination. It must be carried out as much in respect of the pure or *a priori* elements of space and time as in respect of the manifold of sensation, for individual spaces and times contain a multiplicity which, to be apprehended, must be combined.[215] The necessity of this act of synthesis is emphasized in the second edition. "We cannot represent anything as combined in the object without having previously combined it ourselves. Of all representations, *combination* is the only one which cannot be given through ob-

[212] B. 162 note, M. 99 note. Cf. B. 152, M. 93. Similarly at one point in the passage under discussion (B. 102 fin., M. 62 med.) the synthesis is expressly attributed to the spontaneity of thought.

[213] A. 95-104, Mah. 194-8.

[214] Cf. A. 120, Mah. 211.

[215] 'Combine' is used as the verb corresponding to 'synthesis'.

jects,[216] but can be originated only by the subject itself because it is an act of its own activity."[217]

2. Since the data of perception are momentary, and pass away with perception, the act of grasping them together requires that the mind shall reproduce the past data in order to combine them with the present datum. "It is plain that if I draw a line in thought, or wish to think of the time from one midday to another, or even to represent to myself a certain number, I must first necessarily grasp in thought these manifold representations one after another. But if I were continually to lose from my thoughts the preceding representations (the first parts of the line, the preceding parts of time or the units successively represented), and were not to reproduce them, while I proceeded to the succeeding parts, there could never arise a complete representation, nor any of the thoughts just named, not even the first and purest fundamental representations of space and time."[218] This act of reproduction is called 'the synthesis of reproduction in the imagination'.[219]

Further, the necessity of reproduction brings to light a characteristic of the synthesis of apprehension. "It is indeed only an empirical law, according to which representations which have often followed or accompanied one another in the end become associated, and so form a connexion, according to which, even in the absence of the object, one of these representations produces a transition of the mind to another by a fixed rule. But this law of reproduction presupposes that phenomena themselves are actually subject to such a rule, and that in the manifold of their representations there is a concomitance or sequence, according to a fixed rule; for, without this, our empirical imagination would never find anything to do suited to its capacity, and would consequently remain hidden within the depths of the mind as a dead faculty, unknown to ourselves. If cinnabar were now red, now black, now light, now heavy, if a man were changed now into this, now into that animal shape, if our fields were covered on the longest day, now with fruit, now with ice and snow, then my empirical faculty of imagination could not even get an opportunity of thinking of the heavy cinnabar when there occurred the representation of red colour; or if a certain name were given now to one thing, now to another, or if the same thing were called now by one and now by another name, without the control of some rule, to which the phenomena themselves are already subject, no empirical synthesis of reproduction could take place."

"There must then be something which makes this very reproduction of phenomena possible, by being the *a priori* foundation of a necessary synthetical unity of them. But we soon discover it, if we reflect that phenomena are not things in themselves, but the mere play of our representations, which in the end resolve themselves into determinations of our internal sense. For if we can prove that even our purest *a priori* perceptions afford us no knowledge, except so far as they

[216] I. e. given to us through the operation of things in themselves upon our sensibility.

[217] B. 130, M. 80.

[218] A. 102, Mah. 197.

[219] The term 'synthesis' is undeserved, and is due to a desire to find a verbal parallel to the 'synthesis of apprehension in perception'. For the inappropriateness of 'reproduction' and of 'imagination' see pp. 128-129.

contain such a combination of the manifold as renders possible a thoroughgoing synthesis of reproduction, then this synthesis of imagination is based, even before all experience, on *a priori* principles, and we must assume a pure transcendental synthesis of the imagination which lies at the foundation of the very possibility of all experience (as that which necessarily presupposes the reproducibility of phenomena)."[220]

In other words, the faculty of reproduction, if it is to get to work, presupposes that the elements of the manifold are parts of a necessarily related whole; or, as Kant expresses it later, it presupposes the *affinity* of phenomena; and this affinity in turn presupposes that the synthesis of apprehension by combining the elements of the manifold on certain principles makes them parts of a necessarily related whole.[221]

3. Kant introduces the third operation, which he calls 'the synthesis of recognition in the conception',[222] as follows:

"Without consciousness that what we are thinking is identical with what we thought a moment ago, all reproduction in the series of representations would be in vain. For what we are thinking would be a new representation at the present moment, which did not at all belong to the act by which it was bound to have been gradually produced, and the manifold of the same would never constitute a whole, as lacking the unity which only consciousness can give it. If in counting I forget that the units which now hover before my mind have been gradually added by me to one another, I should not know the generation of the group through this successive addition of one to one, and consequently I should not know the number, for this conception consists solely in the consciousness of this unity of the synthesis."

"The word 'conception'[223] might itself lead us to this remark. For it is this *one* consciousness which unites the manifold gradually perceived and then also reproduced into one representation. This consciousness may often be only weak, so that we connect it with the production of the representation only in the result but not in the act itself, i. e. immediately; but nevertheless there must always be one consciousness, although it lacks striking clearness, and without it conceptions, and with them knowledge of objects, are wholly impossible."[224]

Though the passage is obscure and confused, its general drift is clear. Kant, having spoken hitherto only of the operation of the imagination in apprehension and reproduction, now wishes to introduce the understanding. He naturally returns to the thought of it as that which recognizes a manifold as unified by a conception, the manifold, however, being not a group of particulars unified through

[220] A. 100-2, Mah. 195-7.

[221] Cf. A. 113, Mah. 205; A. 121-2, Mah. 211-12; and Caird, i. 362-3. For a fuller account of these presuppositions, and for a criticism of them, cf. Ch. IX, pp. 117-118 and ff.

[222] This title also is a misnomer due to the desire to give parallel titles to the three operations involved in knowledge. There is really only one synthesis referred to, and the title here should be 'the recognition of the synthesis in the conception'.

[223] *Begriff.*

[224] A. 103-4, Mah. 197-8.

the corresponding universal or conception, but the parts of an individual image, e. g. the parts of a line or the constituent units of a number, and the conception which unifies it being the principle on which these parts are combined.[225] His main point is that it is not enough for knowledge that we should combine the manifold of sense into a whole in accordance with a specific principle,[226] but we must also be in some degree conscious of our continuously identical act of combination,[227] this consciousness being at the same time a consciousness of the special unity of the manifold. For the conception which forms the principle of the combination has necessarily two sides; while from our point of view it is the principle according to which we combine and which makes our combining activity one, from the point of view of the manifold it is the special principle[228] by which the manifold is made *one*. If I am to count a group of five units, I must not only add them, but also be conscious of my continuously identical act of addition, this consciousness consisting in the consciousness that I am successively taking units up to, and only up to, five, and being at the same time a consciousness that the units are acquiring the unity of being a group of five. It immediately follows, though Kant does not explicitly say so, that all knowledge implies self-consciousness. For the consciousness that we have been combining the manifold on a certain definite principle is the consciousness of our identity throughout the process, and, from the side of the manifold, it is just that consciousness of the manifold as unified by being brought under a conception which constitutes knowledge. Even though it is Kant's view that the self-consciousness need only be weak and need only arise after the act of combination, when we are aware of its result, still, without it, there will be no consciousness of the manifold as unified through a conception and therefore no knowledge. Moreover, if the self-consciousness be weak, the knowledge will be weak also, so that if it be urged that knowledge in the strictest sense requires the full consciousness that the manifold is unified through a conception, it must be allowed that knowledge in this sense requires a full or clear self-consciousness.

As is to be expected, however, the passage involves a difficulty concerning the respective functions of the imagination and the understanding. Is the understanding represented as only recognizing a principle of unity introduced into the manifold by the imagination, or as also for the first time introducing a principle of unity? At first sight the latter alternative may seem the right interpretation. For he says that unless we were conscious that what we are thinking is identical with what we thought a moment ago, 'what we are thinking would *be* a new repre-

[225] Cf. pp. 87-91.

[226] That the combination proceeds on a specific principle only emerges in this account of the third operation.

[227] Kant's example shows that this consciousness is not the mere consciousness of the act of combination as throughout identical, but the consciousness of it as an identical act of a particular kind.

[228] When Kant says 'this conception [i. e. the conception of the number counted] consists in the consciousness of this unity of the synthesis', he is momentarily and contrary to his usual practice speaking of a conception in the sense of the activity of conceiving a universal, and not in the sense of the universal conceived. Similarly in appealing to the meaning of *Begriff* (conception) he is thinking of 'conceiving' as the activity of combining a manifold through a conception.

sentation which *did not at all belong* to the act by which it was bound to have been gradually produced, and the manifold of the same *would never* constitute a whole, as lacking the unity which only *consciousness can give it*.'[229] Again, in speaking of a conception—which of course implies the understanding—he says that 'it is this one consciousness which *unites* the manifold gradually perceived and then reproduced into *one* representation'.[230] But these statements are not decisive, for he uses the term 'recognition' in his formula for the work of the understanding, and he illustrates its work by pointing out that in counting we must *remember* that we have added the units. Moreover, there is a consideration which by itself makes it necessary to accept the former interpretation. The passage certainly represents the understanding as recognizing the identical action of the mind in combining the manifold on a principle, whether or not it also represents the understanding as the source of this activity. But if it were the understanding which combined the manifold, there would be no synthesis which the imagination could be supposed to have performed,[231] and therefore it could play no part in knowledge at all, a consequence which must be contrary to Kant's meaning. Further if, as the general tenor of the deduction shows, the imagination is really only the understanding working unreflectively,[232] we are able to understand why Kant should for the moment cease to distinguish between the imagination and the understanding, and consequently should use language which implies that the understanding both combines the manifold on a principle and makes us conscious of our activity in so doing. Hence we may say that the real meaning of the passage should be stated thus: 'Knowledge requires one consciousness which, as imagination, combines the manifold on a definite principle constituted by a conception,[233] and, as understanding, is to some extent conscious of its identical activity in so doing, this self-consciousness being, from the side of the whole produced by the synthesis, the consciousness of the conception by which the manifold is unified.'

Hitherto there has been no mention of an *object* of knowledge, and since knowledge is essentially knowledge of an object, Kant's next task is to give such an account of an object of knowledge as will show that the processes already described are precisely those which give our representations, i. e. the manifold of sense, relation to an object, and consequently yield knowledge.

---

[229] The italics are mine. He does not say '*we should not be conscious* of what we are thinking as the same representation and as belonging κτλ., *and we should not be conscious* of the manifold as constituting a whole.

[230] The italics are mine.

[231] There could not, of course, be two syntheses, the one being and the other not being upon a principle.

[232] Cf. pp. 90-91.

[233] In view of Kant's subsequent account of the function of the categories it should be noticed that, according to the present passage, the conception involved in an act of knowledge is the conception not of an 'object in general', but of 'an object of the particular kind which constitutes the individual whole produced by the combination a whole of the particular kind that it is of', and that, in accordance with this, the self-consciousness involved is not the mere consciousness that our combining activity is identical throughout, but the consciousness that it is an identical activity of a particular kind, e. g. that of counting five units. Cf. pp. 99 fin.-100, 102-103, and 110-111.

He begins by raising the question, 'What do we mean by the phrase 'an object of representations'?'[234] He points out that a phenomenon, since it is a mere sensuous representation, and not a thing in itself existing independently of the faculty of representations, is just not an object. To the question, therefore, 'What is meant by an object corresponding to knowledge and therefore distinct from it?' we are bound to answer from the point of view of the distinction between phenomena and things in themselves, that the object is something in general = x, i. e. the thing in itself of which we know only *that* it is and not *what* it is. There is, however, another point of view from which we can say something more about an object of representations and the correspondence of our representations to it, viz. that from which we consider what is involved in the thought of the relation of knowledge or of a representation to its object. "We find that our thought of the relation of all knowledge to its object carries with it something of necessity, since its object is regarded as that which prevents our cognitions[235] being determined at random or capriciously, and causes them to be determined *a priori* in a certain way, because in that they are to relate to an object, they must necessarily also, in relation to it, agree with one another, that is to say, they must have that unity which constitutes the conception of an object."[236]

Kant's meaning seems to be this: 'If we think of certain representations, e. g. certain lines[237] or the representations of extension, impenetrability, and shape,[238] as related to an object, e. g. to an individual triangle or an individual body, we think that they must be mutually consistent or, in other words, that they must have the unity of being parts of a necessarily related whole or system, this unity in fact constituting the conception of an object in general, in distinction from the conception of an object of a particular kind. The latter thought in turn involves the thought of the object of representations as that which prevents them being anything whatever and in fact makes them parts of a system. The thought therefore of representations as related to an object carries with it the thought of a certain necessity, viz. the necessary or systematic unity introduced into the representations by the object. Hence by an object of representations we mean something which introduces into the representations a systematic unity which constitutes the nature of an object in general, and the relatedness of representations to, or their correspondence with, an object involves their systematic unity.'[239]

Certain points, however, should be noticed. In the *first* place, Kant is for the moment tacitly ignoring his own theory of knowledge, in accordance with which the object proper, i. e. the thing in itself, is unknowable, and is reverting to the ordinary conception of knowledge as really *knowledge* of its object. For the ele-

[234] *Vorstellung* in the present passage is perhaps better rendered 'idea', but representation has been retained for the sake of uniformity.

[235] *Erkenntnisse.*

[236] A. 104, Mah. 199.

[237] Cf. A. 105, Mah. 199.

[238] Cf. A. 106, Mah. 200.

[239] It may be noticed that possession of the unity of a system does not really distinguish 'an object' from any other whole of parts, nor in particular from 'a representation'. Any whole of parts must be a systematic unity.

ments which are said, in virtue of being related to an object, to agree and to have the unity which constitutes the conception of an object must be elements of an object which we know; for if the assertion that they agree is to be significant, they must be determinate parts or qualities of the object, e. g. the sides of an individual triangle or the impenetrability or shape of an individual body, and therefore it is implied that we know that the object has these parts or qualities. In the *second* place, both the problem which Kant raises and the clue which he offers for its solution involve an impossible separation of knowledge or a representation from its object. Kant begins with the thought of a phenomenon as a mere representation which, as mental, and as the representation of an object, is just not an object, and asks, 'What is meant by the object of it?' He finds the clue to the answer in the thought that though a representation or idea when considered in itself is a mere mental modification, yet, when considered as related to an object, it is subject to a certain necessity. In fact, however, an idea or knowledge is essentially an idea or knowledge of an object, and we are bound to think of it as such. There is no meaning whatever in saying that the thought of an idea as related to an object carries with it something of necessity, for to say so implies that it is possible to think of it as unrelated to an object. Similarly there is really no meaning in the question, 'What is meant by an object corresponding to knowledge or to an idea?' for this in the same way implies that we can first think of an idea as unrelated to an object and then ask, 'What can be meant by an object corresponding to it?'[240] In the *third* place, Kant only escapes the absurdity involved in the thought of a mere idea or a mere representation by treating representations either as parts or as qualities of an object. For although he speaks of our cognitions,[241] i. e. of our representations, as being determined by the object, he says that they must agree, i. e. they must have that unity which constitutes the conception of an object, and he illustrates representations by the sides of an individual triangle and the impenetrability and shape of an individual body, which are just as 'objective' as the objects to which they relate. The fact is that he really treats a representation not as his problem requires that it should be treated, i. e. as a representation of something, but as something represented,[242] i. e. as something of which we are aware, viz. a part or a quality of an object. In the *fourth* place, not only is that which Kant speaks of as related to an object really not a representation, but also—as we see if we consider the fact which Kant has in mind—that to which he speaks of it as related is really not *an* object but *one and the same object to which another so-called representation is related*. For what Kant says is that representations as related to an object must agree among themselves. But this statement, to be significant, implies that the object to which various representations are related is *one and the same*. Otherwise why should the representations agree? In view, therefore, of these last two considerations we must admit that the real thought underlying Kant's statement should be expressed thus: 'We find that the thought that *two or more parts or qualities of an object* relate to *one and the same object* carries with it a certain necessity, since this object is considered to be that which *prevents these parts or qualities which we know it to possess* from

[240] Cf. pp. 123-125.
[241] *Erkenntnisse.*
[242] *Vorgestellt.*

being determined at random, because by being related to *one and the same object*, they must agree among themselves.' The importance of the correction lies in the fact that what Kant is stating is not what he thinks he is stating. He is really stating the implication of the thought that two or more qualities or parts of some object or other, which, as such, already relate to an object, relate to one and the same object. He thinks he is stating the implication of the thought that a representation which in itself has no relation to an object, has relation to an object. And since his problem is simply to determine what constitutes the relatedness to an object of that which in itself is a mere representation, the distinction is important; for it shows that he really elucidates it by an implication respecting something which already has relation to an object and is not a mental modification at all, but a quality or a part of an object.

Kant continues thus: "But it is clear that, since we have to do only with the manifold of our representations, and the *x*, which corresponds to them (the object), since it is to be something distinct from all our representations, is for us nothing, the unity which the object necessitates can be nothing else than the formal unity of consciousness in the synthesis of the manifold of representations." [I. e. since the object which produces systematic unity in our representations is after all only the unknown thing in itself, viz. *x*,[243] any of the parts or qualities of which it is impossible to know, that to which it gives unity can be only our representations and not its own parts or qualities. For, since we do not know any of its parts or qualities, these representations cannot be its parts or qualities. Consequently, the unity produced by this *x* can only be the formal unity of the combination of the manifold in consciousness.[244]] "Then and then only do we say that we know the object," [i. e. we know that the manifold relates to an object[245]] "if we have produced synthetical unity in the manifold of perception. But this unity would be impossible, if the perception could not be produced by means of such a function of synthesis according to a rule as renders the reproduction of the manifold a priori necessary, and a conception in which the manifold unifies itself possible. Thus we think a triangle as an object, in that we are conscious of the combination of three straight lines in accordance with a rule by which such a perception can at any time be presented. This *unity of the rule* determines all the manifold and limits it to conditions which make the unity of apperception possible, and the conception of this unity is the representation of the object=*x*, which I think through the aforesaid predicates of a triangle." [I. e., apparently, 'to conceive this unity of the rule is to represent to myself the object *x*, i. e. the thing in itself,[246] of which I come to think by means of

[243] Cf. p. 98, note 246.

[244] 'The formal unity' means not the unity peculiar to any particular synthesis, but the character shared by all syntheses of being a systematic whole.

[245] The final sense is the same whether 'object' be here understood to refer to the thing in itself or to a phenomenon.

[246] A comparison of this passage (A. 104-5, Mah. 198-9) with A. 108-9, Mah. 201-2 (which seems to reproduce A. 104-5, Mah. 198-9), B. 522-3, M. 309 and A. 250, Mah. 224, seems to render it absolutely necessary to understand by *x*, and by the transcendental object, the thing in itself. Cf. also B. 236, M. 143 ('so soon as I raise my conception of an object to the transcendental meaning thereof, the house is not a thing in itself but only a phenomenon, i. e. a representation of which the transcendental object is unknown'), A. 372, Mah.

the rule of combination.']

In this passage several points claim attention. In the *first* place, it seems impossible to avoid the conclusion that in the second sentence the argument is exactly reversed. Up to this point, it is the thing in itself which produces unity in our representations. Henceforward it is we who produce the unity by our activity of combining the manifold. The discrepancy cannot be explained away, and its existence can only be accounted for by the exigencies of Kant's position. When he is asking 'What is meant by the object (beyond the mind) corresponding to our representations?' he has to think of the unity of the representations as due to the object. But when he is asking 'How does the manifold of sense become unified?' his view that all synthesis is due to the mind compels him to hold that the unity is produced by us. In the *second* place, the passage introduces a second object in addition to the thing in itself, viz. the phenomenal object, e. g. a triangle considered as a whole of parts unified on a definite principle.[247] It is this object which, as the object that we know, is henceforward prominent in the first edition, and has exclusive attention in the second. The connexion between this object and the thing in itself appears to lie in the consideration that we are only justified in holding that the manifold of sense is related to a thing in itself when we have unified it and therefore know it to be a unity, and that to know it to be a unity is *ipso facto* to be aware of it as related to a phenomenal object; in other words, the knowledge that the manifold is related to an object beyond consciousness is acquired through our knowledge of its relatedness to an object within consciousness. In the *third* place, in view of Kant's forthcoming vindication of the categories, it is important to notice that the process by which the manifold is said to acquire relation to an object is illustrated by a synthesis on a particular principle which constitutes the phenomenal object an object of a particular kind. The synthesis which enables us to recognize three lines as an object is not a synthesis based on general principles constituted by the categories, but a synthesis based on the particular principle that the three lines must be so put together as to form an enclosed space. Moreover, it should be noticed that the need of a particular principle is really inconsistent with his view that relation to an object gives the manifold the systematic unity which constitutes the conception of an object, or that at least a ὕστερον πρότερον is involved. For if the knowledge that certain representations form a systematic unity justifies our holding that they relate to an object, it would seem that in order to know that they relate to an object we need not know the special character of their unity. Yet, as Kant states the facts, we really have to know the special character of their unity in order to know that they possess systematic unity in general.[248] *Lastly*, it is easy to see the connexion of

247 and A. 379, Mah. 253.

[247] Compare 'The object of our perceptions is merely that something of which the conception expresses such a necessity of synthesis' (A. 106, Mah. 200), and 'An object is that in the conception of which the manifold of a given perception is united' (B. 137, M. 84). Cf. also A. 108, Mah. 201.

[248] Kant's position is no doubt explained by the fact that since the object corresponding to our representations is the thing in itself, and since we only know that this is of the same kind in the case of every representation, it can only be thought of as producing systematic unity, and not a unity of a particular kind. The position is also in part due to the fact that the principles of synthesis involved by the phenomenal object are usually thought of by

this account of an object of representations with the preceding account of the synthesis involved in knowledge. Kant had said that knowledge requires a synthesis of the imagination in accordance with a definite principle, and the recognition of the principle of the synthesis by the understanding. From this point of view it is clear that the aim of the present passage is to show that this process yields knowledge of an object; for it shows that this process yields knowledge of a phenomenal object of a particular kind, e. g. of a triangle or of a body, and that this object as such refers to what after all is *the* object, viz. the thing in itself.

The position reached by Kant so far is this. Knowledge, as being knowledge of an object, consists in a process by which the manifold of perception acquires relation to an object. This process again is a process of combination of the manifold into a systematic whole upon a definite principle, accompanied by the consciousness in some degree of the act of combination, and therefore also of the acquisition by the manifold of the definite unity which forms the principle of combination. In virtue of this process there is said to be 'unity of consciousness in the synthesis of the manifold', a phrase which the context justifies us in understanding as a condensed expression for a situation in which (1) the manifold of sense is a unity of necessarily related parts, (2) there is *consciousness* of this unity, and (3) the consciousness which combines and is conscious of combining the manifold, as being necessarily one and the same throughout this process, is itself a unity.

Kant then proceeds to introduce what he evidently considers the keystone of his system, viz. 'transcendental apperception.'

"There is always a transcendental condition at the basis of any necessity. Hence we must be able to find a transcendental ground of the unity of consciousness in the synthesis of the manifold of all our perceptions, and therefore also of the conceptions of objects in general, consequently also of all objects of experience, a ground without which it would be impossible to think any object for our perceptions; for this object is no more than that something, the conception of which expresses such a necessity of synthesis."

"Now this original and transcendental condition is no other than *transcendental apperception*. The consciousness of self according to the determinations of our state in internal sense-perception is merely empirical, always changeable; there can be no fixed or permanent self in this stream of internal phenomena, and this consciousness is usually called *internal sense* or *empirical apperception*. That which is *necessarily* to be represented as numerically identical cannot be thought as such by means of empirical data. The condition which is to make such a transcendental presupposition valid must be one which precedes all experience, and makes experience itself possible."

"Now no cognitions[249] can occur in us, no combination and unity of them with one another, without that unity of consciousness which precedes all data of perception, and by relation to which alone all representation of objects is possible. This pure original unchangeable consciousness I shall call *transcendental appercep-*

Kant as the categories; these of course can only contribute a general kind of unity, and not the special kind of unity belonging to an individual object.

[249] *Erkenntnisse.*

tion. That it deserves this name is clear from the fact that even the purest objective unity, viz. that of *a priori* conceptions (space and time) is only possible by relation of perceptions to it. The numerical unity of this apperception therefore forms the *a priori* foundation of all conceptions, just as the multiplicity of space and time is the foundation of the perceptions of the sensibility."[250]

The argument is clearly meant to be 'transcendental' in character; in other words, Kant continues to argue from the existence of knowledge to the existence of its presuppositions. We should therefore expect the passage to do two things: firstly, to show what it is which is presupposed by the 'unity of consciousness in the synthesis of the manifold'[251]; and secondly, to show that this presupposition deserves the title 'transcendental apperception'. Unfortunately Kant introduces 'transcendental apperception' after the manner in which he introduced the 'sensibility', the 'imagination' and the 'understanding', as if it were a term with which every one is familiar, and which therefore needs little explanation. To interpret the passage, it seems necessary to take it in close connexion with the preceding account of the three 'syntheses' involved in knowledge, and to bear in mind that, as a comparison of passages will show, the term 'apperception', which Kant borrows from Leibniz, always has for Kant a reference to consciousness of self or self-consciousness. If this be done, the meaning of the passage seems to be as follows:

'To vindicate the existence of a self which is necessarily one and the same throughout its representations, and which is capable of being aware of its own identity throughout, it is useless to appeal to that consciousness of ourselves which we have when we reflect upon our successive states. For, although in being conscious of our states we are conscious of ourselves we are not conscious of ourselves as unchanging. The self as going through successive states is changing, and even if in fact its states did not change, its identity would be only contingent; it need not continue unchanged. Consequently, the only course possible is to show that the self-consciousness in question is presupposed in any experience or knowledge. Now it is so presupposed. For, as we have already shown, the relation of representations to an object presupposes one consciousness which combines and unifies them, and is at the same time conscious of the identity of its own action in unifying them. This consciousness is the ground of the unity of consciousness in the synthesis of the manifold. It may fairly be called transcendental, because even a conception which relates to space or time, and therefore is the most remote from sensation, presupposes one consciousness which combines and unifies the manifold of space and time through the conception, and is conscious of the identity of its own action in so doing. It may, therefore, be regarded as the presupposition of *all* conceiving or bringing a manifold under a conception, and therefore of all knowledge. Consequently, since knowledge is possible, i. e. since the manifold of representations can be related to an object, there must be one self capable of being

[250] A. 106-7, Mah. 200-1.

[251] We should have expected this to have been already accomplished. For according to the account already considered, it is we who by our imagination introduce necessity into the synthesis of the manifold and by our understanding become conscious of it. We shall therefore not be surprised to find that 'transcendental apperception' is really only ourselves as exercising imagination and understanding in a new guise.

aware of its own identity throughout its representations.'

At this point of Kant's argument, however, there seems to occur an inversion of the thought. Hitherto, Kant has been arguing from the possibility of knowledge to the possibility of the consciousness of our own identity. But in the next paragraph he appears to reverse this procedure and to argue from the possibility of self-consciousness to the possibility of knowledge.

"But it is just this transcendental unity of apperception[252] which forms, from all possible phenomena which can be together in one experience, a connexion of them according to laws. For this unity of consciousness would be impossible, if the mind in the knowledge of the manifold could not become conscious of the identity of the function whereby it unites the manifold synthetically in one knowledge. Consequently, the original and necessary consciousness of the identity of oneself is at the same time a consciousness of an equally necessary unity of the synthesis of all phenomena according to conceptions, i. e. according to rules which not only make them necessarily reproducible, but thereby determine an object for their perception, i. e. determine the conception of something in which they are necessarily connected. For the mind could not possibly think the identity of itself in the manifold of its representations, and this indeed *a priori*, if it had not before its eyes the identity of its action which subjects all synthesis of apprehension (which is empirical) to a transcendental unity, and first makes possible its connexion according to rules."

The argument seems indisputably to be as follows: 'The mind is necessarily able to be aware of its own identity throughout its manifold representations. To be aware of this, it must be aware of the identity of the activity by which it combines the manifold of representations into a systematic whole. Therefore it must be capable of combining, and of being conscious of its activity in combining, all phenomena which can be its representations into such a whole. But this process, from the point of view of the representations combined, is the process by which they become related to an object and so enter into knowledge. Therefore, since we are capable of being conscious of our identity with respect to all phenomena which can be our representations, the process of combination and consciousness of combination which constitutes knowledge must be possible with respect to them.' Thus the thought of this and the preceding paragraph seems to involve a circle. First the possibility of self-consciousness is deduced from the possibility of knowledge, and then the possibility of knowledge is deduced from the possibility of self-consciousness.

An issue therefore arises, the importance of which can be seen by reference to the final aim of the 'deduction', viz. the vindication of the categories. The categories are 'fundamental conceptions which enable us to think objects in gener-

[252] Kant seems here and elsewhere to use the phrase 'transcendental unity of apperception' as synonymous with 'transcendental apperception', the reason, presumably, being that transcendental apperception is a unity.

al[253] for phenomena'[254]; in other words, they are the principles of the synthesis by which the manifold of sense becomes related to an object. Hence, if this be granted, the proof that the categories are applicable to objects consists in showing that the manifold can be subjected to this synthesis. The question therefore arises whether Kant's real starting-point for establishing the possibility of this synthesis and therefore the applicability of the categories, is to be found in the possibility of knowledge, or in the possibility of self-consciousness, or in both. In other words, does Kant start from the position that all representations must be capable of being related to an object, or from the position that we must be capable of being conscious of our identity with respect to all of them, or from both?

Prima facie the second position is the more plausible basis for the desired conclusion. On the one hand, it does not seem obvious that the manifold *must* be capable of being related to an object; for even if it be urged that otherwise we should have only 'a random play of representations, less than a dream'[255], it may be replied, that this might be or might come to be the case. On the other hand, the fact that our representations are ours necessarily seems to presuppose that we are identical subjects of these representations, and recognition of this fact is the consciousness of our identity.

If we turn to the text for an answer to this question, we find that Kant seems not only to use both starting-points, but even to regard them as equivalents. Thus in introducing the categories[256] Kant begins by appealing to the necessity for knowledge that representations should relate to an object.

"Unity of synthesis according to empirical conceptions would be purely contingent, and were these not based on a transcendental ground of unity, it would be possible for a confused crowd of phenomena to fill our soul, without the possibility of experience ever arising therefrom. But then also all relation of knowledge to objects would fall away, because knowledge would lack connexion according to universal and necessary laws; it would be thoughtless perception but never knowledge, and therefore for us as good as nothing."

"The *a priori* conditions of any possible experience whatever are at the same time conditions of the possibility of the objects of experience. Now I assert that the above mentioned *categories* are nothing but *the conditions of thinking in any possible experience,* just as *space and time* are the *conditions of perception* requisite for the same. The former therefore are also fundamental conceptions by which we think objects in general for phenomena, and are therefore objectively valid *a priori*—which is exactly what we wished to know."

The next sentence, however, bases the necessity of the categories on the possibility of self-consciousness, without giving any indication that a change of standpoint is involved.

---

[253] *Objecte überhaupt,* i. e. objects of any kind in distinction not from objects of a particular kind but from no objects at all.

[254] A. 111, Mah. 204

[255] A. 112, Mah. 204.

[256] A. 110-12, Mah. 203-4.

"But the possibility, nay, even the necessity, of these categories rests on the relation which the whole sensibility, and with it also all possible phenomena, have to original apperception, a relation which forces everything to conform to the conditions of the thoroughgoing unity of self-consciousness, i. e. to stand under universal functions of synthesis, i. e. of synthesis according to conceptions, as that wherein alone apperception can prove *a priori* its thorough-going and necessary identity."

Finally, the conclusion of the paragraph seems definitely to treat both starting-points as really the same.[257] "Thus the conception of a cause is nothing but a synthesis (of the consequent in the time series with other phenomena) *according to conceptions*; and without such a unity, which has its *a priori* rule and subjects phenomena to itself, thorough-going and universal and therefore necessary unity of consciousness in the manifold of sense-perceptions would not be met with. But then also these perceptions would belong to no experience, consequently they would have no object, and would be nothing but a blind play of representations, less than a dream."

The fact is that since for Kant the synthesis of representations in accordance with the categories, accompanied by the consciousness of it, is at once the necessary and sufficient condition of the relatedness of representations to an object and of the consciousness of our identity with respect to them, it seems to him to be one and the same thing whether, in vindicating the synthesis, we appeal to the possibility of knowledge or to the possibility of self-consciousness, and it even seems possible to argue, *via* the synthesis, from knowledge to self-consciousness and vice versa.

Nevertheless, it remains true that the vindication of the categories is different, according as it is based upon the possibility of relating representations to an object or upon the possibility of becoming self-conscious with respect to them. It also remains true that Kant vindicates the categories in both ways. For while, in expounding the three so-called syntheses involved in knowledge, he is vindicating the categories from the point of view of knowledge, when he comes to speak of transcendental apperception, of which the central characteristic is the consciousness of self involved, there is a shifting of the centre of gravity. Instead of treating representations as something which can become related to an object, he now treats them as something of which, as belonging to a self, the self must be capable of being conscious as its own, and argues that a synthesis in accordance with the categories is required for this self-consciousness. It must be admitted then—and the admission is only to be made with reluctance—that when Kant reaches transcendental apperception, he really adopts a new starting-point,[258] and that the passage which introduces transcendental apperception by showing it to be implied in knowledge[259] only serves to conceal from Kant the fact that, from the point of view of the deduction of the categories, he is really assuming without proof the

[257] Cf. A. 113, Mah. 205-6 and A. 108-10, Mah. 202-3.

[258] The existence of this new starting-point is more explicit, A. 116-7 (and note), Mah. 208 (and note), and A. 122, Mah. 212.

[259] A. 107, Mah. 200.

possibility of self-consciousness with respect to all our representations, as a new basis for argument.

The approach to the categories from the side of self-consciousness is, however, more prominent in the second edition, and consequently we naturally turn to it for more light on this side of Kant's position. There Kant vindicates the necessity of the synthesis from the side of self-consciousness as follows:[260]

"[1.] It must be possible that the 'I think' should accompany all my representations; for otherwise something would be represented in me which could not be thought; in other words, the representation would be either impossible or at least for me nothing. [2.] That representation which can be given before all thought is called *perception*. All the manifold of perception has therefore a necessary relation to the 'I think' in the same subject in which this manifold is found. [3.] But this representation[261] [i. e. the 'I think'] is an act of *spontaneity*, i. e. it cannot be regarded as belonging to sensibility. I call it *pure apperception*, to distinguish it from *empirical apperception*, or *original apperception* also, because it is that self-consciousness which, while it gives birth to the representation 'I think', which must be capable of accompanying all others and is one and the same in all consciousness, cannot itself be accompanied by any other.[262] [4.] I also call the unity of it the *transcendental* unity of self-consciousness, in order to indicate the possibility of *a priori* knowledge arising from it. For the manifold representations which are given in a perception would not all of them be *my* representations, if they did not all belong to one self-consciousness, that is, as my representations (even though I am not conscious of them as such), they must necessarily conform to the condition under which alone they *can* stand together in a universal self-consciousness, because otherwise they would not all belong to me. From this original connexion much can be concluded."

[5.] "That is to say, this thorough-going identity of the apperception of a manifold given in perception contains a synthesis of representations,[263] and is possible only through the consciousness of this synthesis.[264] [6.] For the empirical consciousness which accompanies different representations is in itself fragmentary, and without relation to the identity of the subject. [7.] This relation, therefore, takes place not by my merely accompanying every representation with consciousness, but by my *adding* one representation to another, and being conscious of the synthesis of them. [8.] Consequently, only because I can connect a manifold of given representations *in one consciousness*, is it possible for me to represent to

[260] The main clauses have been numbered for convenience of reference.

[261] This is an indisputable case of the use of representation in the sense of something represented or presented.

[262] I. e. consciousness of our identity is final; we cannot, for instance, go further back to a consciousness of the consciousness of our identity.

[263] I understand this to mean 'This through and through identical consciousness of myself as the identical subject of a manifold given in perception involves a synthesis of representations'.

[264] The drift of the passage as a whole (cf. especially § 16) seems to show that here 'the synthesis of representations' means 'their connectedness' and not 'the act of connecting them'.

myself the *identity of consciousness in these representations;* i. e. the *analytical* unity of apperception is possible only under the presupposition of a *synthetical* unity. [9.] The thought, 'These representations given in perception belong all of them to me' is accordingly just the same as, 'I unite them in one self-consciousness, or at least can so unite them;' [10.] and although this thought is not itself as yet the consciousness of the *synthesis* of representations, it nevertheless presupposes the possibility of this synthesis; that is to say, it is only because I can comprehend the manifold of representations in one consciousness, that I call them all *my* representations; for otherwise I should have as many-coloured and varied a self as I have representations of which I am conscious. [11.] Synthetical unity of the manifold of perceptions, as given *a priori,* is therefore the ground of the identity of apperception itself, which precedes *a priori* all *my* determinate thinking. [12.] But connexion does not lie in the objects, nor can it be borrowed from them through perception and thereby first taken up into the understanding, but it is always an operation of the understanding which itself is nothing more than the faculty of connecting *a priori,* and of bringing the manifold of given representations under the unity of apperception, which principle is the highest in all human knowledge."

[13.] "Now this principle of the necessary unity of apperception is indeed an identical, and therefore an analytical, proposition, but nevertheless it declares a synthesis of the manifold given in a perception to be necessary, without which the thorough-going identity of self-consciousness cannot be thought. [14.] For through the Ego, as a simple representation, is given no manifold content; in perception, which is different from it, a manifold can only be given, and through *connexion* in one consciousness it can be thought. An understanding, through whose self-consciousness all the manifold would *eo ipso* be given, would *perceive;* our understanding can only *think* and must seek its perception in the senses. [15.] I am, therefore, conscious of the identical self, in relation to the manifold of representations given to me in a perception, because I call all those representations *mine,* which constitute *one.* [16.] But this is the same as to say that I am conscious *a priori* of a necessary synthesis of them, which is called the original synthetic unity of apperception, under which all representations given to me stand, but also under which they must be brought through a synthesis."[265]

Though this passage involves many difficulties, the main drift of it is clear. Kant is anxious to establish the fact that the manifold of sense must be capable of being combined on principles, which afterwards turn out to be the categories, by showing this to be involved in the fact that we must be capable of being conscious of ourselves as the identical subject of all our representations. To do this, he seeks to prove in the first paragraph that self-consciousness in this sense must be possible, and in the second that this self-consciousness presupposes the synthesis of the manifold.

Examination of the argument, however, shows that the view that self-consciousness must be possible is, so far as Kant is concerned,[266] an assumption for which Kant succeeds in giving no reason at all, and that even if it be true, it cannot

[265] B. 131-5, M. 81-4.

[266] Cf. p. 109, note 277.

form a basis from which to deduce the possibility of the synthesis.

Before, however, we attempt to prove this, it is necessary to draw attention to three features of the argument. In the *first* place, it implies a somewhat different account of self-consciousness to that implied in the passages of the first edition which we have already considered. Self-consciousness, instead of being the consciousness of the identity of our activity in combining the manifold, is now primarily the consciousness of ourselves as identical subjects of all our representations, i. e. it is what Kant calls the analytical unity of apperception; and consequently it is somewhat differently related to the activity of synthesis involved in knowledge. Instead of being regarded as the consciousness of this activity, it is regarded as presupposing the consciousness of the product of this activity, i. e. of the connectedness[267] of the manifold produced by the activity, this consciousness being what Kant calls the synthetical unity of apperception.[268] In the *second* place, it is plain that Kant's view is not that self-consciousness involves the consciousness of our representations as a connected whole, but that it involves the consciousness of them as capable of being connected by a synthesis. Yet, if it is only because I can connect (and therefore apprehend as connected) a manifold of representations in one consciousness, that I can represent to myself the identity of consciousness in these representations, self-consciousness really requires the consciousness of our representations as *already* connected; the mere consciousness of our representations as *capable* of being connected would not be enough. The explanation of the inconsistency seems to lie in the fact that the synthetic unity of which Kant is thinking is the unity of nature. For, as Kant of course was aware, in our ordinary consciousness we do not apprehend the interconnexion of the parts of nature in detail, but only believe that there is such an interconnexion; consequently he naturally weakened the conclusion which he ought to have drawn, viz. that self-consciousness presupposes consciousness of the synthesis, in order to make it conform to the facts of our ordinary consciousness. Yet, if his *argument* is to be defended, its conclusion must be taken in the form that self-consciousness presupposes consciousness of the actual synthesis or connexion and not merely of the possibility of it. In the *third* place, Kant twice in this passage[269] definitely makes the act of synthesis, which his argument maintains to be the condition of *consciousness of the identity* of ourselves, the condition of the *identity* of ourselves. The fact is that, on Kant's view, the act of synthesis of the representations is really a condition of their belonging to one self, the self being presupposed to be a self capable of self-consciousness.[270]

We may now turn to the first of the two main points to be considered, viz. the reason given by Kant for holding that self-consciousness must be possible. In the first paragraph (§§ 1-4) Kant appears twice to state a reason, viz. in §§ 1 and 4. What is meant by the first sentence, "It must be possible that the 'I think' should

[267] More accurately, 'of the possibility of the connectedness'.

[268] The same view seems implied A. 117-8, Mah. 208. Kant apparently thinks of this consciousness as also a self-consciousness (cf. § 9), though it seems that he should have considered it rather as a condition of self-consciousness, cf. p. 109, note 276.

[269] Sections 6 and 10.

[270] Cf. pp. 108-109.

accompany all my representations; for otherwise something would be represented in me which could not be thought; in other words, the representation would either be impossible or at least for me nothing"? It is difficult to hold that 'my representations' here means objects of which I am aware, and that the thesis to be established is that I must be capable of being conscious of my own identity throughout all awareness or thought of objects. For the next sentence refers to perceptions as representations which can be given previously to all thought, and therefore, presumably, as something of which I am not necessarily aware. Again, the ground adduced for the thesis would be in part a mere restatement of it, and in part nonsense. It would be 'otherwise something would be apprehended with respect to which I could not be aware that I was apprehending it; in other words, I could not apprehend it [since otherwise I could be aware that I was apprehending it]', the last words being incapable of any interpretation. It is much more probable that though Kant is leading up to self-consciousness, the phrase 'I think' here refers not to 'consciousness that I am thinking', but to 'thinking'. He seems to mean 'It must be possible to apprehend all my 'affections' (i. e. sensations or appearances in me), for otherwise I should have an affection of which I could not be aware; in other words, there could be no such affection, or at least it would be of no possible importance to me.'[271] And on this interpretation self-consciousness is not introduced till § 3, and then only surreptitiously. On neither interpretation, however, does Kant give the vestige of a *reason* for the possibility of self-consciousness. Again, it seems clear that in § 4 'my representations', and 'representations which belong to me' mean objects of which I am aware (i. e. something presented); for he says of my representations, not that I may not be conscious of them—which he should have said if 'my representations' meant my mental affections of which I could become conscious—but that I may not be conscious of them as my representations. Consequently in § 4 he is merely asserting that I must be able to be conscious of my identity throughout my awareness of objects. So far, then, we find merely the *assertion* that self-consciousness must be possible.[272]

In the next paragraph[273]—which is clearly meant to be the important one—Kant, though he can hardly be said to be aware of it, seems to *assume* that it is the very nature of a knowing self, not only to be identical throughout its thoughts or apprehendings, but to be capable of being conscious of its own identity. § 6 runs: "The empirical consciousness which accompanies different representations is in itself fragmentary, and without relation to the identity of the subject." Kant is saying that if there existed merely a consciousness of A which was not at the same time a consciousness of B and a consciousness of B which was not at the same time a consciousness of A, these consciousnesses would not be the consciousnesses belonging to one self. But this is only true, if the one self to which the consciousness

[271] A third alternative is to understand Kant to be thinking of all thought as self-conscious, i. e. as thinking accompanied by the consciousness of thinking. But since in that case Kant would be arguing from thinking as *thinking*, i. e. as apprehending objects, the possibility of self-consciousness would only be glaringly assumed.

[272] The same is true of A. 116 and A. 117 note, Mah. 208, where Kant also appears to be offering what he considers to be an argument.

[273] §§ 5-11.

of A and the consciousness of B are to belong must be capable of being aware of its own identity. Otherwise it might be one self which apprehended A and then, forgetting A, apprehended B. No doubt in that case the self could not be aware of its own identity in apprehending A and in apprehending B, but none the less it would *be* identical in so doing. We reach the same conclusion if we consider the concluding sentence of § 10. "It is only because I can comprehend the manifold of representations in one consciousness, that I call them all my representations; for otherwise I should have as many-coloured and varied a self as I have representations of which I am conscious." Doubtless if I am to *be aware of* myself as the same in apprehending A and B, then, in coming to apprehend B, I must continue to apprehend A, and therefore must apprehend A and B as related; and such a consciousness on Kant's view involves a synthesis. But if I am merely to *be* the same subject which apprehends A and B, or rather if the apprehension of A and that of B are merely to *be* apprehensions on the part of one and the same subject, no such consciousness of A and B as related and, therefore, no synthesis is involved.

Again, the third paragraph assumes the possibility of self-consciousness as the starting-point for argument. The thought[274] seems to be this: 'For a self to be aware of its own identity, there must be a manifold in relation to which it can apprehend itself as one and the same throughout. An understanding which was perceptive, i. e. which originated objects by its own act of thinking, would necessarily by its own thinking originate a manifold in relation to which it could be aware of its own identity in thinking, and therefore its self-consciousness would need no synthesis. But our understanding, which is not perceptive, requires a manifold to be given to it, in relation to which it can be aware of its own identity by means of a synthesis of the manifold.' If this be the thought, it is clearly presupposed that *any* understanding must be capable of being conscious of its own identity.[275]

Further, it is easy to see how Kant came to take for granted the possibility of self-consciousness, in the sense of the consciousness of ourselves as the identical subject of all our representations. He approaches self-consciousness with the presupposition derived from his analysis of knowledge that our apprehension of a manifold does not consist in separate apprehensions of its elements, but is one apprehension or consciousness of the elements as related.[276] He thinks of this as a general presupposition of all apprehension of a manifold, and, of course, to discover this presupposition is to be self-conscious. To recognize the oneness of our apprehension is to be conscious of our own identity.[277]

[274] Cf. B. 138 fin.-139 init., M. 85 fin.

[275] B. 139 init., M. 85 fin. also assumes that it is impossible for a mind to be a unity without being able to be conscious of its unity.

[276] It is in consequence of this that the statement that 'a manifold of representations belongs to me' means, with the probable exception of § 1, not, 'I am aware of A, I am aware of B, I am aware of C,' but, 'I am aware, in one act of awareness, of A B C as related' (= ABC are 'connected in' or 'belong to' one consciousness). Cf. §§ 4, 8 ('in one consciousness'), 9, 10 ('in one consciousness'), and A. 116, Mah. 208 ('These representations only represent anything in me by belonging with all the rest to one consciousness [accepting Erdmann's emendation *mit allen anderen*], in which at any rate they can be connected').

[277] The above criticism of Kant's thought has not implied that it may not be true that a knowing mind is, as such, capable of being aware of its own unity; the argument has only

Again, to pass to the second main point to be considered,[278] Kant has no justification for arguing from the possibility of self-consciousness to that of the synthesis. This can be seen from the mere form of his argument. Kant, as has been said, seems first to establish the possibility of self-consciousness, and thence to conclude that a synthesis must be possible. But if, as it is his point to urge, consciousness of our identity only takes place through consciousness of the synthesis, this method of argument must be invalid. It would clearly be necessary to know that the synthesis is possible, *before* and *in order that* we could know that self-consciousness is possible. An objector has only to urge that the manifold might be such that it could not be combined into a systematic whole, in order to secure the admission that in that case self-consciousness would not be possible.

Nevertheless, the passage under consideration may be said to lay bare an important presupposition of self-consciousness. It is true that self-consciousness would be impossible, if we merely apprehended the parts of the world in isolation. To be conscious that I who am perceiving C perceived B and A, I must be conscious at once of A, B, and C, in one act of consciousness or apprehension. To be conscious separately of A and B and C is not to be conscious of A and B and C. And, to be conscious of A and B and C in one act of consciousness, I must apprehend A, B, and C as related, i. e. as forming parts of a whole or system. Hence it is only because our consciousness of A, B, and C is never the consciousness of a mere A, a mere B, and a mere C, but is always the consciousness of A B C as elements in one world that we can be conscious of our identity in apprehending A, B, and C. If *per impossibile* our apprehension be supposed to cease to be an apprehension of a plurality of objects in relation, self-consciousness must be supposed to cease also. At the same time, it is impossible to argue from the consciousness of our identity in apprehending to the consciousness of what is apprehended as a unity, and thence to the existence of that unity. For, apart from the consideration that in fact all thinking presupposes the relatedness or—what is the same thing—the necessary relatedness of objects to one another, and that therefore any assertion to the contrary is meaningless, the consciousness of objects as a unity is a condition of the consciousness of our identity, and therefore any doubt that can be raised in regard to the former can be raised equally with regard to the latter.

We may now pass to the concluding portion of the deduction. For the purpose of considering it, we may sum up the results of the preceding discussion by saying that Kant establishes the synthesis of the manifold on certain principles by what are really two independent lines of thought. The manifold may be regarded either as something which, in order to enter into knowledge, must be given relation to an object, or as something with respect to which self-consciousness must be possible. Regarded in either way, the manifold, according to Kant, involves a process of synthesis on certain principles, which makes it a systematic unity. Now Kant introduces the categories by maintaining that they are the principles of synthesis in question. "I assert that the above mentioned *categories* are nothing but the *conditions of thinking in a possible experience*. . . . They are fundamental conceptions by

---

been that Kant's proof is unsuccessful.

[278] Cf. p. 106.

which we think objects in general for phenomena."[279] A synthesis according to the categories is 'that wherein alone apperception can prove *a priori* its thorough-going and necessary identity'.[280] In the first edition this identification is simply asserted, but in the second Kant offers a proof.[281]

Before, however, we consider the proof, it is necessary to refer to a difficulty which seems to have escaped Kant altogether. The preceding account of the synthesis involved in knowledge and in self-consciousness implies, as his illustrations conclusively show, that the synthesis requires a particular principle which constitutes the individual manifold a whole of a particular kind.[282] But, if this be the case, it is clear that the categories, which are merely conceptions of an object in general, and are consequently quite general, cannot possibly be sufficient for the purpose. And since the manifold in itself includes no synthesis and therefore no principle of synthesis, Kant fails to give any account of the source of the particular principles of synthesis required for particular acts of knowledge.[283] This difficulty—which admits of no solution—is concealed from Kant in two ways. In the first place, when he describes what really must be stated as the process by which parts or qualities of an object become related to an object of a particular kind, he thinks that he is describing a process by which representations become related to an object in general.[284] Secondly, he thinks of the understanding as the source of general principles of synthesis, individual syntheses and the particular principles involved being attributed to the imagination; and so, when he comes to consider the part played in knowledge by the understanding, he is apt to ignore the need of particular principles.[285] Hence, Kant's proof that the categories are the principles of synthesis can at best be taken only as a proof that the categories, though not sufficient for the synthesis, are involved in it.

The proof runs thus:

"I could never satisfy myself with the definition which logicians give of a judgement in general. It is, according to them, the representation of a relation between two conceptions. . . ."

"But if I examine more closely the relation of given representations[286] in every judgement, and distinguish it, as belonging to the understanding, from their relation according to the laws of the reproductive imagination (which has only subjective validity), I find that a judgement is nothing but the mode of bringing given representations under the *objective* unity of apperception. This is what is intended by the term of relation 'is' in judgements, which is meant to distinguish the objective unity of given representations from the subjective. For this term indicates the relation of these representations to the original apperception, and also their *neces-*

[279] A. 111, Mah. 204. Cf. A. 119, Mah. 210.

[280] A. 112, Mah. 204.

[281] Cf. p. 87.

[282] Cf. p. 95, note 233, and p. 99.

[283] Cf. pp. 115-117.

[284] Cf. pp. 97-98.

[285] Cf. pp. 116-117.

[286] *Erkenntnisse* here is clearly used as a synonym for representations. Cf. A. 104, Mah. 199.

sary unity, even though the judgement itself is empirical, and therefore contingent, e. g. 'Bodies are heavy.' By this I do not mean that these representations *necessarily* belong *to each other* in empirical perception, but that they belong to each other *by means of the necessary unity* of apperception in the synthesis of perceptions, that is, according to principles of the objective determination of all our representations, in so far as knowledge can arise from them, these principles being all derived from the principle of the transcendental unity of apperception. In this way alone can there arise from this relation *a judgement*, that is, a relation which is *objectively valid*, and is adequately distinguished from the relation of the very same representations which would be only subjectively valid, e. g. according to laws of association. According to these laws, I could only say, 'If I carry a body, I feel an impression of weight', but not 'It, the body, *is* heavy'; for this is tantamount to saying, 'These two representations are connected in the object, that is, without distinction as to the condition of the subject, and are not merely connected together in the perception, however often it may be repeated.'"[287]

This ground for the identification of the categories with the principles of synthesis involved in knowledge may be ignored, as on the face of it unsuccessful. For the argument is that since the activity by which the synthesis is affected is that of judgement, the conceptions shown by the *Metaphysical Deduction* to be involved in judgement must constitute the principles of synthesis. But it is essential to this argument that the present account of judgement and that which forms the basis of the *Metaphysical Deduction* should be the same; and this is plainly not the case.[288] Judgement is now represented as an act by which we relate the manifold of sense in certain necessary ways as parts of the physical world,[289] whereas in the *Metaphysical Deduction* it was treated as an act by which we relate conceptions; and Kant now actually says that this latter account is faulty. Hence even if the metaphysical deduction had successfully derived the categories from the account of judgement which it presupposed, the present argument would not justify the identification of the categories so deduced with the principles of synthesis. The fact is that Kant's vindication of the categories is in substance independent of the *Metaphysical Deduction*. Kant's real thought, as opposed to his formal presentation of it, is simply that when we come to consider what are the principles of synthesis involved in the reference of the manifold to an object, we find that they are the categories.[290] The success, then, of this step in Kant's vindication of the categories

[287] B. 140-2, M. 86-8; cf. *Prol.*, §§ 18-20.

[288] Cf. Caird, i. 348-9 note.

[289] We may notice in passing that this passage renders explicit the extreme difficulty of Kant's view that 'the objective unity of apperception' is the unity of the parts of nature or of the physical world. How can the 'very same representations' stand at once in the subjective relation of association and in the objective relation which consists in their being related as parts of nature? There is plainly involved a transition from representation, in the sense of the apprehension of something, to representation, in the sense of something apprehended. It is objects apprehended which are objectively related; it is our apprehensions of objects which are associated, cf. pp. 125 and 151-152. Current psychology seems to share Kant's mistake in its doctrine of association of ideas, by treating the elements associated, which are really apprehensions of objects, as if they were objects apprehended.

[290] Cf. A. 112, Mah. 204; B. 162, M. 99.

is independent of that of the metaphysical deduction, and depends solely upon the question whether the principles of synthesis involved in knowledge are in fact the categories.

The substance of Kant's vindication of the categories may therefore be epitomized thus: 'We may take either of two starting-points. On the one hand, we may start from the fact that our experience is no mere dream, but an intelligent experience in which we are aware of a world of individual objects. This fact is conceded even by those who, like Hume, deny that we are aware of any necessity of relation between these objects. We may then go on to ask how it comes about that, beginning as we do with a manifold of sense given in succession, we come to apprehend this world of individual objects. If we do so, we find that there is presupposed a synthesis on our part of the manifold upon principles constituted by the categories. To deny, therefore, that the manifold is so connected is implicitly to deny that we have an apprehension of objects at all. But the existence of this apprehension is plainly a fact which even Hume did not dispute. On the other hand, we may start with the equally obvious fact that we must be capable of apprehending our own identity throughout our apprehension of the manifold of sense, and look for the presupposition of this fact. If we do this, we again find that there is involved a combination of the manifold according to the categories.'

In conclusion, attention may be drawn to two points. In the first place, Kant completes his account by at once emphasizing and explaining the paradoxical character of his conclusion. "Accordingly, the order and conformity to law in the phenomena which we call *nature* we ourselves introduce, and we could never find it there, if we, or the nature of our mind, had not originally placed it there."[291] "However exaggerated or absurd then it may sound to say that the understanding itself is the source of the laws of nature and consequently of the formal unity of nature, such an assertion is nevertheless correct and in accordance with the object, i. e. with experience."[292] The explanation of the paradox is found in the fact that objects of nature are phenomena. "But if we reflect that this nature is in itself nothing else than a totality[293] of phenomena and consequently no thing in itself but merely a number of representations of the mind, we shall not be surprised that only in the radical faculty of all our knowledge, viz. transcendental apperception, do we see it in that unity through which alone it can be called object of all possible experience, i. e. nature."[294] "It is no more surprising that the laws of the phenomena in nature must agree with the understanding and with its *a priori* form, that is, its faculty of connecting the manifold in general, than that the phenomena themselves must agree with the *a priori* form of our sensuous perception. For laws exist in the phenomena as little as phenomena exist in themselves; on the contrary, laws exist only relatively to the subject in which the phenomena inhere, so far as it has understanding, just as phenomena exist only relatively to the subject, so far as it has senses. To things in themselves their conformity to law would necessarily also belong independently of an understanding which knows them. But phenomena

[291] A. 125, Mah. 214.
[292] A. 127, Mah. 216.
[293] *Inbegriff.*
[294] A. 114, Mah. 206.

are only representations of things which exist unknown in respect of what they may be in themselves. But, as mere representations, they stand under no law of connexion except that which the connecting faculty prescribes."[295]

In the second place, this last paragraph contains the real reason from the point of view of the deduction[296] of the categories for what may be called the negative side of his doctrine, viz. that the categories only apply to objects of experience and not to things in themselves. According to Kant, we can only say that certain principles of connexion apply to a reality into which we introduce the connexion. Things in themselves, if connected, are connected in themselves and apart from us. Hence there can be no guarantee that any principles of connexion which we might assert them to possess are those which they do possess.

[295] B. 164, M. 100.

[296] The main passage (B. 146-9, M. 90-2), in which he argues that the categories do not apply to things in themselves, ignores the account of a conception as a principle of synthesis, upon which the deduction turns, and returns to the earlier account of a conception as something opposed to a perception, i. e. as that by which an object is thought as opposed to a perception by which an object is given. Consequently, it argues merely that the categories, as conceptions, are empty or without an object, unless an object is given in perception, and that, since things in themselves are not objects of perception, the categories are no more applicable to things in themselves than are any other conceptions.

CHAPTER IX

GENERAL CRITICISM OF THE TRANSCENDENTAL DEDUCTION OF THE CATEGORIES

THE preceding account of Kant's vindication of the categories has included much criticism. But the criticism has been as far as possible restricted to details, and has dealt with matters of principle only so far as has been necessary in order to follow Kant's thought. We must now consider the position as a whole, even though this may involve some repetition.[297] The general difficulties of the position may be divided into two kinds, (1) difficulties involved in the working out of the theory, even if its main principles are not questioned, and (2) difficulties involved in accepting its main principles at all.

The initial difficulty of the first kind, which naturally strikes the reader, concerns the possibility of performing the synthesis. The mind has certain general ways of combining the manifold, viz. the categories. But on general grounds we should expect the mind to possess only one mode of combining the manifold. For the character of the manifold to be combined cannot affect the mind's power of combination, and, if the power of the mind consists in combining, the combining should always be of the same kind. Thus, suppose the manifold given to the mind to be combined consisted of musical notes, we could think of the mind's power of combination as exercised in combining the notes by way of succession, *provided that* this be regarded as the only mode of combination. But if the mind were thought also capable of combining notes by way of simultaneity, we should at once be confronted with the insoluble problem of determining why the one mode of combination was exercised in any given case rather than the other. If, several kinds of synthesis being allowed, this difficulty be avoided by the supposition that, not being incompatible, they are all exercised together, we have the alternative task of explaining how the same manifold can be combined in each of these ways. As a matter of fact, Kant thinks of manifolds of different kinds as combined or related in different ways; thus events are related causally and quantities quantitatively. But since, on Kant's view, the manifold as given is unrelated and all combination comes from the mind, the mind should not be held capable of combining manifolds of different kinds differently. Otherwise the manifold would in its own nature imply the need of a particular kind of synthesis, and would therefore not be unrelated.

---

[297] Difficulties connected with Kant's view of self-consciousness will be ignored, as having been sufficiently considered.

Suppose, however, we waive the difficulty involved in the plurality of the categories. There remains the equally fundamental difficulty that any single principle of synthesis contains in itself no ground for the different ways of its application.[298] Suppose it to be conceded that in the apprehension of definite shapes we combine the manifold in accordance with the conception of figure, and, for the purpose of the argument, that the conception of figure can be treated as equivalent to the category of quantity. It is plain that we apprehend different shapes, e. g. lines[299] and triangles[300], of which, if we take into account differences of relative length of sides, there is an infinite variety, and houses,[301] which may also have an infinite variety of shape. But there is nothing in the mind's capacity of relating the manifold by way of figure to determine it to combine a given manifold into a figure of one kind rather than into a figure of any other kind; for to combine the manifold into a particular shape, there is needed not merely the thought of a figure in general, but the thought of a definite figure. No 'cue' can be furnished by the manifold itself, for any such cue would involve the conception of a particular figure, and would therefore imply that the particular synthesis was implicit in the manifold itself, in which case it would not be true that all synthesis comes from the mind.

This difficulty takes a somewhat different form in the case of the categories of relation. To take the case of cause and effect, the conception of which, according to Kant, is involved in our apprehension of a succession, Kant's view seems to be that we become aware of two elements of the manifold A B as a succession of events in the world of nature by combining them as necessarily successive in a causal order, in which the state of affairs which precedes B and which contains A contains something upon which B must follow (i. e. a cause of B), which therefore makes it necessary that B must follow A.[302] But if we are to do this, we must in some way succeed in selecting or picking out from among the elements of the manifold that element A which is to be thus combined with B. We therefore need something more than the category. It is not enough that we should think that B has a cause; we must think of something in particular as the cause of B, and we must think of it either as coexistent with, or as identical with, A.

Kant fails to notice this second difficulty,[303] and up to a certain point avoids it owing to his distinction between the imagination and the understanding. For he thinks of the understanding as the source of general principles of synthesis, viz. the categories, and attributes individual syntheses to the imagination. Hence the individual syntheses, which involve particular principles, are already effected before the understanding comes into play. But to throw the work of effecting

[298] Cf. p. 111.
[299] B. 137, M. 85.
[300] A. 105, Mah. 199.
[301] B. 162, M. 99.
[302] Cf. pp. 155-158.
[303] We should have expected Kant to have noticed this difficulty in A. 105, Mah. 199, where he describes what is involved in the relation of representations to an object, for his instance of representations becoming so related is the process of combining elements into a triangle, which plainly requires a synthesis of a very definite kind. For the reasons of his failure to notice the difficulty cf. p. 111.

individual syntheses upon the imagination is only to evade the difficulty. For in the end, as has been pointed out,[304] the imagination must be the understanding working unreflectively, and, whether this is so or not, some account must be given of the way in which the imagination furnishes the particular principles of synthesis required.

The third and last main difficulty of the first kind concerns the relation of the elements of the manifold and the kinds of synthesis by which they are combined. This involves the distinction between relating in general and terms to be related. For to perform a synthesis is in general to relate, and the elements to be combined are the terms to be related.[305] Now it is only necessary to take instances to realize that the possibility of relating terms in certain ways involves two presuppositions, which concern respectively the general and the special nature of the terms to be related.

In the first place, it is clear that the general nature of the terms must correspond with or be adapted to the general nature of the relationship to be effected. Thus if two terms are to be related as more or less loud, they must be sounds, since the relation in question is one in respect of sound and not, e. g., of time or colour or space. Similarly, terms to be related as right and left must be bodies in space, right and left being a spatial relation. Again, only human beings can be related as parent and child. Kant's doctrine, however, does not conform to this presupposition. For the manifold to be related consists solely of sensations, and of individual spaces, and perhaps individual times, as elements of pure perception; and such a manifold is not of the kind required. Possibly individual spaces may be regarded as adequate terms to be related or combined into geometrical figures, e. g. into lines or triangles. But a house as a synthesis of a manifold cannot be a synthesis of spaces, or of times, or of sensations. Its parts are bodies, which, whatever they may be, are neither sensations nor spaces nor times, nor combinations of them. In reality they are substances of a special kind. Again, the relation of cause and effect is not a relation of sensations or spaces or times, but of successive states of physical things or substances, the relation consisting in the necessity of their succession.

In the second place, it is clear that the special nature of the relation to be effected presupposes a special nature on the part of the terms to be related. If one sound is to be related to another by way of the octave, that other must be its octave. If one quantity is to be related to another as the double of it, that quantity must be twice as large as the other. In the same way, proceeding to Kant's instances, we see that if we are to combine or relate a manifold into a triangle, and therefore into a triangle of a particular size and shape, the elements of the manifold must be lines, and lines of a particular size. If we are to combine a manifold into a house, and therefore into a house of a certain shape and size, the manifold must consist of bodies of a suitable shape and size. If we are to relate a manifold by way of necessary succession, the manifold must be such that it can be so related; in other words, if

[304] Pp. 90-91.

[305] 'To relate' is used rather than 'to recognize as related', in order to conform to Kant's view of knowledge. But if it be desired to take the argument which follows in connexion with knowledge proper (cf. p. 129), it is only necessary to substitute throughout 'to recognize as related' for 'to relate' and to make the other changes consequent thereon.

we are to relate an element X of the manifold with some other Y as the necessary antecedent of X, there must be some definite element Y which is connected with, and always occurs along with, X. To put the matter generally, we may say that the manifold must be adapted to or 'fit' the categories not only, as has been pointed out, in the sense that it must be of the right kind, but also in the sense that its individual elements must have that orderly character which enables them to be related according to the categories.

Now it is plain from Kant's vindication of what he calls the affinity of phenomena,[306] that he recognizes the existence of this presupposition. But the question arises whether this vindication can be successful. For since the manifold is originated by the thing in itself, it seems prima facie impossible to prove that the elements of the manifold must have affinity, and so be capable of being related according to the categories. Before, however, we consider the chief passage in which Kant tries to make good his position, we may notice a defence which might naturally be offered on his behalf. It might be said that he establishes the conformity of the manifold to the categories at least hypothetically, i. e. upon the supposition that the manifold is capable of entering into knowledge, and also upon the supposition that we are capable of being conscious of our identity with respect to it; for upon either supposition any element of the manifold must be capable of being combined with all the rest into one world of nature. Moreover, it might be added that these suppositions are justified, for our experience is not a mere dream, but is throughout the consciousness of a world, and we are self-conscious throughout our experience; and therefore it is clear that the manifold does in fact 'fit' the categories. But the retort is obvious. Any actual conformity of the manifold to the categories would upon this view be at best but an empirical fact, and, although, if the conformity ceased, we should cease to be aware of a world and of ourselves, no reason has been or can be given why the conformity should not cease.

The passage in which Kant vindicates the affinity of phenomena in the greatest detail is the following:

"We will now try to exhibit the necessary connexion of the understanding with phenomena by means of the categories, by beginning from below, i. e. from the empirical end. The first that is given us is a phenomenon, which if connected with consciousness is called perception[307]. . . . But because every phenomenon contains a manifold, and consequently different perceptions are found in the mind scattered and single, a connexion of them is necessary, which they cannot have in mere sense. There is, therefore, in us an active power of synthesis of this manifold, which we call imagination, and the action of which, when exercised immediately upon perceptions, I call apprehension. The business of the imagination, that is to say, is to bring the manifold of intuition[308] into an *image*; it must, therefore, first receive the impressions into its activity, i. e. apprehend them."

"But it is clear that even this apprehension of the manifold would not by itself produce an image and a connexion of the impressions, unless there were a subjec-

[306] Cf. A. 100-2, Mah. 195-7 (quoted pp. 92-93); A. 113, Mah. 205; A. 121-2, Mah. 211-2.
[307] *Wahrnehmung.*
[308] *Anschauung.*

tive ground in virtue of which one perception, from which the mind has passed to another, is summoned to join that which follows, and thus whole series of perceptions are presented, i. e. a reproductive power of imagination, which power, however, is also only empirical."

"But if representations reproduced one another at haphazard just as they happened to meet together, once more no determinate connexion would arise, but merely chaotic heaps of them, and consequently no knowledge would arise; therefore the reproduction of them must have a rule, according to which a representation enters into connexion with this rather than with another in the imagination. This subjective and *empirical* ground of reproduction according to rules is called the *association* of representations."

"But now, if this unity of association had not also an objective ground, so that it was impossible that phenomena should be apprehended by the imagination otherwise than under the condition of a possible synthetic unity of this apprehension, it would also be a pure accident that phenomena were adapted to a connected system of human knowledge. For although we should have the power of associating perceptions, it would still remain wholly undetermined and accidental whether they were associable; and in the event of their not being so, a multitude of perceptions and even perhaps a whole sensibility would be possible, in which much empirical consciousness would be met with in my mind, but divided and without belonging to *one* consciousness of myself, which however is impossible. For only in that I ascribe all perceptions to one consciousness (the original apperception) can I say of all of them that I am conscious of them. There must therefore be an objective ground, i. e. a ground to be recognized *a priori* before all empirical laws of the imagination, on which rests the possibility, nay even the necessity, of a law which extends throughout all phenomena, according to which we regard them without exception as such data of the senses, as are in themselves associable and subjected to universal rules of a thorough-going connexion in reproduction. This objective ground of all association of phenomena I call the *affinity* of phenomena. But we can meet this nowhere else than in the principle of the unity of apperception as regards all cognitions which are to belong to me. According to it, all phenomena without exception must so enter into the mind or be apprehended as to agree with the unity of apperception, which agreement would be impossible without synthetical unity in their connexion, which therefore is also objectively necessary."

"The objective unity of all (empirical) consciousness in one consciousness (the original apperception) is therefore the necessary condition even of all possible perception, and the affinity of all phenomena (near or remote) is a necessary consequence of a synthesis in the imagination, which is *a priori* founded upon rules."

"The imagination is therefore also a power of *a priori* synthesis, for which reason we give it the name of the productive imagination; and so far as it, in relation to all the manifold of the phenomenon, has no further aim than the necessary unity in the synthesis of the phenomenon, it can be called the transcendental function of the imagination. It is therefore strange indeed, but nevertheless clear from the preceding, that only by means of this transcendental function of the imagination does even the affinity of phenomena, and with it their association and, through this, lastly their reproduction according to laws, and consequently experience itself become possible, because without it no conceptions of objects would ever come together into one experience."[309]

If it were not for the last two paragraphs[310], we should understand this difficult passage to be substantially identical in meaning with the defence of the affinity of phenomena just given.[311] We should understand Kant to be saying (1) that the synthesis which knowledge requires presupposes not merely a faculty of association on our part by which we reproduce elements of the manifold according to rules, but also an affinity on the part of the manifold to be apprehended, which enables our faculty of association to get to work, and (2) that this affinity can be vindicated as a presupposition at once of knowledge and of self-consciousness.

In view, however, of the fact that, according to the last two paragraphs, the affinity is due to the imagination,[312] it seems necessary to interpret the passage thus:

'Since the given manifold of sense consists of isolated elements, this manifold, in order to enter into knowledge, must be combined into an image. This combination is effected by the imagination, which however must first apprehend the elements one by one.'

'But this apprehension of the manifold by the imagination could produce no image, unless the imagination also possessed the power of reproducing past elements of the manifold, and, if knowledge is to arise, of reproducing them according to rules. This faculty of reproduction by which, on perceiving the element A, we are led to think of or reproduce a past element B—B being reproduced according to some rule—rather than C or D is called the faculty of association; and since the rules according to which it works depend on empirical conditions, and therefore cannot be anticipated *a priori,* it may be called the subjective ground of reproduction.'

'But if the image produced by association is to play a part in knowledge, the empirical faculty of reproduction is not a sufficient condition or ground of it. A further condition is implied, which may be called objective in the sense that it is *a priori* and prior to all empirical laws of imagination. This condition is that the act by which the data of sense enter the mind or are apprehended, i. e. the act by which the imagination *apprehends and combines* the data of sense into a sensuous image, must *make* the elements such that they have affinity, and therefore such that they can subsequently be recognized as parts of a necessarily related whole.[313]

[309] A. 119-23, Mah. 210-3.

[310] And also the first and last sentence of the fourth paragraph, where Kant speaks not of 'phenomena which are to be apprehended', but of the 'apprehension of phenomena' as necessarily agreeing with the unity of apperception.

[311] p. 118.

[312] It should be noted that in the last paragraph but one Kant does not say '*our knowledge* that phenomena must have affinity is a consequence of *our knowledge* that there must be a synthesis of the imagination', but 'the affinity of all phenomena is a consequence of a synthesis in the imagination'. And the last paragraph precludes the view that in making the latter statement he meant the former. Cf. also A. 101, Mah. 196.

[313] On this interpretation 'entering the mind' or 'being apprehended' in the fourth

Unless this condition is satisfied, even if we possessed the faculty of association, our experience would be a chaos of disconnected elements, and we could not be self-conscious, which is impossible. Starting, therefore, with the principle that we must be capable of being self-conscious with respect to all the elements of the manifold, we can lay down *a priori* that this condition is a fact.'

'It follows, then, that the affinity or connectedness of the data of sense presupposed by the *re*production which is presupposed in knowledge, is actually produced by the *pro*ductive faculty of imagination, which, in combining the data into a sensuous image, gives them the unity required.'

If, as it seems necessary to believe, this be the correct interpretation of the passage,[314] Kant is here trying to carry out to the full his doctrine that *all* unity or connectedness comes from the mind's activity. He is maintaining that the imagination, acting *pro*ductively on the data of sense and thereby combining them into an image, gives the data a connectedness which the understanding can subsequently recognize. But to maintain this is, of course, only to throw the problem one stage further back. If reproduction, in order to enter into knowledge, implies a manifold which has such connexion that it is capable of being reproduced according to rules, so the production of sense-elements into a coherent image in turn implies sense-elements capable of being so combined. The act of combination cannot confer upon them or introduce into them a unity which they do not already possess.

The fact is that this step in Kant's argument exhibits the final breakdown of his view that all unity or connectedness or relatedness is conferred upon the data of sense by the activity of the mind. Consequently, this forms a convenient point at which to consider what seems to be the fundamental mistake of this view. The mistake stated in its most general form appears to be that, misled by his theory of perception, he regards 'terms' as given by things in themselves acting on the sensibility, and 'relations' as introduced by the understanding,[315] whereas the fact is that in the sense in which terms can be said to be given, relations can and must also be said to be given.

To realize that this is the case, we need only consider Kant's favourite instance of knowledge, the apprehension of a straight line. According to him, this presupposes that there is given to us a manifold, which—whether he admits it or not—must really be parts of the line, and that we combine this manifold on a principle

paragraph does not refer merely to the apprehension of elements one by one, which is preliminary to the act of combining them, but includes the act by which they are combined. If so, Kant's argument formally involves a circle. For in the second and third paragraphs he argues that the synthesis of perceptions involves reproduction according to rules, and then, in the fourth paragraph, he argues that this reproduction presupposes a synthesis of perceptions. We may, however, perhaps regard his argument as being in substance that knowledge involves *re*production by the imagination of elements capable of connexion, and that this reproduction involves *pro*duction by the imagination of the data of sense, which are to be reproduced, into an image.

[314] If the preceding interpretation (pp. 119-120) be thought the correct one, it must be admitted that Kant's vindication of the affinity breaks down for the reason given, p. 118.

[315] The understanding being taken to include the imagination, as being the faculty of *spontaneity* in distinction from the *passive* sensibility.

involved in the nature of straightness. Now suppose that the manifold given is the parts AB, BC, CD, DE of the line AE. It is clearly only possible to recognize AB and BC as contiguous parts of a straight line, if we immediately apprehend that AB and BC form one line of which these parts are identical in direction. Otherwise, we might just as well join AB and BC at a right angle, and in fact at any angle; we need not even make AB and BC contiguous.[316] Similarly, the relation of BC to CD and of CD to DE must be just as immediately apprehended as the parts themselves. Is there, however, any relation of which it could be said that it is not given, and to which therefore Kant's doctrine might seem to apply? There is. Suppose AB, BC, CD to be of such a size that, though we can see AB and BC, or BC and CD, together, we cannot see AB and CD together. It is clear that in this case we can only learn that AB and CD are parts of the same straight line through an inference. We have to infer that, because each is in the same straight line with BC, the one is in the same straight line with the other. Here the fact that AB and CD are in the same straight line is not immediately apprehended. This relation, therefore, may be said not to be given; and, from Kant's point of view, we could say that we introduce this relation into the manifold through our activity of thinking, which combines AB and CD together in accordance with the principle that two straight lines which are in the same line with a third are in line with one another. Nevertheless, this case is no exception to the general principle that relations must be given equally with terms; for we only become aware of the relation between AB and CD, which is not given, because we are already aware of other relations, viz. those between AB and BC, and BC and CD, which are given. Relations then, or, in Kant's language, particular syntheses must be said to be given, in the sense in which the elements to be combined can be said to be given.

Further, we can better see the nature of Kant's mistake in this respect, if we bear in mind that Kant originally and rightly introduced the distinction between the sensibility and the understanding as that between the passive faculty by which an individual is given or presented to us and the active faculty by which we bring an individual under, or recognize it as an instance of a universal.[317] For we then see that Kant in the *Transcendental Deduction*, by treating what is given by the sensibility as terms and what is contributed by the understanding as relations, is really confusing the distinction between a relation and its terms with that between universal and individual; in other words, he says of terms what ought to be said of individuals, and of relations what ought to be said of universals. That the confusion is a confusion, and not a legitimate identification, it is easy to see. For, on the one hand, a relation between terms is as much an individual as either of the terms. That a body A is to the right of a body B is as much an individual fact as either A or B.[318] And if terms, as being individuals, belong to perception and are given, in the sense that they are in an immediate relation to us, relations, as being

[316] In order to meet a possible objection, it may be pointed out that if AB and BC be given in isolation, the contiguity implied in referring to them as *AB* and *BC* will not be known.

[317] Cf. pp. 14-15.

[318] I can attach no meaning to Mr. Bertrand Russell's assertion that relations have no instances. See *The Principles of Mathematics*, § 55.

individuals, equally belong to perception and are given. On the other hand, individual terms just as much as individual relations imply corresponding universals. An individual body implies 'bodiness', just as much as the fact that a body A is to the right of a body B implies the relationship of 'being to the right of something'. And if, as is the case, thinking or conceiving in distinction from perceiving, is that activity by which we recognize an individual, given in perception, as one of a kind, conceiving is involved as much in the apprehension of a term as in the apprehension of a relation. The apprehension of 'this red body' as much involves the recognition of an individual as an instance of a kind, i. e. as much involves an act of the understanding, as does the apprehension of the fact that it is brighter than some other body.

Kant has failed to notice this confusion for two reasons. In the first place, beginning in the *Analytic* with the thought that the thing in itself, by acting on our sensibility, produces isolated sense data, he is led to adopt a different view of the understanding from that which he originally gave, and to conceive its business as consisting in relating these data. In the second place, by distinguishing the imagination from the understanding, he is able to confine the understanding to being the source of universals or principles of relation in distinction from individual relations.[319] Since, however, as has been pointed out, and as Kant himself sees at times, the imagination is the understanding working unreflectively, this limitation cannot be successful.

There remain for consideration the difficulties of the second kind, i. e. the difficulties involved in accepting its main principles at all. These are of course the most important. Throughout the deduction Kant is attempting to formulate the nature of knowledge. According to him, it consists in an activity of the mind by which it combines the manifold of sense on certain principles and is to some extent aware that it does so, and by which it thereby gives the manifold relation to an object. Now the fundamental and final objection to this account is that what it describes is not knowledge at all. The justice of this objection may be seen by considering the two leading thoughts underlying the view, which, though closely connected, may be treated separately. These are the thought of knowledge as a process by which representations acquire relation to an object, and the thought of knowledge as a process of synthesis.

It is in reality meaningless to speak of 'a process by which representations or ideas acquire relation to an object'.[320] The phrase must mean a process by which a mere apprehension, which, as such, is not the apprehension of an object, becomes the apprehension of an object. Apprehension, however, is essentially and from the very beginning the apprehension of an object, i. e. of a reality apprehended. If there is no object which the apprehension is 'of', there is no apprehension. It is therefore wholly meaningless to speak of a process by which an apprehension *becomes* the apprehension of an object. If when we reflected we were not aware of an object, i. e. a reality apprehended, we could not be aware of our apprehension; for our apprehension is the apprehension of it, and is itself only apprehended in

[319] Cf. pp. 116-117.
[320] Cf. p. 97, and pp. 151-153.

relation to, though in distinction from, it. It is therefore impossible to suppose a condition of mind in which, knowing what 'apprehension' means, we proceed to ask, 'What is meant by an object of it?' and 'How does an apprehension become related to an object?'; for both questions involve the thought of a mere representation, i. e. of an apprehension which as yet is not the apprehension of anything.

These questions, when their real nature is exhibited, are plainly absurd. Kant's special theory, however, enables him to evade the real absurdity involved. For, according to his view, a representation is the representation or apprehension of something only from the point of view of the thing in itself. As an appearance or perhaps more strictly speaking as a sensation, it has also a being of its own which is not relative[321]; and from this point of view it *is* possible to speak of 'mere' representations and to raise questions which presuppose their reality.[322]

But this remedy, if remedy it can be called, is at least as bad as the disease. For, in the first place, the change of standpoint is necessarily illegitimate. An appearance or sensation is not from any point of view a representation in the proper sense, i. e. a representation or apprehension of something. It is simply a reality to be apprehended, of the special kind called mental. If it be called a representation, the word must have a new meaning; it must mean something represented, or presented,[323] i. e. object of apprehension, with the implication that what is presented, or is object of apprehension, is mental or a modification of the mind. Kant therefore only avoids the original absurdity by an illegitimate change of standpoint, the change being concealed by a tacit transition in the meaning of representation. In the second place, the change of standpoint only saves the main problem from being absurd by rendering it insoluble. For if a representation be taken to be an appearance or a sensation, the main problem becomes that of explaining how it is that, beginning with the apprehension of mere appearances or sensations, we come to apprehend an object, in the sense of an object in nature, which, as such, is not an appearance or sensation but a part of the physical world. But if the immediate object of apprehension were in this way confined to appearances, which are, to use Kant's phrase, determinations of our mind, our apprehension would be limited to these appearances, and any apprehension of an object in nature would be impossible.[324] In fact, it is just the view that the immediate object of apprehension consists in a determination of the mind which forms the basis of the solipsist position. Kant's own solution involves an absurdity at least as great as that involved in the thought of a mere representation, in the proper sense of representation. For the solution is that appearances or sensations become related to an object, in the sense of an object in nature, by being combined on certain principles. Yet it is plainly impossible to combine appearances or sensations into an object in nature. If a triangle, or a house, or 'a freezing of water'[325] is the result of any process of combination, the elements combined must be respectively lines, and bricks, and physical

[321] Cf. p. 73 init.

[322] The absurdity of the problem really propounded is also concealed from Kant in the way indicated, pp. 97 fin.-98 init.

[323] *Vorgestellt.*

[324] Cf. p. 66.

[325] B. 162, M. 99.

events; these are objects in the sense in which the whole produced by the combination is an object, and are certainly not appearances or sensations. Kant conceals the difficulty from himself by the use of language to which he is not entitled. For while his instances of objects are always of the kind indicated, he persists in calling the manifold combined 'representations', i. e. presented mental modifications. This procedure is of course facilitated for him by his view that nature is a phenomenon or appearance, but the difficulty which it presents to the reader culminates when he speaks of the very same representations as having both a subjective and an objective relation, i. e. as being both modifications of the mind and parts of nature.[326]

We may now turn to Kant's thought of knowledge as a process of synthesis. When Kant speaks of synthesis, the kind of synthesis of which he usually is thinking is that of spatial elements into a spatial whole; and although he refers to other kinds, e. g. of units into numbers, and of events into a temporal series, nevertheless it is the thought of spatial synthesis which guides his view. Now we must in the end admit that the spatial synthesis of which he is thinking is really the *construction* or *making* of spatial objects in the literal sense. It would be rightly illustrated by making figures out of matches or spelicans, or by drawing a circle with compasses, or by building a house out of bricks. Further, if we extend this view of the process of which Kant is thinking, we have to allow that the process of synthesis in which, according to Kant, knowledge consists is that of making or constructing parts of the physical world, and in fact the physical world itself, out of elements given in perception.[327] The deduction throughout presupposes that the synthesis is really *manufacture*, and Kant is at pains to emphasize the fact. "The order and conformity to law in the phenomena which we call *nature* we ourselves introduce, and we could not find it there, if we or the nature of our mind had not originally placed it there."[328] He naturally rejoices in the manufacture, because it is just this which makes the categories valid. If knowing is really making, the principles of synthesis must apply to the reality known, because it is by these very principles that the reality is made. Moreover, recognition of this fact enables us to understand certain features of his view which would otherwise be inexplicable. For if the synthesis consists in literal construction, we are able to understand why Kant should think (1) that in the process of knowledge the mind *introduces* order into the manifold, (2) that the mind is limited in its activity of synthesis by having to conform to certain principles of construction which constitute the nature of the understanding, and (3) that the manifold of phenomena must possess affinity. If, for example, we build a house, it can be said (1) that we introduce into the materials a plan or principle of arrangement which they do not possess in themselves, (2) that the particular plan is limited by, and must conform to, the laws of spatial relation and to the general presuppositions of physics, such as the uniformity of nature, and (3) that only such materials are capable of the particular combination

[326] B. 139-42, M. 87-8. Cf. 112, note 289, and pp. 151-152.

[327] It is for this reason that the mathematical illustrations of the synthesis are the most plausible for his theory. While we can be said to construct geometrical figures, and while the construction of geometrical figures can easily be mistaken for the apprehension of them, we cannot with any plausibility be said to construct the physical world.

[328] A. 125, Mah. 214. Cf. the other passages quoted pp. 113-114.

as possess a nature suitable to it. Moreover, if, for Kant, knowing is really making, we are able to understand two other prominent features of his view. We can understand why Kant should lay so much stress upon the 'recognition' of the synthesis, and upon the self-consciousness involved in knowledge. For if the synthesis of the manifold is really the making of an object, it results merely in the existence of the object; knowledge of it is still to be effected. Consequently, knowledge of the object only finds a place in Kant's view by the *recognition* (on the necessity of which he insists) of the manifold as combined on a principle. This recognition, which Kant considers only an element in knowledge, is really the knowledge itself. Again, since the reality to be known is a whole of parts which we construct on a principle, we know that it is such a whole, and therefore that 'the manifold is related to one object', because, and only because, we know that we have combined the elements on a principle. Self-consciousness therefore *must* be inseparable from consciousness of an object.

The fundamental objection to this account of knowledge seems so obvious as to be hardly worth stating; it is of course that knowing and making are not the same. The very nature of knowing presupposes that the thing known is already made, or, to speak more accurately, already exists.[329] In other words, knowing is essentially the discovery of what already is. Even if the reality known happens to be something which we make, e. g. a house, the knowing it is distinct from the making it, and, so far from being identical with the making, presupposes that the reality in question is already made. Music and poetry are, no doubt, realities which in some sense are 'made' or 'composed', but the apprehension of them is distinct from and presupposes the process by which they are composed.

How difficult it is to resolve knowing into making may be seen by consideration of a difficulty in the interpretation of Kant's phrase 'relation of the manifold to an object', to which no allusion has yet been made. When it is said that a certain manifold is related to, or stands[330] in relation to, an object, does the relatedness referred to consist in the fact that the manifold is combined into a whole, or in the fact that we are conscious of the combination, or in both? If we accept the first alternative we must allow that, while relatedness to an object implies a process of synthesis, yet the relatedness, and therefore the synthesis, have nothing to do with knowledge. For the relatedness of the manifold to an object will be the combination of the elements of the manifold as parts of an object constructed, and the process of synthesis involved will be that by which the object is constructed. This process of synthesis will have nothing to do with knowledge; for since it is merely the process by which the object is constructed, knowledge so far is not effected at all, and no clue is given to the way in which it comes about. If, however, we accept the second alternative, we have to allow that while relatedness to an object has to do with knowledge, yet it in no way implies a process of synthesis. For since in that case it consists in the fact that we are conscious of the manifold as together forming an object, it in no way implies that the object has been produced by a process of synthesis. Kant, of course, would accept the third alternative. For, firstly, since it is knowledge which he is describing, the phrase 'relatedness to an object'

[329] Cf. Ch. VI.

[330] A. 109, Mah. 202.

cannot refer simply to the *existence* of a combination of the manifold, and of a process by which it has been produced; its meaning must include *consciousness* of the combination. In the second place, it is definitely his view that we cannot represent anything as combined in the object without having previously combined it ourselves.[331] Moreover, it is just with respect to this connexion between the synthesis and the consciousness of the synthesis that his reduction of knowing to making helps him; for to make an object, e. g. a house, is to make it consciously, i. e. to combine materials on a principle of which we are aware. Since, then, the combining of which he speaks is really making, it seems to him impossible to combine a manifold without being aware of the nature of the act of combination, and therefore of the nature of the whole thereby produced.[332] But though this is clearly Kant's view, it is not justified. In the first place, 'relatedness of the manifold to an object' ought not to refer *both* to its combination in a whole *and* to our consciousness of the combination; and in strictness it should refer to the former only. For as referring to the former it indicates a relation of the manifold *to the object*, as being the parts of the object, and as referring to the latter it indicates a relation of the manifold *to us*, as being apprehended by us as the parts of the object. But two relations which, though they are of one and the same thing, are nevertheless relations of it to two different things, should not be referred to by the same phrase. Moreover, since the relatedness is referred to as relatedness to an object, the phrase properly indicates the relation of the manifold to an object, and not to us as apprehending it. Again, in the second place, Kant cannot successfully maintain that the phrase is primarily a loose expression for our consciousness of the manifold as related to an object, and that since this implies a process of synthesis, the phrase may fairly include in its meaning the thought of the combination of the manifold by us into a whole. For although Kant asserts—and with some plausibility—that we can only apprehend as combined what we have ourselves combined, yet when we consider this assertion seriously we see it to be in no sense true.

The general conclusion, therefore, to be drawn is that the process of synthesis by which the manifold is said to become related to an object is a process not of knowledge but of construction in the literal sense, and that it leaves knowledge of the thing constructed still to be effected. But if knowing is obviously different from making, why should Kant have apparently felt no difficulty in resolving knowing into making? Three reasons may be given.

In the first place, the very question, 'What does the process of knowing consist in?' at least suggests that knowing can be resolved into and stated in terms of

[331] B. 130, M. 80.

[332] To say that 'combining', in the sense of making, *really* presupposes consciousness of the nature of the whole produced, would be inconsistent with the previous assertion that even where the reality known is something made, the knowledge of it presupposes that the reality is already made. Strictly speaking, the activity of combining presupposes consciousness not of the whole which we *succeed* in producing, but of the whole which we *want* to produce.

It may be noted that, from the point of view of the above argument, the activity of combining presupposes actual consciousness of the act of combination and of its principle, and does not imply merely the possibility of it. Kant, of course, does not hold this.

something else. In this respect it resembles the modern phrase '*theory* of knowledge'. Moreover, since it is plain that in knowing we are active, the question is apt to assume the form, 'What do we *do* when we know or think?' and since one of the commonest forms of doing something is to perform a physical operation on physical things, whereby we effect a recombination of them on some plan, it is natural to try to resolve knowing into this kind of doing, i. e. into making in a wide sense of the word.

In the second place, Kant never relaxed his hold upon the thing in itself. Consequently, there always remained for him a reality which existed in itself and was not made by us. This was to him the fundamental reality, and the proper object of knowledge, although unfortunately inaccessible to *our* faculties of knowing. Hence to Kant it did not seriously matter that an inferior reality, viz. the phenomenal world, was made by us in the process of knowing.

In the third place, it is difficult, if not impossible, to read the *Deduction* without realizing that Kant failed to distinguish knowing from that formation of mental imagery which accompanies knowing. The process of synthesis, if it is even to seem to constitute knowledge and to involve the validity of the categories, must really be a process by which we construct, and recognize our construction of, an individual reality in nature out of certain physical data. Nevertheless, it is plain that what Kant normally describes as the process of synthesis is really the process by which we construct an imaginary picture of a reality in nature not present to perception, i. e. by which we imagine to ourselves what it would look like if we were present to perceive it. This is implied by his continued use of the terms 'reproduction' and 'imagination' in describing the synthesis. To be aware of an object of past perception, it is necessary, according to him, that the object should be *re*produced. It is thereby implied that the object of our present awareness is not the object of past perception, but a mental image which copies or reproduces it. The same implication is conveyed by his use of the term 'imagination' to describe the faculty by which the synthesis is effected; for 'imagination' normally means the power of making a mental image of something not present to perception, and this interpretation is confirmed by Kant's own description of the imagination as 'the faculty of representing an object even without its presence in perception'.[333] Further, that Kant really fails to distinguish the construction of mental imagery from literal construction is shown by the fact that, although he insists that the formation of an image and reproduction are both necessary for knowledge, he does not consistently adhere to this. For his general view is that the elements combined and recognized as combined are the original data of sense, and not reproductions of them which together form an image, and his instances imply that the elements retained in thought, i. e. the elements of which we are aware subsequently to perception, are the elements originally perceived, e. g. the parts of a line or the units counted.[334] Moreover, in one passage Kant definitely describes certain *objects* of

[333] B. 152, M. 93; cf. also Mah. 211, A. 120.

[334] Cf. A. 102-3, Mah. 197-8. The fact is that the appeal to reproduction is a useless device intended by Kant—and by 'empirical psychologists'—to get round the difficulty of allowing that in the apprehension (in memory or otherwise) of a reality not present to perception, we are really aware of the reality. The difficulty is in reality due to a sensationalistic

perception taken together as an *image* of that 'kind' of which, when taken together, they are an instance. "If I place five points one after another, ... this is an image of the number five."[335] Now, if it be granted that Kant has in mind normally the process of imagining, we can see why he found no difficulty in the thought of knowledge as construction. For while we cannot reasonably speak of making *an object of knowledge*, we can reasonably speak of making *a mental image* through our own activity, and also of making it in accordance with the categories and the empirical laws which presuppose them. Moreover, the ease with which it is possible to take the imagining which accompanies knowing for knowing[336]—the image formed being taken to be the object known and the forming it being taken to be the knowing it—renders it easy to transfer the thought of construction to the knowledge itself. The only defect, however, under which the view labours is the important one that, whatever be the extent to which imagination must accompany knowledge, it is distinct from knowledge. To realize the difference we have only to notice that the process by which we present to ourselves in imagination realities not present to perception presupposes, and is throughout guided by, the knowledge of them. It should be noted, however, that, although the process of which Kant is normally thinking is doubtless that of constructing mental imagery, his real view must be that knowledge consists in constructing a world out of the data of sense, or, more accurately, as his instances show, out of the objects of isolated perceptions, e. g. parts of a line or units to be counted. Otherwise the final act of recognition would be an apprehension not of the world of nature, but of an image of it.

'This criticism,' it may be said, 'is too sweeping. It may be true that the process which Kant describes is really making in the literal sense and not knowing, but Kant's mistake may have been merely that of thinking of the wrong kind of synthesis. For both ordinary language and that of philosophical discussion imply that synthesis plays some part in knowledge. Thus we find in ordinary language the phrases '*putting* 2 and 2 *together*' and '2 and 2 *make* 4'. Even in philosophical discussions we find it said that a complex conception, e. g. gold, is a *synthesis* of simple conceptions, e. g. yellowness, weight, &c.; that in judgement we *relate* or *refer* the predicate to the subject; and that in inference we *construct* reality, though only mentally or ideally. Further, in any case it is by thinking or knowing that the world comes to be *for us*; the more we think, the more of reality there is for us. Hence at least the world *for us* or *our* world is due to our activity of knowing, and so is in some sense made by us, i. e. by our relating activity.'

This position, however, seems in reality to be based on a simple but illegitimate transition, viz. the transition to the assertion that in knowing we relate, or combine, or construct from the assertion that in knowing we recognize as related, or combined, or constructed—the last two terms being retained to preserve the

standpoint, avowed or unavowed, and the device is useless, because the assumption has in the end to be made, covertly or otherwise, that we are really aware of the reality in question.

[335] B. 179, M. 109. Cf. the whole passage B. 176-81, M. 107-10 (part quoted pp. 133-134), and pp. 134-135.

[336] Cf. Locke and Hume.

parallelism.[337] While the latter assertion may be said to be true, although the terms 'combined' and 'constructed' should be rejected as misleading, the former assertion must be admitted to be wholly false, i. e. true in no sense whatever. Moreover, the considerations adduced in favour of the position should, it seems, be met by a flat denial of their truth or, if not, of their relevance. For when it is said that *our* world, or the world *for us*, is due to our activity of thinking, and so is in some sense *made* by us, all that should be meant is that our *apprehending* the world as whatever we apprehend it to be *presupposes* activity on our part. But since the activity is after all only the activity itself of apprehending or knowing, this assertion is only a way of saying that apprehending or knowing is not a condition of mind which can be produced in us *ab extra*, but is something which we have to do for ourselves. Nothing is implied to be made. If anything is to be said to be made, it must be not our world but our activity of apprehending the world; but even we and our activity of apprehending the world are not related as maker and thing made. Again, to speak of a complex conception, e. g. gold, and to say that it involves a synthesis of simple conceptions by the mind is mere 'conceptualism'. If, as we ought to do, we replace the term 'conception' by 'universal', and speak of gold as a synthesis of universals, any suggestion that the mind performs the synthesis will vanish, for a 'synthesis of universals' will mean simply a connexion of universals. All that is mental is our apprehension of their connexion. Again, in judgement we cannot be said to *relate* predicate to subject. Such an assertion would mean either that we relate a conception to a conception, or a conception to a reality[338], or a reality to a reality; and, on any of these interpretations, it is plainly false. To retain the language of 'relation' or of 'combination' at all, we must say that in judgement we recognize real elements as related or combined. Again, when we infer, we do not construct, ideally or otherwise. 'Ideal construction'[339] is a contradiction in terms, unless it refers solely to mental imagining, in which case it is not inference. Construction which is not 'ideal', i. e. literal construction, plainly cannot constitute the nature of inference; for inference would cease to be inference, if by it we made, and did not apprehend, a necessity of connexion. Again, the phrase '2 and 2 *make* 4' does not justify the view that in some sense we 'make' reality. It of course suggests that 2 and 2 are not 4 until they are added, i. e. that the addition makes them 4.[340] But the language is only appropriate when we are literally making a group of 4 by physically placing 2 pairs of bodies in one group. Where we are counting, we should say merely that 2 and 2 *are* 4. Lastly, it must be allowed that the use of the phrase 'putting two and two together', to describe an inference from facts not quite obviously connected, is loose and inexact. If we meet a dog with a blood-stained mouth and shortly afterwards see a dead fowl, we may be said to put two and two together and to conclude thereby that the dog killed the fowl. But, strictly speaking, in drawing the inference we do not put anything together. We certainly do not put

[337] Cf. Caird, i. 394, where Dr. Caird speaks of 'the distinction of the activity of thought from the matter which it *combines or recognizes as combined* in the idea of an object'. (The italics are mine.) The context seems to indicate that the phrase is meant to express the truth, and not merely Kant's view.

[338] Cf. the account of judgement in Mr. Bradley's *Logic*.

[339] Cf. the account of inference in Mr. Bradley's *Logic*.

[340] Cf. Bradley, *Logic*, pp. 370 and 506.

together the facts that the mouth of the dog is blood-stained and that the fowl has just been killed. We do not even put the premises together, i. e. our apprehensions of these facts. What takes place should be described by saying simply that seeing that the fowl is killed, we also remember that the dog's mouth was stained, and then apprehend a connexion between these facts.

The fact seems to be that the thought of synthesis in no way helps to elucidate the nature of knowing, and that the mistake in principle which underlies Kant's view lies in the implicit supposition that it is possible to elucidate the nature of knowledge by means of something other than itself. Knowledge is *sui generis* and therefore a 'theory' of it is impossible. Knowledge is simply knowledge, and any attempt to state it in terms of something else must end in describing something which is not knowledge.[341]

[341] Cf. pp. 66-67.

CHAPTER X

THE SCHEMATISM OF THE CATEGORIES

As has already been pointed out,[342] the *Analytic* is divided into two parts, the *Analytic of Conceptions*, of which the aim is to discover and vindicate the validity of the categories, and the *Analytic of Principles*, of which the aim is to determine the use of the categories in judgement. The latter part, which has now to be considered, is subdivided into two. It has, according to Kant, firstly to determine the sensuous conditions under which the categories are used, and secondly to discover the *a priori* principles involved in the categories, as exercised under these sensuous conditions, such, for instance, as the law that all changes take place according to the law of cause and effect. The first problem is dealt with in the chapter on the 'schematism of the pure conceptions of the understanding', the second in the chapter on the 'system of all principles of the pure understanding'.

We naturally feel a preliminary difficulty with respect to the existence of this second part of the *Analytic* at all. It seems clear that if the first part is successful, the second must be unnecessary. For if Kant is in a position to lay down that the categories must apply to objects, no special conditions of their application need be subsequently determined. If, for instance, it can be laid down that the category of quantity must apply to objects, it is implied either that there are no special conditions of its application, or that they have already been discovered and shown to exist. Again, to assert the applicability of the categories is really to assert the existence of principles, and in fact of just those principles which it is the aim of the *System of Principles* to prove. Thus to assert the applicability of the categories of quantity and of cause and effect is to assert respectively the principles that all objects of perception are extensive quantities, and that all changes take place according to the law of cause and effect. The *Deduction of the Categories* therefore, if successful, must have already proved the principles now to be vindicated; and it is a matter for legitimate surprise that we find Kant in the *System of Principles* giving proofs of these principles which make no appeal to the *Deduction of the Categories*.[343] On the other hand, for the existence of the account of the schematism of the categories Kant has a better show of reason. For the conceptions derived in the *Metaphysical Deduction* from the nature of formal judgement are in themselves too abstract to be the conceptions which are to be shown applicable to the sensible world, since all the latter involve the thought of time. Thus, the conception of

[342] pp. 75-76.

[343] The cause of Kant's procedure is, of course, to be found in the unreal way in which he isolates conception from judgement.

cause and effect derived from the nature of the hypothetical judgement includes no thought of time, while the conception of which he wishes to show the validity is that of necessary succession in time. Hence the conceptions discovered by analysis of formal judgement have in some way to be rendered more concrete in respect of time. The account of the schematism, therefore, is an attempt to get out of the false position reached by appealing to Formal Logic for the list of categories. Nevertheless, the mention of a sensuous condition under which alone the categories can be employed[344] should have suggested to Kant that the transcendental deduction was defective, and, in fact, in the second version of the transcendental deduction two paragraphs[345] are inserted which take account of this sensuous condition.

The beginning of Kant's account of schematism may be summarized thus: 'Whenever we subsume an individual object of a certain kind, e. g. a plate, under a conception, e. g. a circle, the object and the conception must be homogeneous, that is to say, the individual must possess the characteristic which constitutes the conception, or, in other words, must be an instance of it. Pure conceptions, however, and empirical perceptions, i. e. objects of empirical perception, are quite heterogeneous. We do not, for instance, perceive cases of cause and effect. Hence the problem arises, 'How is it possible to subsume objects of empirical perception under pure conceptions?' The possibility of this subsumption presupposes a *tertium quid,* which is homogeneous both with the object of empirical perception and with the conception, and so makes the subsumption mediately possible. This *tertium quid* must be, on the one side, intellectual and, on the other side, sensuous. It is to be found in a 'transcendental determination of time', i. e. a conception involving time and involved in experience. For in the first place this is on the one side intellectual and on the other sensuous, and in the second place it is so far homogeneous with the category which constitutes its unity that it is universal and rests on an *a priori* rule, and so far homogeneous with the phenomenon that all phenomena are in time.[346] Such transcendental determinations of time are the schemata of the pure conceptions of the understanding.' Kant continues as follows:

"The schema is in itself always a mere product of the imagination. But since the synthesis of the imagination has for its aim no single perception, but merely unity in the determination of the sensibility, the schema should be distinguished from the image. Thus, if I place five points one after another, ... this is an image of the number five. On the other hand, if I only just think a number in general—no matter what it may be, five or a hundred—this thinking is rather the representation of a method of representing in an image a group (e. g. a thousand), in conformity with a certain conception, than the image itself, an image which, in the instance given, I should find difficulty in surveying and comparing with the conception. Now this representation of a general procedure of the imagination to supply its

[344] B. 175, M. 106.

[345] B. §§ 24 and 26, M. §§ 20 and 22.

[346] It may be noted that the argument here really fails. For though phenomena as involving temporal relations, might possibly be said to be instances of a transcendental determination of time, the fact that the latter agrees with the corresponding category by being universal and *a priori* does not constitute it homogeneous with the category, in the sense required for subsumption, viz. that it is an instance of or a species of the category.

image to a conception, I call the schema of this conception."

"The fact is that it is not images of objects, but schemata, which lie at the foundation of our pure sensuous conceptions. No image could ever be adequate to our conception of a triangle in general. For it would not attain the generality of the conception which makes it valid for all triangles, whether right-angled, acute-angled, &c., but would always be limited to one part only of this sphere. The schema of the triangle can exist nowhere else than in thought, and signifies a rule of the synthesis of the imagination in regard to pure figures in space. An object of experience or an image of it always falls short of the empirical conception to a far greater degree than does the schema; the empirical conception always relates immediately to the schema of the imagination as a rule for the determination of our perception in conformity with a certain general conception. The conception of 'dog' signifies a rule according to which my imagination can draw the general outline of the figure of a four-footed animal, without being limited to any particular single form which experience presents to me, or indeed to any possible image that I can represent to myself *in concreto*. This schematism of our understanding in regard to phenomena and their mere form is an art hidden in the depths of the human soul, whose true modes of action we are not likely ever to discover from Nature and unveil. Thus much only can we say: the *image* is a product of the empirical faculty of the productive imagination, while the *schema* of sensuous conceptions (such as of figures in space) is a product and, as it were, a monogram of the pure *a priori* imagination, through which, and according to which, images first become possible, though the images must be connected with the conception only by means of the schema which they express, and are in themselves not fully adequate to it. On the other hand, the schema of a pure conception of the understanding is something which cannot be brought to an image; on the contrary, it is only the pure synthesis in accordance with a rule of unity according to conceptions in general, a rule of unity which the category expresses, and it is a transcendental product of the imagination which concerns the determination of the inner sense in general according to conditions of its form (time) with reference to all representations, so far as these are to be connected *a priori* in one conception according to the unity of apperception."[347]

Now, in order to determine whether schemata can constitute the desired link between the pure conceptions or categories and the manifold of sense, it is necessary to follow closely this account of a schema. Kant unquestionably in this passage treats as a mental image related to a conception what really is, and what on his own theory ought to have been, an individual object related to a conception, i. e. an instance of it. In other words, he takes a mental image of an individual for the individual itself.[348] On the one hand, he treats a schema of a conception throughout as the thought of a procedure of the imagination to present to the conception its *image*, and he opposes schemata not to objects but to *images;* on the other hand, his problem concerns subsumption under a conception, and what is subsumed must be an instance of the conception, i. e. an individual object of the kind in ques-

[347] B. 179-81, M. 109-10.

[348] Cf. pp. 128-129. The mistake is, of course, facilitated by the fact that 'objects in nature', being for Kant only 'appearances', resemble mental images more closely than they do as usually conceived.

tion.[349] Again, in asserting that if I place five points one after another, ... this is an image of the number five, he is actually saying that an individual group of five points is an image of a group of five in general.[350] Further, if the process of schematizing is to enter—as it must—into knowledge of the phenomenal world, what Kant here speaks of as the images related to a conception must be taken to be individual instances of the conception, whatever his language may be. For, in order to enter into knowledge, the process referred to must be that by which *objects of experience* are constructed. Hence the passage should be interpreted as if throughout there had been written for 'image' 'individual instance' or more simply 'instance'. Again, the process of schematizing, although *introduced* simply as a process by which an individual is to be subsumed indirectly under a conception, is assumed in the passage quoted to be a process of *synthesis*. Hence we may say that the process of schematizing is a process by which we combine the manifold of perception into an individual whole in accordance with a conception, and that the schema of a conception is the thought of the rule of procedure on our part by which we combine the manifold in accordance with the conception, and so bring the manifold under the conception. Thus the schema of the conception of 100 is the thought of a process of synthesis by which we combine say 10 groups of 10 units into 100, and the schematizing of the conception of 100 is the process by which we do so. Here it is essential to notice three points. In the first place, the schema is a conception which relates not to the reality apprehended but to us. It is the thought of a rule of procedure on our part by which an instance of a conception is constructed, and not the thought of a characteristic of the reality constructed. For instance, the thought of a rule by which we can combine points to make 100 is a thought which concerns us and not the points; it is only the conception corresponding to this schema, viz. the thought of 100, which concerns the points. In the second place, although the thought of time is involved in the schema, the succession in question lies not in the object, but in our act of construction or apprehension. In the third place, the schema presupposes the corresponding conception and the process of schematizing directly brings the manifold of perception under the conception. Thus the thought of combining 10 groups of 10 units to make 100 presupposes the thought of 100, and the process of combination brings the units under the conception of 100.

If, however, we go on to ask what is required of schemata and of the process of schematizing, if they are to enable the manifold to be subsumed under the categories, we see that each of these three characteristics makes it impossible for them to fulfil this purpose. For firstly, an individual manifold A has to be brought under a category B. Since *ex hypothesi* this cannot be effected directly, there is needed a mediating conception C. C, therefore, it would seem, must be at once a species of

[349] Cf. B. 176, M. 107. That individuals are really referred to is also implied in the assertion that 'the synthesis of imagination has for its aim no single *perception,* but merely unity in the determination of sensibility'. (The italics are mine.)

[350] Two sentences treat individual objects and images as if they might be mentioned indifferently. "An object of experience or an image of it always falls short of the empirical conception to a far greater degree than does the schema." "The conception of a 'dog' signifies a rule according to which my imagination can draw the general outline of the figure of a four-footed animal without being limited to any single particular form which experience presents to me, or indeed to any possible image that I can represent to myself *in concreto.*"

B and a conception of which A is an instance. In any case C must be a conception relating to the reality to be known, and not to any process of knowing on our part, and, again, it must be more concrete than B. This is borne out by the list of the schemata of the categories. But, although a schema may be said to be more concrete than the corresponding conception, in that it presupposes the conception, it neither is nor involves a more concrete conception of an *object* and in fact, as has been pointed out, relates not to the reality to be known but to the process on our part by which we construct or apprehend it.[351] In the second place, the time in respect of which the category B has to be made more concrete must relate to the object, and not to the successive process by which we apprehend it, whereas the time involved in a schema concerns the latter and not the former. In the third place, from the point of view of the categories, the process of schematizing should be a process whereby we combine the manifold into a whole A in accordance with the conception C, and thereby render *possible* the subsumption of A under the category B. If it be a process which actually subsumes the manifold under B, it will *actually* perform that, the very impossibility of which has made it necessary to postulate such a process at all. For, according to Kant, it is just the fact that the manifold cannot be subsumed directly under the categories that renders schematism necessary. Yet, on Kant's general account of a schema, the schematizing must actually bring a manifold under the corresponding conception. If we present to ourselves an individual triangle by successively joining three lines according to the conception of a triangle, i. e. so that they enclose a space, we are directly bringing the manifold, i. e. the lines, under the conception of a triangle. Again, if we present to ourselves an instance of a group of 100 by combining 10 groups of 10 units of any kind, we are directly bringing the units under the conception of 100. If this consideration be applied to the schematism of a category, we see that the process said to be necessary because a certain other process is impossible is the very process said to be impossible.

If, therefore, Kant succeeds in finding schemata of the categories in detail in the sense in which they are required for the solution of his problem, i. e. in the sense of more concrete conceptions involving the thought of time and relating to objects, we should expect either that he ignores his general account of a schema, or that if he appeals to it, the appeal is irrelevant. This we find to be the case. His account of the first two transcendental schemata makes a wholly irrelevant appeal to the temporal process of synthesis on our part, while his account of the remaining schemata makes no attempt to appeal to it at all.

"The pure *schema* of *quantity*, as a conception of the understanding, is *number*, a representation which comprises the successive addition of one to one (homogeneous elements). Accordingly, number is nothing else than the unity of the synthesis of the manifold of a homogeneous perception in general, in that I generate time

[351] It may be objected that, from Kant's point of view, the thought of a rule of construction, and the thought of the principle of the whole to be constructed, are the same thing from different points of view. But if this be insisted on, the schema and its corresponding conception become the same thing regarded from different points of view; consequently the schema will not be a more concrete conception of an object than the corresponding conception, but it will be the conception itself.

itself in the apprehension of the perception."[352]

It is clear that this passage, whatever its precise interpretation may be,[353] involves a confusion between the thought of counting and that of number. The thought of number relates to objects of apprehension and does not involve the thought of time. The thought of counting, which presupposes the thought of number, relates to our apprehension of objects and involves the thought of time; it is the thought of a successive process on our part by which we count the number of units contained in what we already know to consist of units.[354] Now we must assume that the schema of quantity is really what Kant says it is, viz. number, or to express it more accurately, the thought of number, and not the thought of counting, with which he wrongly identifies it. For his main problem is to find conceptions which at once are more concrete than the categories and, at the same time, like the categories, relate to objects, and the thought of counting, though more concrete than that of number, does not relate to objects. Three consequences follow. In the first place, although the schema of quantity, i. e. the thought of number, is more concrete than the thought of quantity,[355] it is not, as it should be, more concrete in respect of time; for the thought of number does not include the thought of time. Secondly, the thought of time is only introduced into the schema of quantity irrelevantly by reference to the temporal process of *counting*, by which we come to apprehend the number of a given group of units. Thirdly, the schema of quantity is only in appearance connected with the nature of a schema in general, as Kant describes it, by a false identification of the thought of number with the thought of the process on our part by which we count groups of units, i. e. numbers.

The account of the schema of reality, the second category, runs as follows: "Reality is in the pure conception of the understanding that which corresponds

[352] B. 182, M. 110.

[353] The drift of the passage would seem to be this: 'If we are to present to ourselves an instance of a quantity, we must successively combine similar units until they form a quantity. This process involves the thought of a successive process by which we add units according to the conception of a quantity. This thought is the thought of number, and since by it we present to ourselves an instance of a quantity, it is the schema of quantity.' But if this be its drift, considerations of sense demand that it should be rewritten, at least to the following extent: 'If we are to present to ourselves an instance of a *particular* quantity [which will really be a particular number, for it must be regarded as discrete, (cf. B. 212, M. 128 fin., 129 init.)] e. g. three, we must successively combine units until they form *that* quantity. This process involves the thought of a successive process, by which we add units according to the conception of *that* quantity. This thought is the thought of a particular number, and since by it we present to ourselves an instance of *that* quantity, this thought is the schema of *that* quantity.' If this rewriting be admitted to be necessary, it must be allowed that Kant has confused (*a*) the thoughts of particular quantities and of particular numbers with those of quantity and of number in general respectively, (*b*) the thought of a particular quantity with that of a particular number (for the process referred to presupposes that the particular quantity taken is known to consist of a number of equal units) and (*c*) the thought of counting with that of number.

[354] This statement is, of course, not meant as a definition of counting, but as a means of bringing out the distinction between a process of counting and a number.

[355] For the thought of a number is the thought of a quantity of a special kind, viz. of a quantity made up of a number of similar units without remainder.

to a sensation in general, that therefore of which the conception in itself indicates a being (in time), while negation is that of which the conception indicates a not being (in time). Their opposition, therefore, arises in the distinction between one and the same time as filled or empty. Since time is only the form of perception, consequently of objects as phenomena, that which in objects corresponds to sensation is the transcendental matter of all objects as things in themselves (thinghood, reality).[356] Now every sensation has a degree or magnitude by which it can fill the same time, i. e. the internal sense, in respect of the same representation of an object, more or less, until it vanishes into nothing (= 0 = *negatio*). There is, therefore, a relation and connexion between reality and negation, or rather a transition from the former to the latter, which makes every reality representable as a *quantum*; and the schema of a reality, as the quantity of something so far as it fills time, is just this continuous and uniform generation of the reality in time, as we descend in time from the sensation which has a certain degree, down to the vanishing thereof, or gradually ascend from negation to the magnitude thereof."[357]

This passage, if it be taken in connexion with the account of the anticipations of perception,[358] seems to have the following meaning: 'In thinking of something as a reality, we think of it as that which corresponds to, i. e. produces, a sensation, and therefore as something which, like the sensation, is in time; and just as every sensation, which, as such, occupies time, has a certain degree of intensity, so has the reality which produces it. Now to produce for ourselves an instance of a reality in this sense, we must add units of reality till a reality of the required degree is produced, and the thought of this method on our part of constructing an individual reality is the schema of reality.' But if this represents Kant's meaning, the schema of reality relates only to our process of apprehension, and therefore is not a conception which relates to objects and is more concrete than the corresponding category in respect of time. Moreover, it is matter for surprise that in the case of this category Kant should have thought schematism necessary, for time is actually included in his own statement of the category.

The account of the schemata of the remaining categories need not be considered. It merely *asserts* that certain conceptions relating to objects and involving the thought of time are the schemata corresponding to the remaining categories, without any attempt to connect them with the nature of a schema. Thus, the schema of substance is asserted to be the *permanence* of the real *in time*, that of cause the *succession* of the manifold, in so far as that succession is subjected to a rule, that of interaction the *coexistence* of the determinations or accidents of one substance with those of another according to a universal rule.[359] Again, the schemata of possibility, of actuality and of necessity are said to be respectively the accordance of the synthesis of representations with the conditions of time in general, existence in a determined time, and existence of an object in all time.

The main confusion pervading the chapter is of course that between temporal

[356] It is difficult to see how Kant could meet the criticism that here, contrary to his intention, he is treating physical objects as things in themselves. Cf. pp. 142-143.

[357] B. 182-3, M. 110-11.

[358] B. 207-18, M. 125-32.

[359] The italics are mine.

relations which concern the process of apprehension and temporal relations which concern the realities apprehended. Kant is continually referring to the former as if they were the latter. The cause of this confusion lies in Kant's reduction of physical realities to representations. Since, according to him, these realities are only our representations, all temporal relations are really relations of our representations, and these relations have to be treated at one time as relations of our apprehensions, and at another as relations of the realities apprehended, as the context requires.

CHAPTER XI

THE MATHEMATICAL PRINCIPLES

As has been pointed out,[360] the aim of the second part of the *Analytic of Principles* is to determine the *a priori* principles involved in the use of the categories under the necessary sensuous conditions. These principles Kant divides into four classes, corresponding to the four groups of categories, and he calls them respectively 'axioms of perception', 'anticipations of sense-perception', 'analogies of experience', and 'postulates of empirical thought'. The first two and the last two classes are grouped together as 'mathematical' and 'dynamical' respectively, on the ground that the former group concerns the perception of objects, i. e. their nature apprehended in perception, while the latter group concerns their existence, and that consequently, since assertions concerning the existence of objects presuppose the realization of empirical conditions which assertions concerning their nature do not, only the former possesses an absolute necessity and an immediate evidence such as is found in mathematics.[361] These two groups of principles are not, as their names might suggest, principles within mathematics and physics, but presuppositions of mathematics and physics respectively. Kant also claims appropriateness for the special terms used of each minor group to indicate the kind of principles in question, viz. 'axioms', 'anticipations', 'analogies', 'postulates'. But it may be noted as an indication of the artificiality of the scheme that each of the first two groups contains only one principle, although Kant refers to them in the plural as axioms and anticipations respectively, and although the existence of three categories corresponding to each group would suggest the existence of three principles.

The axiom of perception is that 'All perceptions are extensive quantities'. The proof of it runs thus:

[360] p. 132.

[361] The assertion that all perceptions (i. e. all objects of perception) are extensive quantities relates, according to Kant, to the nature of objects, while the assertion that an event must have a necessary antecedent affirms that such an antecedent must exist, but gives no clue to its specific nature. Compare "But the existence of phenomena cannot be known *a priori*, and although we could be led in this way to infer the fact of some existence, we should not know this existence determinately, i. e. we could not anticipate the respect in which the empirical perception of it differed from that of other existences". (B. 221, M. 134). Kant seems to think that the fact that the dynamical principles relate to the existence of objects is a sufficient justification of their name.

It needs but little reflection to see that the distinctions which Kant draws between the mathematical and the dynamical principles must break down.

"An extensive quantity I call that in which the representation of the parts renders possible the representation of the whole (and therefore necessarily precedes it). I cannot represent to myself any line, however small it may be, without drawing it in thought, that is, without generating from a point all its parts one after another, and thereby first drawing this perception. Precisely the same is the case with every, even the smallest, time. . . . Since the pure perception in all phenomena is either time or space, every phenomenon as a perception is an extensive quantity, because it can be known in apprehension only by a successive synthesis (of part with part). All phenomena, therefore, are already perceived as aggregates (groups of previously given parts), which is not the case with quantities of every kind, but only with those which are represented and apprehended by us as *extensive*."[362]

Kant opposes an extensive quantity to an intensive quantity or a quantity which has a degree. "That quantity which is apprehended only as unity and in which plurality can be represented only by approximation to negation = 0, I call *intensive quantity*."[363] The aspect of this ultimate distinction which underlies Kant's mode of stating it is that only an extensive quantity is a whole, i. e. something made up of parts. Thus a mile can be said to be made up of two half-miles, but a velocity of one foot per second, though comparable with a velocity of half a foot per second, cannot be said to be made up of two such velocities; it is essentially one and indivisible. Hence, from Kant's point of view, it follows that it is only an extensive magnitude which can, and indeed must, be apprehended through a successive synthesis of the parts. The proof of the axiom seems to be simply this: 'All phenomena as objects of perception are subject to the forms of perception, space and time. Space and time are [homogeneous manifolds, and therefore] extensive quantities, only to be apprehended by a successive synthesis of the parts. Hence phenomena, or objects of experience, must also be extensive quantities, to be similarly apprehended.' And Kant goes on to add that it is for this reason that geometry and pure mathematics generally apply to objects of experience.

We need only draw attention to three points. Firstly, no justification is given of the term 'axiom'. Secondly, the argument does not really appeal to the doctrine of the categories, but only to the character of space and time as forms of perception. Thirdly, it need not appeal to space and time as forms of perception in the proper sense of ways in which we apprehend objects, but only in the sense of ways in which objects are related[364]; in other words, it need not appeal to Kant's theory of knowledge. The conclusion follows simply from the nature of objects as spatially and temporally related, whether they are phenomena or not. It may be objected that Kant's thesis is that *all* objects of perception are extensive quantities, and that unless space and time are allowed to be ways in which *we must perceive* objects, we cannot say that all objects will be spatially and temporally related, and so extensive quantities. But to this it may be replied that it is only true that all objects of perception are extensive quantities if the term 'object of perception' be restricted to parts of the physical world, i. e. to just those realities which Kant is thinking of as

[362] B. 203-4, M. 123.
[363] B. 210, M. 127.
[364] Cf. pp. 19-21.

spatially and temporally related,[365] and that this restriction is not justified, since a sensation or a pain which has only intensive quantity is just as much entitled to be called an object of perception.

The anticipation of sense-perception consists in the principle that 'In all phenomena, the real, which is an object of sensation, has intensive magnitude, i. e. a degree'. The proof is stated thus:

"Apprehension merely by means of sensation fills only one moment (that is, if I do not take into consideration the succession of many sensations). Sensation, therefore, as that in the phenomenon the apprehension of which is not a successive synthesis advancing from parts to a complete representation, has no extensive quantity; the lack of sensation in one and the same moment would represent it as empty, consequently = 0. Now that which in the empirical perception corresponds to sensation is reality (*realitas phaenomenon*); that which corresponds to the lack of it is negation = 0. But every sensation is capable of a diminution, so that it can decrease and thus gradually vanish. Therefore, between reality in the phenomenon and negation there exists a continuous connexion of many possible intermediate sensations, the difference of which from each other is always smaller than that between the given sensation and zero, or complete negation. That is to say, the real in the phenomenon has always a quantity, which, however, is not found in apprehension, since apprehension takes place by means of mere sensation in one moment and not by a successive synthesis of many sensations, and therefore does not proceed from parts to the whole. Consequently, it has a quantity, but not an extensive quantity."

"Now that quantity which is apprehended only as unity, and in which plurality can be represented only by approximation to negation = 0, I call an *intensive quantity*. Every reality, therefore, in a phenomenon has intensive quantity, that is, a degree."[366]

In other words, 'We can lay down *a priori* that all sensations have a certain degree of intensity, and that between a sensation of a given intensity and the total absence of sensation there is possible an infinite number of sensations varying in intensity from nothing to that degree of intensity. Therefore the real, which corresponds to sensation, can also be said *a priori* to admit of an infinite variety of degree.'

Though the principle established is of little intrinsic importance, the account of it is noticeable for two reasons. In the first place, although Kant clearly means by the 'real corresponding to sensation' a body in space, and regards it as a phenomenon, it is impossible to see how he can avoid the charge that he in fact treats it as a thing in itself.[367] For the correspondence must consist in the fact that the real causes or excites sensation in us, and therefore the real, i. e. a body in space, is implied to be a thing in itself. In fact, Kant himself speaks of considering the real in the

[365] The context shows that Kant is thinking only of such temporal relations as belong to the physical world, and not of those which belong to us as apprehending it. Cf. p. 74.

[366] B. 209-10, M. 127.

[367] Cf. p. 138 note 356.

phenomenon as the cause of sensation,[368] and, in a passage added in the second edition, after proving that sensation must have an intensive quantity, he says that, corresponding to the intensive quantity of sensation, an intensive quantity, i. e. *a degree of influence on sense,* must be attributed to all objects of sense-perception.[369] The difficulty of consistently maintaining that the real, which corresponds to sensation, is a phenomenon is, of course, due to the impossibility of distinguishing between reality and appearance within phenomena.[370]

In the second place, Kant expressly allows that in this anticipation we succeed in discovering *a priori* a characteristic of sensation, although sensation constitutes that empirical element in phenomena, which on Kant's general view cannot be apprehended *a priori.*

"Nevertheless, this anticipation of sense-perception must always be somewhat surprising to an inquirer who is used to transcendental reflection, and is thereby rendered cautious. It leads us to feel some misgiving as to whether the understanding can anticipate such a synthetic proposition as that respecting the degree of all that is real in phenomena, and consequently respecting the possibility of the internal distinction of sensation itself, if we abstract from its empirical quality. There remains, therefore, a problem not unworthy of solution, viz. 'How can the understanding pronounce synthetically and *a priori* upon phenomena in this respect, and thus anticipate phenomena even in that which is specially and merely empirical, viz. that which concerns sensations?'"[371] But although Kant recognizes that the anticipation is surprising, he is not led to revise his general theory, as being inconsistent with the existence of the anticipation. He indeed makes an attempt[372] to deal with the difficulty; but his solution consists not in showing that the anticipation is consistent with his general theory—as he should have done, if the theory was to be retained—but in showing that, in the case of the degree of sensation, we do apprehend the nature of sensation *a priori.*

Strangely enough, Hume finds himself face to face with what is in principle the same difficulty, and treats it in a not dissimilar way. "There is, however, one contradictory phenomenon, which may prove, that 'tis not absolutely impossible for ideas to go before their correspondent impressions. I believe it will readily be allow'd, that the several distinct ideas of colours, which enter by the eyes, or those of sounds, which are convey'd by the hearing, are really different from each other, tho' at the same time resembling. Now if this be true of different colours, it must be no less so of the different shades of the same colour, that each of them produces a distinct idea, independent of the rest. For if this shou'd be deny'd, 'tis possible, by the continual gradation of shades, to run a colour insensibly into what is most

[368] B. 210, M. 128.

[369] B. 208, M. 126. The italics are mine. Cf. from the same passage, "Phenomena contain, over and above perception, the materials for some object (through which is represented something existing in space and time), i. e. they contain the real of sensation as a merely subjective representation of which we can only become conscious that *the subject is affected,* and which we relate *to an object in general.*" (The italics are mine.)

[370] Cf. pp. 49-52.

[371] B. 217, M. 131; cf. B. 209, M. 127.

[372] B. 217-18, M. 132.

remote from it; and if you will not allow any of the means to be different, you cannot without absurdity deny the extremes to be the same. Suppose therefore a person to have enjoyed his sight for thirty years, and to have become perfectly well acquainted with colours of all kinds, excepting one particular shade of blue, for instance, which it never has been his fortune to meet with. Let all the different shades of that colour, except that single one, be plac'd before him, descending gradually from the deepest to the lightest; 'tis plain that he will perceive a blank, where that shade is wanting, and will be sensible, that there is a greater distance in that place betwixt the contiguous colours, than in any other. Now I ask, whether 'tis possible for him, from his own imagination, to supply this deficiency, and raise up to himself the idea of that particular shade, tho' it had never been conveyed to him by his senses? I believe there are few but will be of opinion that he can; and this may serve as a proof, that the simple ideas are not always derived from the correspondent impressions; tho' the instance is so particular and singular, that 'tis scarce worth our observing, and does not merit that for it alone we should alter our general maxim."[373]

[373] Hume, *Treatise*, Bk. I, Part 1, § 1.

CHAPTER XII

THE ANALOGIES OF EXPERIENCE

EACH of the three categories of relation, i. e. those of substance and accident, of cause and effect, and of interaction between agent and patient involves, according to Kant, a special principle, and these special principles he calls 'analogies of experience'. They are stated thus:[374] (1) In all changes of phenomena the substance is permanent, and its quantity in nature is neither increased nor diminished. (2) All changes take place according to the law of the connexion of cause and effect. (3) All substances, so far as they can be perceived in space as coexistent, are in complete interaction. The justification of the term *analogy* of experience is as follows. In mathematics an analogy is a formula which asserts the equality of two *quantitative* relations, and is such that, if three of the terms are given, we can discover the fourth, e. g. if we know that $a : b = c : d$, and that $a = 2$, $b = 4$, $c = 6$ we can discover that $d = 12$. But in philosophy an analogy is the assertion of the equality of two *qualitative* relations and is such that, if three of the terms are given, we can discover, not the fourth, but only the relation of the third to the fourth, though at the same time we are furnished with a clue whereby to search for the fourth in experience. In this philosophical sense, the principles involved in the categories of relation are analogies. For instance, the principles of causality can be stated in the form 'Any known event X is to *some other* event Y, whatever it be, as effect to cause'; so stated, it clearly informs us not of the character of Y but only of the fact that there must be a Y, i. e. a necessary antecedent, though at the same time this knowledge enables us to search in experience for the special character of Y.

The principles to be established relate to the two kinds of temporal relation apprehended in the world of nature, viz. coexistence and succession. The *method* of proof, which is to be gathered from the proofs themselves rather than from Kant's general remarks[375] on the subject, is the same in each case. Kant expressly rejects any proof which is 'dogmatical' or 'from conceptions', e. g. any attempt to show that the very conception of change presupposes the thought of an identical subject of change.[376] The proof is transcendental in character, i. e. it argues that the principle to be established is a condition of the possibility of *apprehending* the temporal relation in question, e. g. that the existence of a permanent subject of change is presupposed in any *apprehension* of change. It assumes that we become aware of sequences and coexistences in the world of nature by a process which begins with

[374] The formulation of them in the first edition is slightly different.

[375] B. 218-24, M. 132-6; and B. 262-5, M. 159-61.

[376] B. 263-4, M. 160-1; B. 289, M. 174-5.

a succession of mere perceptions, i. e. perceptions which are so far not the perceptions of a sequence or of a coexistence or indeed of anything;[377] and it seeks to show that this process involves an appeal to one of the principles in question—the particular principle involved depending on the temporal relation apprehended—and consequently, that since we do apprehend this temporal relation, which, as belonging to the world of nature, must be distinct from any temporal relation of our perceptions, the principle appealed to is valid.

The proof of the first analogy is given somewhat differently in the first edition, and in a passage added in the second. The earlier version, which is a better expression of the attitude underlying Kant's general remarks on the analogy, is as follows:

"Our *apprehension* of the manifold of a phenomenon is always successive, and is therefore always changing. By it alone, therefore, we can never determine whether this manifold, as an object of experience, is coexistent or successive, unless there lies at the base of it something that exists *always*, that is, something *enduring* and *permanent*, of which all succession and coexistence are nothing but so many ways (*modi* of time) in which the permanent exists. Only in the permanent, then, are time relations possible (for simultaneity and succession are the only relations in time); i. e. the permanent is the *substratum* of the empirical representation of time itself, in which alone all time-determination is possible. Permanence expresses in general time, as the persisting correlate of all existence of phenomena, of all change, and of all concomitance. . . . Only through the permanent does *existence* in different parts of the successive series of time gain a *quantity* which we call *duration*. For, in mere succession, existence is always vanishing and beginning, and never has the least quantity. Without this permanent, then, no time relation is possible. Now, time in itself cannot be perceived[378]; consequently this permanent in phenomena is the substratum of all time-determination, and therefore also the condition of the possibility of all synthetic unity of sense-perceptions, that is, of experience, and in this permanent all existence and all change in time can only be regarded as a mode of the existence of that which endures and is permanent. Therefore in all phenomena the permanent is the object itself, i. e. the substance (*phenomenon*); but all that changes or can change belongs only to the way in which this substance or substances exist, consequently to their determinations."[379] "Accordingly since substance cannot change in existence, its quantity in nature can neither be increased nor diminished."[380] The argument becomes plainer if it be realized that in the

[377] This assumption is of course analogous to the assumption which underlies the *Transcendental Deduction of the Categories*, that knowledge begins with the successive origination in us of isolated data of sense.

[378] *Wahrgenommen.*

[379] A. 182-4 and B. 225-7, M. 137-8. This formulation of the conclusion is adapted only to the form in which the first analogy is stated in the first edition, viz. "All phenomena contain the permanent (*substance*) as the object itself and the changeable as its mere determination, i. e. as a way in which the object exists." Hence a sentence from the conclusion of the proof added in the second edition is quoted to elucidate Kant's meaning; its doctrine is as legitimate a conclusion of the argument given in the first edition as of that peculiar to the second.

[380] B. 225, M. 137.

interval between the two editions, Kant came to think that the permanent in question was matter or bodies in space.[381] "We find that in order to give something *permanent* in perception corresponding to the conception of *substance* (and thereby to exhibit the objective reality of this conception), we need a perception *in space* (of matter), because space alone has permanent determinations, while time, and consequently everything which is in the internal sense, is continually flowing."[382]

Kant's thought appears to be as follows: 'Our apprehension of the manifold consists of a series of successive acts in which we apprehend its elements one by one and in isolation. This apprehension, therefore, does not enable us to determine that its elements are temporally related either as successive or as coexistent.[383] In order to determine this, we must apprehend the elements of the manifold as related to something permanent. For a succession proper, i. e. a change, is a succession of states or determinations of something permanent or unchanging. A mere succession which is not a succession of states of something which remains identical is an unconnected series of endings and beginnings, and with respect to it, 'duration', which has meaning with regard to changes, i. e. successions proper, has no meaning at all. Similarly, coexistence is a coexistence of states of two permanents. Hence, to apprehend elements of the manifold as successive or coexistent, we must apprehend them in relation to a permanent or permanents. Therefore, to apprehend a coexistence or a succession, we must perceive something permanent. But this permanent something cannot be time, for time cannot be perceived. It must therefore be a permanent in phenomena; and this must be the object itself or the substance of a phenomenon, i. e. the substratum of the changes which it undergoes, or that of which the elements of the manifold are states or modifications.[384] Consequently, there must be a permanent substance of a phenomenon, and the quantity of substances taken together must be constant.'

Now, if Kant's thought has been here represented fairly, it is open to the following comments. In the first place, even if his position be right in the main, Kant should not introduce the thought of the *quantity* of substance, and speak of the quantity as constant. For he thereby implies that in a plurality of substances—if such a plurality can in the end be admitted—there may be total extinction of, or partial loss in, some, if only there be a corresponding compensation in others;

[381] Cf. Caird, i. 541-2.

[382] B. 291, M. 176 (in 2nd ed. only). Cf. B. 277 fin.-278 init., M. 168 (in 2nd ed. only).

[383] The account of the first analogy as a whole makes it necessary to think that Kant in the first two sentences of the proof quoted does not mean exactly what he says, what he says being due to a desire to secure conformity with his treatment of the second and third analogies. What he *says* suggests (1) that he is about to discuss the implications, not of the process by which we come to apprehend the manifold as temporally related in one of the two ways possible, i. e. either as successive or as coexistent, but of the process by which we decide whether the relation of the manifold which we already know to be temporal is that of succession or that of coexistence, and (2) that the necessity for this process is due to the fact that our *apprehension* of the manifold is always successive. The context, however, refutes both suggestions, and in any case it is the special function of the processes which involve the second and third analogies to determine the relations of the manifold as that of succession and that of coexistence respectively.

[384] Cf. B. 225, M. 137 (first half).

whereas such extinction and creation would be inconsistent with the nature of a substance.[385] Even Kant himself speaks of having established the impossibility of the origin and extinction of substance.[386]

In the second place, it is impossible to see how it can be legitimate for Kant to speak of a permanent substratum of change at all.[387] For phenomena or appearances neither are nor imply the substratum of which Kant is thinking. They might be held to imply ourselves as the identical substratum of which they are successive states, but this view would be irrelevant to, if not inconsistent with, Kant's doctrine. It is all very well to *say* that the substratum is to be found in matter, i. e. in bodies in space,[388] but the assertion is incompatible with the phenomenal character of the world; for the sensations or appearances produced in us by the thing in itself cannot be successive states of bodies in space. In the third place, in spite of Kant's protests against any proof which is 'dogmatical' or 'from conceptions', such a proof really forms the basis of his thought. For if the argument is to proceed not from the nature of change as such but from the possibility of perceiving change, it must not take into account any implications of the possibility of perceiving change which rest upon implications of the nature of change as such. Yet this is what the argument does. For the reason really given for the view that the apprehension of change involves the apprehension of the manifold as related to a permanent substratum is that a change, as such, implies a permanent substratum. It is only because change is held to imply a substratum that we are said to be able to apprehend a change only in relation to a substratum. Moreover, shortly afterwards, Kant, apparently without realizing what he is doing, actually uses what is, on the very face of it, the dogmatic method, and in accordance with it develops the implications of the perception of change. "Upon this permanence is based the justification of the conception of *change*. Coming into being and perishing are not changes of that which comes to be or perishes. Change is but a mode of existence, which follows on another mode of existence of the same object. Hence everything which changes *endures* and only its *condition changes*. . . . Change, therefore, can be perceived only in substances, and absolute coming to be or perishing, which does not concern merely a determination of the permanent, cannot be a possible perception."[389] Surely the fact that Kant is constrained in spite of himself to use the dogmatic method is some indication that it is the right method. It is in reality impossible to make any discoveries about change, or indeed about anything, except by consideration of the nature of the thing itself; no study of the conditions under which it can be apprehended can throw any light upon its nature.[390] Lastly, although the supposition is not so explicit as the corresponding supposition made in the case of the other analogies, Kant's argument really assumes, and assumes wrongly, the existence of a process by which, starting with the successive appre-

[385] I owe this comment to Professor Cook Wilson.

[386] B. 232-3, M. 141 fin.

[387] The term 'permanent' is retained to conform to Kant's language. Strictly speaking, only a state of that which changes can be said to persist or to be permanent; for the substratum of change is not susceptible of any temporal predicates. Cf. p. 164.

[388] B. 291, M. 176.

[389] B. 230-1, M. 176.

[390] Cf. pp. 161-162.

hension of elements of the manifold in isolation, we come to apprehend them as temporally related.

The deduction of the second and third analogies argues that the principles of causality and reciprocal action are involved respectively in the processes by which we become aware of successions and of coexistences in the world of nature. From this point of view it would seem that the first analogy is a presupposition of the others, and that the process which involves the first is presupposed by the process which involves the others. It would seem that it is only upon the conclusion of a process by which, beginning with the successive apprehension of elements of the manifold in isolation, we come to apprehend them as *either* successive or coexistent elements in the world of nature, that there can arise a process by which we come to decide *whether* the specific relation is that of succession or of coexistence. For if the latter process can take place independently of the former, i. e. if it can start from the successive apprehension of the manifold, the former process will be unnecessary, and in that case the vindication of the first analogy will be invalid. It is necessary, however, to distinguish between Kant's nominal and his actual procedure. Though he nominally regards the first analogy as the presupposition of the others,[391] he really does not. For he does not in fact treat the process which involves the validity of the first analogy as an antecedent condition of the processes which involve the validity of the others. On the contrary, the latter processes begin *ab initio* with the mere successive apprehension of the manifold, i. e. they begin at a stage where we are not aware of any relation in the physical world at all; and Kant, in his account of them, nowhere urges that they involve the first analogy.[392]

Moreover, just because Kant does not face the difficulties involved in the thought of a process which begins in this way until he comes to vindicate causality, it is only when we come to this vindication that we realize the real nature of his deduction of the analogies, and, in particular, of that of the first.

Kant, prompted no doubt by his desire to answer Hume, treats the principle of causality very fully. The length of the discussion, however, is due not so much to the complication of the argument as to Kant's desire to make his meaning unmistakable; his account consists mainly in a repetition of what is substantially the same argument no less than five times. Hence it will suffice to consider those passages which best express Kant's meaning. At the same time, the prominence of the principle of causality in Kant's theory, and in the history of philosophy generally, and also the way in which Kant's treatment of it reveals the true nature of his general position, makes it necessary to consider these passages in some detail.

Hume had denied that we are justified in asserting any causal connexion, i. e. any necessity of succession in the various events which we perceive, but even this denial presupposed that we do apprehend particular sequences in the world of nature, and therefore that we succeed in distinguishing between a sequence of events in nature and a mere sequence of perceptions, such as is also to be found when we apprehend a coexistence of bodies in space. Kant urges, in effect, that this

[391] Cf. B. 229, M. 140; B. 232-3, M. 141-2; and Caird, i. 545 and ff.

[392] This is not disproved by B. 247-51, M. 150-2, which involves a different conception of cause and effect.

denial renders it impossible to explain, as we should be able to do, the possibility of making the distinction in question, which even the denial itself presupposes that we make. Holding, with Hume, that in all cases of perception what we are directly aware of is a succession of perceptions, he contends that it is necessary to explain how in certain cases we succeed in passing from the knowledge of our successive perceptions to the knowledge of a succession in what we perceive. How is it that we know, when, as we say, we see a boat going down stream, that there is a succession in what we perceive, and not merely a succession in our perception of it, as is the case when, as we say, we see the parts of a house? Hume, according to Kant, cannot answer this question; he has only the right to say that in all cases we have a succession of perceptions; for in reality an answer to the question will show that the acquisition of this knowledge involves an appeal to the principle of causality. Since, then, we do in fact, as even Hume implicitly allowed, succeed in distinguishing between a succession in objects in nature and a succession in our apprehension of them, the law of causality must be true. "It is only under this presupposition (i. e. of causality) that even the experience of an event is possible."[393]

Kant begins[394] his proof as follows: "Our apprehension of the manifold of a phenomenon is always successive. The representations of the parts succeed one another. Whether they succeed one another in the object also is a second point for reflection which is not contained in the first."[395] But, before he can continue, the very nature of these opening sentences compels him to consider a general problem which they raise. The distinction referred to between a succession in our apprehensions or representations and a succession in the object implies an object distinct from the apprehensions or representations. What, then, can be meant by such an object? For prima facie, if we ignore the thing in itself as unknowable, there is no object; there are only representations. But, in that case, what can be meant by a succession in the object? Kant is therefore once more[396] forced to consider the question 'What is meant by object of representations?' although on this occasion with special reference to the meaning of a succession in the object; and the vindication of causality is bound up with the answer. The answer is stated thus:

"Now we may certainly give the name of object to everything, and even to every representation, so far as we are conscious thereof; but what this word may mean in the case of phenomena, not in so far as they (as representations) are objects, but in so far as they only indicate an object, is a question requiring deeper consideration. So far as they, as representations only, are at the same time objects of consciousness, they are not to be distinguished from apprehension, i. e. reception into the synthesis of imagination, and we must therefore say, 'The manifold of phenomena is always produced successively in the mind'. If phenomena were things in themselves, no man would be able to infer from the succession of the representations of their manifold how this manifold is connected in the object. For after all we have to do only with our representations; how things may be in themselves, without regard to the representations through which they affect us, is

[393] B. 240, M. 146. For the general view, cf. Caird, i. 556-61.

[394] The preceding paragraph is an addition of the second edition.

[395] B. 234, M. 142.

[396] Cf. A. 104-5, Mah. 198-9, and pp. 96-100 and 123-125.

wholly outside the sphere of our knowledge. Now, although phenomena are not things in themselves, and are nevertheless the only thing which can be given to us as data for knowledge, it is my business to show what kind of connexion in time belongs to the manifold in phenomena themselves, while the representation of this manifold in apprehension is always successive. Thus, for example, the apprehension of the manifold in the phenomenon of a house which stands before me is successive. Now arises the question, whether the manifold of this house itself is in itself also successive, which of course no one will grant. But, so soon as I raise my conceptions of an object to the transcendental meaning thereof, the house is not a thing in itself, but only a phenomenon, i. e. a representation, the transcendental object of which is unknown. What, then, am I to understand by the question, 'How may the manifold be connected in the phenomenon itself (which is nevertheless nothing in itself)?' Here that which lies in the successive apprehension is regarded as representation, while the phenomenon which is given me, although it is nothing more than a complex of these representations, is regarded as the object thereof, with which my conception, drawn from the representations of apprehension, is to agree. It is soon seen that, since agreement of knowledge with the object is truth, we can ask here only for the formal conditions of empirical truth, and that the phenomenon, in opposition to the representations of apprehension, can only be represented as the object of the same, distinct therefrom, if it stands under a rule, which distinguishes it from every other apprehension, and which renders necessary a mode of conjunction of the manifold. That in the phenomenon which contains the condition of this necessary rule of apprehension is the object."[397]

This passage is only intelligible if we realize the *impasse* into which Kant has been led by his doctrine that objects, i. e. realities in the physical world, are only representations or ideas. As has already been pointed out,[398] an apprehension is essentially inseparable from a reality of which it is the apprehension. In other words, an apprehension is always the apprehension of a reality, and a reality apprehended, i. e. an object of apprehension, cannot be stated in terms of the apprehension of it. We never confuse an apprehension and its object; nor do we take the temporal relations which belong to the one for the temporal relations which belong to the other, for these relations involve different terms which are never confused, viz. apprehensions and the objects apprehended. Now Kant, by his doctrine of the unknowability of the thing in itself, has really deprived himself of an object of apprehension or, in his language, of an object of representations. For it is the thing in itself which is, properly speaking, the object of the representations of which he is thinking, i. e. representations of a reality in nature; and yet the thing in itself, being on his view inapprehensible, can never be for him an object in the proper sense, i. e. a reality apprehended. Hence he is only able to state the fact of knowledge in terms of mere apprehensions, or ideas, or representations—the particular name is a matter of indifference—and consequently his efforts to recover an object of apprehension are fruitless. As a matter of fact, these efforts only result in the assertion that the object of representations consists in the representations themselves related in a certain necessary way. But this view is open to two fatal

[397] B. 234-6, M. 143-4. Cf. B. 242, M. 147.

[398] pp. 71-72; cf. pp. 97 and 123-124.

objections. In the first place, a complex of representations is just not an object in the proper sense, i. e. a reality apprehended. It essentially falls on the subject side of the distinction between an apprehension and the reality apprehended. The *complexity* of a complex of representations in no way divests it of the character which it has as a complex of *representations*. In the second place, on this view the same terms have to enter at once into two incompatible relations. Representations have to be related successively as our representations or apprehensions—as in fact they are related—and, at the same time, successively or otherwise, as the case may be, as parts of the object apprehended, viz. a reality in nature. In other words, the same terms have to enter into both a subjective and an objective relation, i. e. both a relation concerning us, the knowing subjects, and a relation concerning the object which we know.[399] "A phenomenon in opposition to the representations of apprehension can only be represented as the object of the same, distinct therefrom, if it stands under a rule which distinguishes it from *every other* apprehension, and renders necessary a mode of conjunction of the manifold."[400] A representation, however, cannot be so related by a rule to another representation, for the rule meant relates to realities in nature, and, however much Kant may try to maintain the contrary, two representations, not being realities in nature, cannot be so related. Kant is in fact only driven to treat rules of nature as relating to representations, because there is nothing else to which he can regard them as relating. The result is that he is unable to justify the very distinction, the implications of which it is his aim to discover, and he is unable to do so for the very reason which would have rendered Hume unable to justify it. Like Hume, he is committed to a philosophical vocabulary which makes it meaningless to speak of relations of objects at all in distinction from relations of apprehensions. It has been said that for Kant the road to objectivity lay through necessity.[401] But whatever Kant may have thought, in point of fact there is no road to objectivity, and, in particular, no road through necessity. No necessity in the relation between two representations can render the relation objective, i. e. a relation between objects. No doubt the successive acts in which we come to apprehend the world are necessarily related; we certainly do not suppose their order to be fortuitous. Nevertheless, their relations are not in consequence a relation of realities apprehended.

Kant only renders his own view plausible by treating an apprehension or representation as if it consisted in a sensation or an appearance. A sensation or an appearance, so far from being the apprehension of anything, is in fact a reality which can be apprehended, of the kind called mental. Hence it can be treated as an object, i. e. something apprehended or presented, though not really as an object in nature. On the other hand, from the point of view of the thing in itself it can be treated as only an apprehension, even though it is an unsuccessful apprehension. Thus, for Kant, there is something which can with some plausibility be treated as an object as well as an apprehension, and therefore as capable of standing in both a subjective and an objective relation to other realities of the same kind.[402]

[399] Cf. p. 112, note 289, and p. 125.

[400] The italics are mine.

[401] Caird, i. 557.

[402] Cf. pp. 73 and 124.

If we now turn to the passage under discussion, we find it easy to vindicate the justice of the criticism that Kant, inconsistently with the distinction which he desires to elucidate, treats the same thing as at once the representation of an object and the object represented. He is trying to give such an account of 'object of representations' as will explain what is meant by a succession in an object in nature, i. e. a phenomenon, in distinction from the succession in our apprehension of it. In order to state this distinction at all, he has to speak of what enters into the two successions as different. "It is my business to show what sort of connexion in time belongs to the *manifold* in phenomena themselves, while the *representation* of this manifold in apprehension is always successive."[403] Here an element of the manifold is distinguished from the representation of it. Yet Kant, though he thus distinguishes them, repeatedly identifies them; in other words, he identifies a representation with that of which it is a representation, viz. an element in or part of the object itself. "*Our apprehension* of the manifold of the phenomenon is always successive. *The representations* of the parts succeed one another. Whether *they* [i. e. *the representations*[404]] succeed one another *in the object* also, is a second point for reflection. . . . So far as they [i. e. phenomena], as representations only, are at the same time objects of consciousness, they are not to be distinguished from apprehension, i. e. reception into the synthesis of imagination, and we must therefore say, *'The manifold of phenomena* is always produced successively in the mind'. If phenomena were things in themselves, no man would be able to infer from the succession of the representations how *this manifold* is connected *in the object*. . . . The phenomenon, in opposition to the representations of apprehension, can only be represented as the object of the same, distinct therefrom, if it stands under a rule, which distinguishes *it* from every *other* representation and which renders necessary a mode of conjunction of the manifold."[405]

Since Kant in introducing his vindication of causality thus identifies elements in the object apprehended (i. e. the manifold of phenomena) with the apprehensions of them, we approach the vindication itself with the expectation that he will identify a causal rule, which consists in a necessity in the succession of objects, viz. of events in nature, with the necessity in the succession of our apprehensions of them. This expectation turns out justified. The following passage adequately expresses the vindication:

"Let us now proceed to our task. That something happens, i. e. that something or some state comes to be which before was not, cannot be empirically perceived, unless a phenomenon precedes, which does not contain in itself this state; for a reality which follows upon an empty time, and therefore a coming into existence preceded by no state of things, can just as little be apprehended as empty time itself. Every apprehension of an event is therefore a perception which follows upon another perception. But because this is the case with all synthesis of apprehension, as I have shown above[406] in the phenomenon of a house, the apprehension of an event is thereby not yet distinguished from other apprehensions. But I notice also,

[403] The italics are mine.

[404] This is implied both by the use of 'also' and by the context.

[405] The italics are mine.

[406] B. 235-6, M. 143 (quoted pp. 150-151).

that if in a phenomenon which contains an event, I call the preceding state of my perception A, and the following state B, B can only follow A in apprehension, while the perception A cannot follow B but can only precede it. For example, I see a ship float down a stream. My perception of its place lower down follows upon my perception of its place higher up the course of the river, and it is impossible that in the apprehension of this phenomenon the vessel should be perceived first below and afterwards higher up the stream. Here, therefore, the order in the sequence of perceptions in apprehension is determined, and apprehension is bound to this order. In the former example of a house, my perceptions in apprehension could begin at the roof and end at the foundation, or begin below and end above; in the same way they could apprehend the manifold of the empirical perception from left to right, or from right to left. Accordingly, in the series of these perceptions, there was no determined order, which necessitated my beginning at a certain point, in order to combine the manifold empirically. But this rule is always to be found in the perception of that which happens, and it makes the order of the successive perceptions (in the apprehension of this phenomenon) *necessary*."

"In the present case, therefore, I shall have to derive the *subjective sequence* of apprehension from the *objective sequence* of phenomena, for otherwise the former is wholly undetermined, and does not distinguish one phenomenon from another. The former alone proves nothing as to the connexion of the manifold in the object, for it is wholly arbitrary. The latter, therefore [i. e. the objective sequence of phenomena[407]], will consist in that order of the manifold of the phenomenon, according to which the apprehension of the one (that which happens) follows that of the other (that which precedes) *according to a rule*. In this way alone can I be justified in saying of the phenomenon itself, and not merely of my apprehension, that a sequence is to be found therein, which is the same as to say that I cannot arrange my apprehension otherwise than in just this sequence."

"In conformity with such a rule, therefore, there must exist in that which in general precedes an event the condition of a rule, according to which this event follows always and necessarily, but I cannot conversely go back from the event, and determine (by apprehension) that which precedes it. For no phenomenon goes back from the succeeding point of time to the preceding point, although it does certainly relate to *some preceding point of time*; on the other hand, the advance from a given time to the determinate succeeding time is necessary. Therefore, because there certainly is something which follows, I must relate it necessarily to something else in general, which precedes, and upon which it follows in conformity with a rule, that is necessarily, so that the event, as the conditioned, affords certain indication of some condition, while this condition determines the event."

"If we suppose that nothing precedes an event, upon which this event must follow in conformity with a rule, all sequence of perception would exist only in apprehension, i. e. would be merely subjective, but it would not thereby be objectively determined which of the perceptions must in fact be the preceding and which the succeeding one. We should in this manner have only a play of represen-

[407] The sense is not affected if 'the latter' be understood to refer to the connexion of the manifold in the object.

tations, which would not be related to any object, i. e. no phenomenon would be distinguished through our perception in respect of time relations from any other, because the succession in apprehension is always of the same kind, and so there is nothing in the phenomenon to determine the succession, so as to render a certain sequence objectively necessary. I could therefore not say that in the phenomenon two states follow each other, but only that one apprehension follows on another, a fact which is merely *subjective* and does not determine any object, and cannot therefore be considered as knowledge of an object (not even in the phenomenon)."

"If therefore we experience that something happens, we always thereby presuppose that something precedes, on which it follows according to a rule. For otherwise, I should not say of the object, that it follows, because the mere sequence in my apprehension, if it is not determined by a rule in relation to something preceding, does not justify the assumption of a sequence in the object. It is therefore always in reference to a rule, according to which phenomena are determined in their sequence (i. e. as they happen) by the preceding state, that I make my subjective synthesis (of apprehension) objective, and it is solely upon this presupposition that even the experience of something which happens is possible."[408]

The meaning of the first paragraph is plain. Kant is saying that when we reflect upon the process by which we come to apprehend the world of nature, we can lay down two propositions. The first is that the process is equally successive whether the object apprehended be a succession in nature or a coexistence of bodies in space, so that the knowledge that we have a succession of apprehensions would not by itself enable us to decide whether the object of the apprehensions is a sequence or not. The second proposition is that, nevertheless, there is this difference between the succession of our apprehensions where we apprehend a succession and where we apprehend a coexistence, that in the former case, and in that only, the succession of our apprehensions is irreversible or, in other words, is the expression of a rule of order which makes it a necessary succession. So far we find no mention of causality, i. e. of a necessity of succession in objects, but only a necessity of succession in our apprehension of them. So far, again, we find no contribution to the problem of explaining how we distinguish between successive perceptions which are the perceptions of an event and those which are not. For it is reasonable to object that it is only possible to say that the order of our perceptions is irreversible, if and because we already know that what we have been perceiving is an event, and that therefore any attempt to argue from the irreversibility of our perceptions to the existence of a sequence in the object must involve a **ὕστερον πρότερον**. And it is clear that, if irreversibility in our perceptions were the only irreversibility to which appeal could be made, even Kant would not have supposed that the apprehension of a succession was reached through belief in an irreversibility.

The next paragraph, of which the interpretation is difficult, appears to introduce a causal rule, i. e. an irreversibility in objects, by identifying it with the irreversibility in our perceptions of which Kant has been speaking. The first step to this identification is taken by the assertion: "In the present case, therefore, I shall

[408] B. 236-41, M. 144-6.

have to derive the subjective sequence of perceptions from the objective sequence of phenomena. . . . The latter will consist in the order of the *manifold of the phenomenon*, according to which *the apprehension* of the one (that which happens) follows that of the other (that which precedes) according to a rule."[409] Here Kant definitely implies that an objective sequence, i. e. an order or sequence of the *manifold* of a phenomenon, consists in a sequence of *perceptions or apprehensions* of which the order is necessary or according to a rule; in other words, that a succession of perceptions in the special case where the succession is necessary is a succession of events perceived.[410] This implication enables us to understand the meaning of the assertion that 'we must therefore derive the subjective sequence of perceptions from the objective sequence of phenomena', and to see its connexion with the preceding paragraph. It means, 'in view of the fact that in all apprehensions of a succession, and in them alone, the sequence of perceptions is irreversible, we are justified in saying that a given sequence of perceptions is the apprehension of a succession, if we know that the sequence is irreversible; in that case we must be apprehending a real succession, for an irreversible sequence of perceptions *is* a sequence of events perceived.' Having thus implied that irreversibility of perceptions constitutes them events perceived, he is naturally enough able to go on to speak of the irreversibility of perceptions as if it were the same thing as an irreversibility of events perceived, and thus to bring in a causal rule. "In this way alone [i. e. only by deriving the subjective from the objective sequence] can I be justified in saying of the phenomenon itself, and not merely of my apprehension, that a sequence is to be found therein, *which is the same as to say* that I cannot *arrange* my apprehension otherwise than in just this sequence. In conformity with *such a rule*, therefore, there must exist in that which in general precedes *an event* the condition of a rule, according to which *this event follows always and necessarily*."[411] Here the use of the word 'arrange'[412] and the statement about the rule in the next sentence imply that Kant has now come to think of the rule of succession as a causal rule relating to the objective succession. Moreover, if any doubt remains as to whether Kant really confuses the two irreversibilities or necessities of succession, it is removed by the last paragraph of the passage quoted. "If therefore we experience that something happens, we always thereby presuppose that something precedes on which *it* follows according to a rule. For otherwise I should not say of the object that *it* follows; because the mere succession of my apprehension, if *it* is not determined by a rule in relation to something preceding, does not justify the assumption of a succession in the object. It is therefore always in reference to a rule, according to which *phenomena* are determined in their sequence (i. e. as they happen) by the preceding state, that I make my subjective sequence (of apprehension) objective."[413] The fact is simply that Kant *must* identify the two irreversibilities, because, as has been pointed out, he has only one set of terms to be related as irreversible, viz. the elements of the manifold, which have to be, from one point of view, elements of an

[409] The italics are mine. 'According to which' does not appear to indicate that the two orders referred to are different.

[410] Cf. B. 242 fin., M. 147 fin.

[411] The italics are mine

[412] *Anstellen.*

[413] The italics are mine.

object and, from another, representations or apprehensions of it.

As soon, therefore, as the real nature of Kant's vindication of causality has been laid bare, it is difficult to describe it as an argument at all. He is anxious to show that in apprehending A B as a real or objective succession we presuppose that they are elements in a causal order of succession. Yet in support of his contention he points only to the quite different fact that where we apprehend a succession A B, we think of the *perception* of A and the *perception* of B as elements in a necessary but subjective succession.

Before we attempt to consider the facts with which Kant is dealing, we must refer to a feature in Kant's account to which no allusion has been made. We should on the whole expect from the passage quoted that, in the case where we regard two perceptions A B as necessarily successive and therefore as constituting an objective succession, the necessity of succession consists in the fact that A is the cause of B. This, however, is apparently not Kant's view; on the contrary, he seems to hold that, in thinking of A B as an objective succession, we presuppose not that A causes B, but only that the state of affairs which precedes B, and which therefore includes A, contains a cause of B, the coexistence or identity of this cause with A rendering the particular succession A B necessary. "Thus [if I perceive that something happens] it arises that there comes to be an order among our representations in which the present (so far as it has taken place) points to some preceding state as a correlate, *though a still undetermined correlate,*[414] of this event which is given, and this correlate relates to the event by determining the event as its consequence, and connects the event with itself necessarily in the series of time."[415]

The fact is that Kant is in a difficulty which he feels obscurely himself. He seems driven to this view for two reasons. If he were to maintain that A was necessarily the cause of B, he would be maintaining that all observed sequences are causal, i. e. that in them the antecedent and consequent are always cause and effect, which is palpably contrary to fact. Again, his aim is to show that we become aware of a succession by presupposing the law of causality. This law, however, is quite general, and only asserts that *something* must precede an event upon which it follows always and necessarily. Hence by itself it palpably gives no means of determining whether this something is A rather than anything else.[416] Therefore if he were to maintain that the antecedent member of an apprehended objective succession must be thought of as its cause, the analogy would obviously provide no means of determining the antecedent member, and therefore the succession itself, for the succession must be the sequence of B upon some definite antecedent. On the other hand, the view that the cause of B need not be A only incurs the

[414] The italics are mine.

[415] B. 244, M. 148. Cf. B. 243, M. 148 (first half) and B. 239, M. 145 (second paragraph). The same implication is to be found in his formulation of the rule involved in the perception of an event, e. g. "In conformity with such a rule, there must exist in that which in general precedes an event, the condition of a rule, according to which this event follows always and necessarily." Here the condition of a rule is the necessary antecedent of the event, whatever it may be.

[416] Cf. B. 165, M. 101, where Kant points out that the determination of particular laws of nature requires experience.

same difficulty in a rather less obvious form. For, even on this view, the argument implies that in order to apprehend two individual perceptions A B as an objective succession, we must know that A *must* precede B, and the presupposition that B implies a cause in the state of affairs preceding B in no way enables us to say either that A coexists with the cause, or that it is identical with it, and therefore that it must precede B.

Nevertheless, it cannot be regarded as certain that Kant did not think of A, the apprehended antecedent of B, as necessarily the cause of B, for his language is both ambiguous and inconsistent. When he considers the apprehension of a succession from the side of the successive perceptions, he at least tends to think of A B as cause and effect;[417] and it may well be that in discussing the problem from the side of the law of causality, he means the cause of B to be A, although the generality of the law compels him to refer to it as *something* upon which B follows according to a rule.

Further, it should be noticed that to allow as Kant, in effect, does elsewhere[418], that experience is needed to determine the cause of B is really to concede that the apprehension of objective successions is *prior to*, and *presupposed by*, any process which appeals to the principle of causality; for if the principle of causality does not by itself enable us to determine the cause of B, it cannot do more than enable us to pick out the cause of B among events known to precede B independently of the principle. Hence, from this point of view, there can be no process such as Kant is trying to describe, and therefore its precise nature is a matter of indifference.

We may now turn to the facts. There is, it seems, no such thing as a process by which, beginning with the knowledge of successive apprehensions or representations, of the object of which we are unaware, we come to be aware of their object. Still less is there a process—and it is really this which Kant is trying to describe—by which, so beginning, we come to apprehend these successive representations as objects, i. e. as parts of the physical world, through the thought of them as necessarily related. We may take Kant's instance of our apprehension of a boat going down stream. We do not first apprehend two perceptions of which the object is undetermined and then decide that their object is a succession rather than a coexistence. Still less do we first apprehend two perceptions or representations and then decide that they are related as successive events in the physical world. From the beginning we apprehend a real sequence, viz. the fact that the boat having left one place is arriving at another; there is no process *to* this apprehension. In other words, from the beginning we are aware of real elements, viz. of events in nature, and we are aware of them as really related, viz. as successive in nature. This must be so. For if we begin with the awareness of two mere perceptions, we could never thence reach the knowledge that their object was a succession, or even the knowledge that they had an object; nor, so beginning, could we become aware of the perceptions themselves as successive events in the physical world. For suppose, *per impossibile*, the existence of a process by which we come to be aware of

[417] He definitely implies this, B. 234, M. 142.

[418] Cf. B. 165, M. 101, where Kant points out that the determination of particular laws of nature requires experience.

two elements A and B as standing in a relation of sequence in the physical world. In the first place, A and B, with the awareness of which we begin, must be, and be known to be, real or objective, and not perceptions or apprehensions; otherwise we could never come to apprehend them as related in the physical world. In the second place, A and B must be, and be known to be, real with the reality of a physical event, otherwise we could never come to apprehend them as related by way of succession in the physical world. If A and B were bodies, as they are when we apprehend the parts of a house, they could never be apprehended as successive. In other words, the process by which, on Kant's view, A and B become, and become known to be, events presupposes that they already are, and are known to be, events. Again, even if it be granted that A and B are real events, it is clear that there can be no process by which we come to apprehend them as successive. For if we apprehended events A and B separately, we could never thence advance to the apprehension of their relation, or, in other words, we could never discover which came first. Kant himself saw clearly that the perception of A followed by the perception of B does not by itself yield the perception that B follows A. In fact it was this insight which formed the starting-point of his discussion.[419] Unfortunately, instead of concluding that the apprehension of a succession is ultimate and underivable from a more primitive apprehension, he tried to formulate the nature of the process by which, starting from such a succession of perceptions, we reach the apprehension of a succession. The truth is simply that there is and can be no *process to* the apprehension of a succession; in other words, that we do and must apprehend a real succession immediately or not at all. The same considerations can of course be supplied *mutatis mutandis* to the apprehension of the coexistence of bodies in space, e. g. of the parts of a house.

It may be objected that this denial of the existence of the process which Kant is trying to describe must at least be an overstatement. For the assertion that the apprehension of a succession or of a coexistence is immediate may seem to imply that the apprehension of the course of a boat or of the shape of a house involves no process at all; yet either apprehension clearly takes time and so must involve a process. But though a process is obviously involved, it is not a process from the apprehension of what is not a succession to the apprehension of a succession, but a process from the apprehension of one succession to that of another. It is the process by which we pass from the apprehension of one part of a succession which may have, and which it is known may have, other parts to the apprehension of what is, and what is known to be, another part of the same succession. Moreover, the assertion that the apprehension of a succession must be immediate does not imply that it may not be reached by a process. It is not inconsistent with the obvious fact that to apprehend that the boat is now turning a corner is really to apprehend that what before was going straight is now changing its course, and therefore presupposes a previous apprehension of the boat's course as straight. It only implies that the apprehension of a succession, if reached by a process at all, is not reached by a process of which the starting-point is not itself the apprehension of a succession.

Nevertheless, a plausible defence of Kant's treatment of causality can be found,

[419] Cf. B. 237, M. 144.

which may be formulated thus: 'Time, just as much as space, is a sphere within which we have to distinguish between appearance and reality. For instance, when moving in a lift, we see, as we say, the walls moving, while the lift remains stationary. When sitting in a train which is beginning to move out of a station, we see, as we say, another train beginning to move, although it is in fact standing still. When looking at distant trees from a fast train, we see, as we say, the buildings in the intermediate space moving backwards. In these cases the events seen are not real, and we only succeed in determining what is really happening, by a process which presupposes the law of causality. Thus, in the last case we only believe that the intermediate buildings do not move, by realizing that, given the uniformity of nature, belief in their motion is incompatible with what we believe on the strength of experience of these buildings on other occasions and of the rest of the world. These cases prove the existence of a process which enables us, and is required to enable us, to decide whether a given change is objective or subjective, i. e. whether it lies in the reality apprehended or in our apprehension of it; and this process involves an appeal to causality. Kant's mistake lay in his choice of illustrations. His illustrations implied that the process which involves causality is one by which we distinguish a succession in the object apprehended from another relation in the object, viz. a coexistence of bodies. But he ought to have taken illustrations which implied that the process is one by which we distinguish a succession in the object from a succession in our perception of it. In other words, the illustrations should, like those just given, have illustrated the process by which we distinguish an objective from a subjective change, and not a process by which we distinguish an objective change from something else also objective. Consequently, Kant's conclusion and his *general* method of treatment are right, even if, misled by his instances, he supports his position by arguments which are wrong.'

This defence is, however, open to the following reply: 'At first sight the cases taken undoubtedly seem to illustrate a process in which we seek to discover whether a certain change belongs to objects or only to our apprehension of them, and in which we appeal to causality in arriving at a decision. But this is only because we ignore the relativity of motion. To take the third case: our first statement of the facts is that we saw the intermediate buildings moving, but that subsequent reflection on the results of other experience forced us to conclude that the change perceived was after all only in our apprehension and not in the things apprehended. The statement, however, that we saw the buildings moving really assumes that we, the observers, were stationary; and it states too much. What we really perceived was a relative changing of position between us, the near buildings, and the distant trees. This is a fact, and the apprehension of it, therefore, does not afterwards prove mistaken. It is equally compatible with motion on the part of the trees, or of the buildings, or of the observers, or of a combination of them; and that for which an appeal to causality is needed is the problem of deciding which of these alternatives is correct. Moreover, the perceived relative change of position is objective; it concerns the things apprehended. Hence, in this case too, it can be said that we perceive an objective succession from the beginning, and that the appeal to causality is only needed to determine something further about it. It is useless to urge that to be aware of an event is to be aware of it in all its definiteness, and that this awareness admittedly involves an appeal to causality; for it is easy to see that unless our awareness of the relative motion formed the starting-point of any subsequent process in which we appealed to the law of causality, we could never use the law to determine which body really moved.'

Two remarks may be made in conclusion. In the first place, the basis of Kant's account, viz. the view that in our apprehension of the world we advance from the apprehension of a succession of perceptions to the apprehension of objects perceived, involves a ὕστερον πρότερον. As Kant himself in effect urges in the *Refutation of Idealism,*[420] self-consciousness, in the sense of the consciousness of the successive process in which we apprehend the world, is plainly only attained by reflecting upon our apprehension of the world. We first apprehend the world and only by subsequent reflection become aware of our activity in apprehending it. Even if consciousness of the world must lead to, and so is in a sense inseparable from, self-consciousness, it is none the less its presupposition.

In the second place, it seems that the true vindication of causality, like that of the first analogy, lies in the dogmatic method which Kant rejects. It consists in insight into the fact that it is of the very nature of a physical event to be an element in a process of change undergone by a system of substances in space, this process being through and through necessary in the sense that any event (i. e. the attainment of any state by a substance) is the outcome of certain preceding events (i. e. the previous attainment of certain states by it and other substances), and is similarly the condition of certain subsequent events.[421] To attain this insight, we have only to reflect upon what we really mean by a 'physical event'. The vindication can also be expressed in the form that the very *thought* of a physical event presupposes the *thought* of it as an element in a necessary process of change—provided, however, that no distinction is implied between the nature of a thing and what we think its nature to be. But to vindicate causality in this way is to pursue the dogmatic method; it is to argue from the nature, or, to use Kant's phrase, from the conception, of a physical event. On the other hand, it seems that the method of arguing transcendentally, or from the possibility of perceiving events, must be doomed to failure in principle. For if, as has been argued to be the case,[422] apprehension is essentially the apprehension of a reality as it exists independently of the apprehension of it, only those characteristics can be attributed to it, as characteristics which it must have if it is to be apprehended, which belong to it in its own nature or in virtue of its being what it is. It can only be because we think that a thing has some characteristic in virtue of its own nature, and so think 'dogmatically', that we can think that in apprehending it we must apprehend it as having that characteristic.[423]

There remains to be considered Kant's proof of the third analogy, i. e. the principle that all substances, so far as they can be perceived in space as coexistent, are in thorough-going interaction. The account is extremely confused, and it is difficult to extract from it a consistent view. We shall consider here the version added

[420] Cf. pp. 172-173.
[421] This statement of course includes the third analogy.
[422] Cf. Chh. IV and VI.
[423] Cf. pp. 148-149.

in the second edition, as being the fuller and the less unintelligible.

"Things are *coexistent*, when in empirical intuition[424] the perception[425] of the one can follow upon the perception of the other, and vice versa (which cannot occur in the temporal succession of phenomena, as we have shown in the second principle). Thus I can direct my perception first to the moon and afterwards to the earth, or conversely, first to the earth and then to the moon, and because the perceptions of these objects can reciprocally follow each other, I say that they coexist. Now coexistence is the existence of the manifold in the same time. But we cannot perceive time itself, so as to conclude from the fact that things are placed in the same time that the perceptions of them can follow each other reciprocally. The synthesis of the imagination in apprehension, therefore, would only give us each of these perceptions as existing in the subject when the other is absent and vice versa; but it would not give us that the objects are coexistent, i. e. that, if the one exists, the other also exists in the same time, and that this is necessary in order that the perceptions can follow each other reciprocally. Hence there is needed a conception-of-the-understanding[426] of the reciprocal sequence of the determinations of these things coexisting externally to one another, in order to say that the reciprocal succession of perceptions is grounded in the object, and thereby to represent the coexistence as objective. But the relation of substances in which the one contains determinations the ground of which is contained in the other is the relation of influence, and if, reciprocally, the former contains the ground of the determinations in the latter, it is the relation of community or interaction. Consequently, the coexistence of substances in space cannot be known in experience otherwise than under the presupposition of their interaction; this is therefore also the condition of the possibility of things themselves as objects of experience."[427]

The proof begins, as we should expect, in a way parallel to that of causality. Just as Kant had apparently argued that we learn that a succession of perceptions is the perception of a sequence when we find the order of the perceptions to be irreversible, so he now definitely asserts that we learn that certain perceptions are the perceptions of a coexistence of bodies in space when we find that the order of the perceptions is reversible, or, to use Kant's language, that there can be a reciprocal sequence of the perceptions. This beginning, if read by itself, seems as though it should also be the end. There seems nothing more which need be said. Just as we should have expected Kant to have completed his account of the apprehension of a succession when he pointed out that it is distinguished by the irreversibility of the perceptions, so here we should expect him to have said enough when he points out that the earth and the moon are said to be coexistent because our perceptions of them can follow one another reciprocally.

The analogy, however, has in some way to be brought in, and to this the rest of the proof is devoted. In order to consider how this is done, we must first consider the nature of the analogy itself. Kant speaks of 'a conception-of-the-understanding

[424] *Anschauung.*

[425] *Wahrnehmung.*

[426] *Verstandesbegriff.*

[427] B. 257-8, M. 156-7.

of the reciprocal sequence of the determinations of things which coexist externally to one another'; and he says that 'that relation of substances in which the one contains determinations, the ground of which is contained in the other substance, is the relation of influence'. His meaning can be illustrated thus. Suppose two bodies, A, a lump of ice, and B, a fire, close together, yet at such a distance that they can be observed in succession. Suppose that A passes through changes of temperature a_1 a_2 a_3 . . . in certain times, the changes ending in states α_1 α_2 α_3 . . ., and that B passes through changes of temperature b_1 b_2 b_3 . . . in the same times, the changes ending in states β_1 β_2 β_3. Suppose also, as we must, that A and B interact, i. e. that A in passing through its changes conditions the changes through which B passes, and therefore also the states in which B ends, and vice versa, so that a_2 and α_2 will be the outcome not of a_1 and α_1 alone, but of a_1 and α_1, and b_1 and β_1 jointly. Then we can say (1) that A and B are in the relation of influence, and also of interaction or reciprocal influence, in the sense that they *mutually* (not alternately) determine one another's states. Again, if we first perceive A in the state α_1 by a perception A_1, then B in the state β_2 by a perception B_2, then A in the state α_3 by a perception A_3 and so on, we can speak (2) of a reciprocal sequence of perceptions, in the sense of a sequence of perceptions in which alternately a perception of B follows a perception of A and a perception of A follows a perception of B; for first a perception of B, viz. B_2, follows a perception of A, viz. A_1, and then a perception of A, viz. A_3, follows a perception of B, viz. B_2. We can also speak (3) of a reciprocal sequence of the determinations of two things in the sense of a necessary succession of states which *alternately* are states of A and of B; for α_1, which is perceived first, can be said to contribute to determine β_2, which is perceived next, and β_2 can be said to contribute to determine α_3, which is perceived next, and so on; and this reciprocal sequence can be said to be involved in the very nature of interaction. Further, it can be said (4) that if we perceive A and B alternately, and so only in the states α_1 α_3 . . . β_2 β_4 . . . respectively, we can only fill in the blanks, i. e. discover the states α_2 α_4 . . . β_1 β_3 . . . *coexistent* with β_2 β_4 . . . and α_1 α_3 . . . respectively, if we presuppose the thought of interaction. For it is only possible to use the observed states as a clue to the unobserved states, if we presuppose that the observed states are members of a necessary succession of which the unobserved states are also members and therefore have partially determined and been determined by the observed states. Hence it may be said that the determination of the unobserved states coexistent with the observed states presupposes the thought of interaction.

How then does Kant advance from the assertion that the apprehension of a coexistence requires the knowledge that our *perceptions* can be reciprocally sequent to the assertion that it presupposes the thought that the *determinations of phenomena* are reciprocally sequent? The passage in which the transition is effected is obscure and confused, but it is capable of interpretation as soon as we see that it is intended to run parallel to the proof of the second analogy which is added in the second edition.[428] Kant apparently puts to himself the question, 'How are we to know when we have a reciprocal sequence of perceptions from which we can infer a coexistence in what we perceived?' and apparently answers it thus: 'Since we cannot perceive time, and therefore cannot perceive objects as dated in time with

[428] B. 233-4, M. 142.

respect to one another, we cannot begin with the apprehension of the coexistence of two objects, and thence infer the possibility of reciprocal sequence in our perceptions. This being so, the synthesis of imagination in apprehension can indeed combine these perceptions [these now being really considered as determinations or states of an object perceived] in a reciprocal sequence, but there is so far no guarantee that the sequence produced by the synthesis is not an arbitrary product of the imagination, and therefore we cannot think of it as a reciprocal sequence in objects. In order to think of such a reciprocal sequence as not arbitrary but as constituting a real sequence in objects [= 'as grounded in the object'], we must think of the states reciprocally sequent [as necessarily related and therefore] as successive states of two coexisting substances which interact or mutually determine one another's successive states. Only then shall we be able to think of the coexistence of objects involved in the reciprocal sequence as an objective fact, and not merely as an arbitrary product of the imagination.' But, if this fairly expresses Kant's meaning, his argument is clearly vitiated by two confusions. In the first place, it confuses a subjective sequence of perceptions which are alternately perceptions of A and of B, two bodies in space, with an objective sequence of perceived states of bodies, α_1 β_2 α_3 β_4, which are alternately states of two bodies A and B, the same thing being regarded at once as a perception and as a state of a physical object. In the second place, mainly in consequence of the first confusion, it confuses the necessity that the perceptions of A and of B can follow one another alternately with the necessity of succession in the alternately perceived states of A and B as interacting. Moreover, there is really a change in the cases under consideration. The case with which he begins, i. e. when he is considering merely the reciprocal sequence of perceptions, is the successive perceptions of two *bodies in space* alternately, e. g. of the moon and the earth, the nature of their states at the time of perception not being in question. But the case with which he ends is the successive perception of the *states of two bodies* alternately, e. g. of the states of the fire and of the lump of ice. Moreover, it is only in the latter case that the objective relation apprehended is that of coexistence in the proper sense, and in the sense which Kant intends throughout, viz. that of being contemporaneous in distinction from being successive. For when we say that two bodies, e. g. the moon and the earth, coexist, we should only mean that both exist, and not, as Kant means, that they are contemporaneous. For to a substance, being as it is the substratum of changes, we can ascribe no temporal predicates. That which changes cannot be said either to begin, or to end, or to exist at a certain moment of time, or, therefore, to exist contemporaneously with, or after, or before anything else; it cannot even be said to persist through a portion of time or, to use the phrase of the first analogy, to be permanent. It will be objected that, though the cases are different, yet the transition from the one to the other is justified, for it is precisely Kant's point that the existence together of two substances in space can only be discovered by consideration of their successive states under the presupposition that they mutually determine one another's states. "Besides the mere fact of existence there must be something by which A determines the place in time for B, and conversely B the place for A, because only under this condition can these substances be empirically represented as coexistent."[429]

[429] B. 259, M. 157.

The objection, however, should be met by two considerations, each of which is of some intrinsic importance. In the first place, the apprehension of a body in space in itself involves the apprehension that it exists together with all other bodies in space, for the apprehension of something as spatial involves the apprehension of it as spatially related to, and therefore as existing together with, everything else which is spatial. No process, therefore, such as Kant describes is required in order that we may learn that it exists along with some other body. In the second place, that for which the principle of interaction is really required is not, as Kant supposes, the determination of the coexistence of an unperceived body with a perceived body, but the determination of that unperceived state of a body already known to exist which is coexistent with a perceived state of a perceived body. As has been pointed out, if we perceive A and B alternately in the states $\alpha_1\ \beta_2\ \alpha_3\ \beta_4 \ldots$ we need the thought of interaction to determine the nature of $\beta_1\ \alpha_2\ \beta_3\ \alpha_4 \ldots$ Thus it appears that Kant in his vindication of the third analogy omits altogether to notice the one process which really presupposes it.

CHAPTER XIII

THE POSTULATES OF EMPIRICAL THOUGHT

THE postulates of empirical thought, which correspond to the categories of modality, are stated as follows:

> "1. That which agrees with the formal conditions of experience (according to perception and conceptions) is *possible*.
>
> 2. That which is connected with the material conditions of experience (sensation) is *actual*.
>
> 3. That of which the connexion with the actual is determined according to universal conditions of experience is *necessary* (exists necessarily)."[430]

These principles, described as only 'explanations of the conceptions of possibility, actuality, and necessity as employed in experience', are really treated as principles by which we decide what is possible, what is actual, and what is necessary. The three conceptions involved do not, according to Kant, enlarge our knowledge of the nature of objects, but only 'express their relation to the faculty of knowledge'[431]; i. e. they only concern our ability to apprehend an object whose nature is already determined for us otherwise as at least possible, or as real, or as even necessary. Moreover, it is because these principles do not enlarge our knowledge of the nature of objects that they are called postulates; for a postulate in geometry, from which science the term is borrowed (e. g. that it is possible with a given line to describe a circle from a given point), does not augment the conception of the figure to which it relates, but only asserts the possibility of the conception itself.[432] The discussion of these principles is described, contrary to the terminology adopted in the case of the preceding principles, as 'explanation' and not as 'proof'. The discussion, however, certainly includes a proof of them, for it is Kant's main object to *prove* that these principles constitute the general character of what can be asserted to be possible, actual, or necessary respectively. Again, as before, the basis of proof lies in a theory of knowledge, and in particular in Kant's theory of knowledge; for it consists in the principle that everything knowable must conform to the conditions involved in its being an object of possible experience.

To understand these principles and the proof of them, we must notice certain preliminary considerations. In the *first* place, the very problem of distinguishing

[430] B. 265-6, M. 161.
[431] B. 266, M. 161. Cf. B. 286-7, M. 173-4.
[432] B. 286-7, M. 173-4.

the possible, the actual, and the necessary presupposes the existence of distinctions which may prove open to question. It presupposes that something may be possible without being actual, and again that something may be actual without being necessary. In the *second* place, Kant's mode of approaching the problem assumes that we can begin with a conception of an object, e. g. of a man with six toes, and then ask whether the object of it is possible, whether, if possible, it is also actual, and whether, if actual, it is also necessary. In other words, it assumes the possibility of separating what is conceived from what is possible, and therefore *a fortiori* from what is actual,[433] and from what is necessary. *Thirdly*, in this context, as in most others, Kant in speaking of a conception is thinking, to use Locke's phraseology, not of a 'simple' conception, such as that of equality or of redness, but of a 'complex' conception, such as that of a centaur, or of a triangle in the sense of a three-sided three-angled figure. It is the apprehension of a 'complex' of elements.[434] *Fourthly*, what is said to be possible, real, or necessary is not the conception but the corresponding object. The question is not, for instance, whether the conception of a triangle or of a centaur is possible, actual, or necessary, but whether a triangle or a centaur is possible, actual, or necessary. Kant sometimes speaks loosely of conceptions as possible,[435] but the terms which he normally and, from the point of view of his theory, rightly applies to conceptions are 'objectively real' and 'fictitious'.[436] *Lastly*, Kant distinguishes 'objectively real' and 'fictitious' conceptions in two ways. He speaks of establishing the objective reality of a conception as consisting in establishing the possibility of a corresponding object,[437] implying therefore that a fictitious conception is a conception of which the corresponding object is not known to be possible. Again, he describes as fictitious new conceptions of substances, powers, and interactions, which we might form from the material offered to us by perception without borrowing from experience itself the example of their connexions, e. g. the conception of a power of the mind to perceive the future; and he says that the possibility of these conceptions (i. e. the possibility of corresponding objects) cannot, like that of the categories, be acquired *a priori* through their being conditions on which all experience depends, but must be discovered empirically or not at all. Of such conceptions he says that, without being based upon experience and its known laws, they are arbitrary syntheses which, although they contain no contradiction, have no claim to objective reality, and therefore to the possibility of corresponding objects.[438] He implies, therefore, that the object of a conception can be said to be possible only when the conception is the apprehension of a complex of elements together with the apprehension—which, if not *a priori*, must be based upon experience—that they are connected.

[433] The view that 'in the mere conception of a thing no sign of its existence is to be found' (B. 272, M. 165) forms, of course, the basis of Kant's criticism of the ontological argument for the existence of God. Cf. *Dialectic*, Bk. II, Ch. III, § 4.

[434] Cf. 'a conception which includes in itself a synthesis' (B. 267 med., M. 162 med.).

[435] E. g. B. 269 fin., M. 163 fin.; B. 270 med., M. 164 init. The formulation which really expresses Kant's thought is to be found B. 266 med., M. 161 fin.; B. 268 init., M. 162 fin.; B. 268 med., M. 163 init.; and B. 270 med., M. 164 init.

[436] *Gedichtete*.

[437] B. 268 init., M. 162 fin.

[438] B. 269-70, M. 163-4.

Hence a conception may be regarded as 'objectively real', or as 'fictitious' according as it is the apprehension of a complex of elements accompanied by the apprehension that they are connected, or the apprehension of a complex of elements not so accompanied.

It is now possible to state Kant's problem more precisely. With regard to a given complex conception he wishes to determine the way in which we can answer the questions (1) 'Has the conception a possible object to correspond to it', or, in other words, 'Is the conception 'objectively real' or 'fictitious'?' (2) 'Given that a corresponding object is possible, is it also real?' (3) 'Given that it is real, is it also necessary?'

The substance of Kant's answer to this problem may be stated thus: 'The most obvious guarantee of the objective reality of a conception, i. e. of the possibility of a corresponding object, is the experience of such an object. For instance, our experience of water guarantees the objective reality of the conception of a liquid which expands as it solidifies. This appeal to experience, however, takes us beyond the possibility of the object to its reality, for the experience vindicates the possibility of the object only through its reality. Moreover, here the basis of our assertion of possibility is only empirical, whereas our aim is to discover the conceptions of which the objects can be determined *a priori* to be possible. What then is the answer to this, the real problem? To take the case of cause and effect, we cannot reach any conclusion by the mere study of the conception of cause and effect. For although the conception of a necessary succession contains no contradiction, the necessary succession of events is a mere arbitrary synthesis as far as our thought of it is concerned; we have no direct insight into the necessity. Therefore we cannot argue from this conception to the possibility of a corresponding object, viz. a necessarily successive series of events in nature. We can, however, say that that synthesis is not arbitrary but necessary to which any object must conform, if it is to be an object of experience. From this point of view we can say that there must be a possible object corresponding to the conception of cause and effect, because only as subjected to this synthesis are there objects of experience at all. Hence, if we take this point of view, we can say generally that all spatial and temporal conceptions, as constituting the conditions of perceiving in experience, and all the categories, as constituting the conditions of conceiving in experience, must have possible objects. In other words, 'that which agrees with the formal conditions of experience (according to perception and conceptions) is *possible*'. Again, if we know that the object of a conception is possible, how are we to determine whether it is also actual? It is clear that, since we cannot advance from the mere conception, objectively real though it may be, to the reality of the corresponding object, we need perception. The case, however, where the corresponding object is directly perceived may be ignored, for it involves no inference or process of thought; the appeal is to experience alone. Therefore the question to be considered is, 'How do we determine the actuality of the object of a conception comparatively *a priori*, i. e. without direct experience of it[439]?' The answer must be that we do so by finding it to be 'connected with an actual perception in accordance with the analogies of

[439] Cf. B. 279, M. 169 and p. 2, note 4.

experience'[440]. For instance, we must establish the actuality of an object corresponding to the conception of a volcanic eruption by showing it to be involved, in accordance with the analogies (and with particular empirical laws), in the state of a place which we are now perceiving. In other words, we can say that 'that which is connected with the material conditions of existence (sensation) is *actual*'. Finally, since we cannot learn the existence of any object of experience wholly *a priori*, but only relatively to another existence already given, the necessity of the existence of an object can never be known from conceptions, but only from its connexion with what is perceived; this necessity, however, is not the necessity of the existence of a substance, but only the necessity of connexion of an unobserved state of a substance with some observed state of a substance. Therefore we can (and indeed must) say of an unobserved object corresponding to a conception, not only that it is real, but also that it is necessary, when we know it to be connected with a perceived reality 'according to universal conditions of experience'; but the necessity can be attributed only to states of substances and not to substances themselves.'

Throughout this account there runs one fatal mistake, that of supposing that we can separate our knowledge of things as possible, as actual, and as necessary. Even if this supposition be tenable in certain cases,[441] it is not tenable in respect of the objects of a complex conception, with which Kant is dealing. If we know the object of a complex conception to be possible, we already know it to be actual, and if we know it to be actual, we already know it to be necessary. A complex conception in the proper sense is the apprehension of a complex of elements together with the apprehension of, or insight into, their connexion.[442] Thus, in the case of the conception of a triangle we see that the possession of three sides necessitates the possession of three angles. From such a conception must be distinguished Kant's 'fictitious' conception, i. e. the apprehension of a complex of elements without the apprehension of connexion between them. Thus, in the case of the conception of a man with six toes, there is no apprehension of connexion between the possession of the characteristics indicated by the term 'man' and the possession of six toes. In such a case, since we do not apprehend any connexion between the elements, we do not really 'conceive' or 'think' the object in question, e. g. a man with six toes. Now in the case of a complex conception proper, it is impossible to think of a corresponding individual as only possible. The question 'Is a triangle, in the sense of a figure with three sides and three angles, possible?' really means 'Is it possible for a three-sided figure to have three angles?' To this question we can only answer that we see that a three-sided figure can have three angles, because we see that it must have, and therefore has, and can have, three angles; in other words, that we see a triangle in the sense in question to be possible, because we see it to be necessary, and, therefore, actual, and possible. It cannot be argued that our insight is limited to the fact that if there are three-sided figures they must be three-angled, and that therefore we only know a triangle in the sense in question to be possible. Our apprehension of the fact that the possession of three sides necessitates the possession

[440] B. 273, M. 165.

[441] For instance, it might at least be *argued* that we know space to be actual without knowing it to be necessary.

[442] *Not* 'together with the apprehension *that* the elements are connected'. Cf. p. 168.

of three angles presupposes knowledge of the existence of three-sided figures, for it is only in an actual three-sided figure that we can apprehend the necessity. It may, however, be objected that the question ought to mean simply 'Is a three-sided figure possible?' and that, understood in this sense, it cannot be answered in a similar way. Nevertheless, a similar answer is the right answer. For the question 'Is a three-sided figure possible?' really means 'Is it possible for three straight lines to form a figure, i. e. to enclose a space?' and we can only answer it for ourselves by seeing that a group of three straight lines or directions, no two of which are parallel, must, as such, enclose a space, this insight presupposing the apprehension of an actual group of three straight lines. It may be said, therefore, that we can only determine the possibility of the object of a complex conception in the proper sense, through an act in which we apprehend its necessity and its actuality at once. It is only where conceptions are 'fictitious', and so not properly conceptions, that appeal to experience is necessary. The question 'Is an object corresponding to the conception of a man with six toes possible?' presupposes the reality of man and asks whether any man can have six toes. If we understood the nature of man and could thereby apprehend either that the possession of six toes was, or that it was not, involved in one of the possible differentiations of man, we could decide the question of possibility *a priori*, i. e. through our conceiving alone without an appeal to experience; but we could do so only because we apprehended either that a certain kind of man with six toes was necessary and actual, or that such a man was impossible and not actual. If, however, as is the case, we do not understand the nature of man, we can only decide the question of possibility by an appeal to experience, i. e. to the experience of a corresponding object, or of an object from which the existence of such an object could be inferred. Here, therefore—assuming the required experience to be forthcoming—we can appeal to Kant's formula and say that we know that such a man, i. e. an object corresponding to the conception, is actual, as being connected with the material conditions of experience. But the perception which constitutes the material conditions of experience in the case in question is only of use because it carries us beyond possibility to actuality, and appeal to it is only necessary because the object is not really conceived or, in other words, because the so-called conception is not really a conception.

Kant really treats his 'objectively real' conceptions as if they were 'fictitious', even though he speaks of them as complete. Consequently, his conceptions not being conceptions proper, he is necessarily led to hold that an appeal to experience is needed in order to establish the reality of a corresponding object. Yet, this being so, he should have asked himself whether, without an appeal to perception, we could even say that a corresponding object was possible. That he did not ask this question is partly due to the fact that he attributes the form and the matter of knowledge to different sources, viz. to the mind and to things in themselves. While the conceptions involved in the forms of perception, space, and time, and also the categories are the manifestations of the mind's own nature, sensations, which form the matter of knowledge, are due to the action of things in themselves on our sensibility, and of this activity we can say nothing. Hence, from the point of view of our mind—and since we do not know things in themselves, this is the only point of view we can take—the existence of sensations, and therefore of objects, which must be given in perception, is wholly contingent and only to be discovered through experience. On the other hand, since the forms of perception and conception necessarily determine in certain ways the nature of objects, *if* there prove to be any objects, the conceptions involved may be thought to determine what objects are possible, even though the very existence of the objects is uncertain. Nevertheless, on his own principles, Kant should have allowed that, apart from perception, we could discover *a priori* at least the reality, even if not the necessity, of the objects of these conceptions. For his general view is that the forms of perception and the categories are only actualized on the occasion of the stimulus afforded by the action of things in themselves on the sensibility. Hence the fact that the categories and forms of perception are actualized—a fact implied in the very existence of the *Critique*—involves the existence of objects corresponding to the categories and to the conceptions involved in the forms of perception. On Kant's own principles, therefore, we could say *a priori* that there must be objects corresponding to these conceptions, even though their nature in detail could only be filled in by experience.[443]

[443] Cf. Caird, i. 604-5.

NOTE

THE REFUTATION OF IDEALISM

THIS well-known passage[444] practically replaces a long section,[445] contained only in the first edition, on the fourth paralogism of pure reason. Its aim is to vindicate against 'idealism' the reality of objects in space, and it is for this reason inserted after the discussion of the second postulate. The interest which it has excited is due to Kant's use of language which at least seems to imply that bodies in space are things in themselves, and therefore that here he really abandons his main thesis.

Idealism is the general name which Kant gives to any view which questions or denies the reality of the physical world; and, as has been pointed out before,[446] he repeatedly tries to defend himself against the charge of being an idealist in this general sense. This passage is the expression of his final attempt. Kant begins by distinguishing two forms which idealism can take according as it regards the existence of objects in space as false and *impossible,* or as doubtful and *indemonstrable*. His own view, which regards their existence as certain and demonstrable, and which he elsewhere[447] calls transcendental idealism, constitutes a third form. The first form is the dogmatic idealism of Berkeley. This view, Kant says, is unavoidable, if space be regarded as a property of things in themselves, and the basis of it has been destroyed in the *Aesthetic*. The second form is the problematic idealism of Descartes, according to which we are immediately aware only of our own existence, and belief in the existence of bodies in space can be only an inference, and an uncertain inference, from the immediate apprehension of our own existence. This view, according to Kant, is the outcome of a philosophical attitude of mind, in that it demands that a belief should be proved, and apparently—to judge from what Kant says of Berkeley—it does not commit Descartes to the view that bodies in space, if their reality can be vindicated, are things in themselves.

The assertion that the *Aesthetic* has destroyed the basis of Berkeley's view, taken together with the drift of the *Refutation* as a whole, and especially of Remark I, renders it clear that the *Refutation* is directed against Descartes and not Berkeley. Kant regards himself as having already refuted Berkeley's view, as he here states it, viz. that the existence of objects in space is *impossible*, on the ground that it arose from the mistake of supposing that space, if real at all, must be a property of things

[444] B. 274-9, M. 167-9. Cf. B. xxxix (note), M. xl (note).

[445] A. 367-80, Mah. 241-53.

[446] Cf. pp. 40-41.

[447] A. 369, Mah. 243; cf. B. 44, M. 27.

in themselves, whereas the *Aesthetic* has as he thinks, shown that space can be, and in point of fact is, a property of phenomena. He now wants to prove—compatibly with their character as phenomena—that the existence of bodies in space is not even, as Descartes contends, *doubtful*. To prove this he seeks to show that Descartes is wrong in supposing that we have no immediate experience of these objects. His method is to argue that reflection shows that internal experience presupposes external experience, i. e. that unless we were directly aware of spatial objects, we could not be aware of the succession of our own states, and consequently that it is an inversion to hold that we must reach the knowledge of objects in space, if at all, by an inference from the immediate apprehension of our own states.

An examination of the proof itself, however, forces us to allow that Kant, without realizing what he is doing, really abandons the view that objects in space are phenomena, and uses an argument the very nature of which implies that these objects are things in themselves. The proof runs thus:

Theorem. "The mere but empirically determined consciousness of my own existence proves the existence of objects in space external to me."

"*Proof.* I am conscious of my own existence as determined in time. All time-determination presupposes something permanent in perception.[448] This permanent, however, cannot be an intuition[449] in me. For all grounds of determination of my own existence, which can be found in me, are representations, and as such themselves need a permanent different from them, in relation to which their change and consequently my existence in the time in which they change can be determined.[450] The perception of this permanent, therefore, is possible only through a *thing* external to me, and not through the mere *representation* of a thing external to me. Consequently, the determination of my existence in time is possible only through the existence of actual things, which I perceive external to me. Now consciousness in time is necessarily connected with the consciousness of the possibility of this time-determination; hence it is necessarily connected also with the existence of things external to me, as the condition of time-determination, i. e. the consciousness of my own existence, is at the same time an immediate consciousness of the existence of other things external to me."[451]

The nature of the argument is clear. 'In order to be conscious, as I am, of a determinate succession of my states, I must perceive something permanent as that in relation to which alone I can perceive my states as having a definite order.[452] But this permanent cannot be a perception in me, for in that case it would only be a representation of mine, which, as such, could only be apprehended in relation to another permanent. Consequently, this permanent must be a thing external to me and not a representation of a thing external to me. Consequently, the consciousness of my own existence, which is necessarily a consciousness of my successive

[448] *Wahrnehmung.*

[449] *Anschauung.*

[450] The text has been corrected in accordance with Kant's note in the preface to the second edition, B. xxxix, M. xl.

[451] B. 275-6, M. 167.

[452] Cf. Kant's proof of the first analogy.

states, involves the immediate consciousness of things external to me.'

Here there is no way of avoiding the conclusion that Kant is deceived by the ambiguity of the phrase 'a thing external to me' into thinking that he has given a proof of the existence of bodies in space which is compatible with the view that they are only phenomena, although in reality the proof presupposes that they are things in themselves. In the 'proof', the phrase 'a thing external to me' must have a double meaning. It must mean a thing external to my body, i. e. any body which is not my body; in other words, it must be a loose expression for a body in space. For, though the 'proof' makes us appeal to the spatial character of things external to me, the *Refutation* as a whole, and especially Remark II, shows that it is of bodies in space that he is thinking throughout. The phrase must also, and primarily, mean a thing external to, in the sense of independent of, my mind, i. e. a thing in itself. For the nerve of the argument consists in the contention that the permanent the perception of which is required for the consciousness of my successive states must be a *thing* external to me in opposition to the representation of a thing external to me, and a thing external to me in opposition to a thing external to me can only be a thing in itself. On the other hand, in Kant's conclusion, 'a thing external to me' can only mean a body in space, this being supposed to be a phenomenon; for his aim is to establish the reality of bodies in space compatibly with his general view that they are only phenomena. The proof therefore requires that things external to me, in order that they may render possible the consciousness of my successive states, should have the very character which is withheld from them in the conclusion, viz. that of existing independently of me; in other words, if Kant establishes the existence of bodies in space at all, he does so only at the cost of allowing that they are things in themselves.[453]

Nevertheless, the *Refutation* may be considered to suggest the proper refutation of Descartes. It is possible to ignore Kant's demand for a permanent as a condition of the apprehension of our successive states, and to confine attention to his remark that he has shown that external experience is really immediate, and that only by means of it is the consciousness of our existence as determined in time possible.[454] If we do so, we may consider the *Refutation* as suggesting the view that Descartes' position is precisely an inversion of the truth; in other words, that our consciousness of the world, so far from being an uncertain inference from the consciousness of our successive states, is in reality a presupposition of the latter consciousness, in that this latter consciousness only arises through reflection upon the former, and that therefore Descartes' admission of the validity of self-consciousness implicitly involves the admission *a fortiori* of the validity of our consciousness of the world.[455]

---

[453] The ambiguity of the phrase 'external to me' is pointed out in the suppressed account of the fourth paralogism, where it is expressly declared that objects in space are only representations. (A. 372-3, Mah. 247). Possibly the introduction of an argument which turns on the view that they are not representations may have had something to do with the suppression.

[454] B. 277, M. 167 fin.

[455] Cf. Caird, i. 632 and ff.

Printed by Libri Plureos GmbH in Hamburg,
Germany

9 789356 148543